Gentleman Radical

The International Library of Historical Studies
Series ISBN 1 86064 079 6

The International Library of Historical Studies (ILHS) brings together the work of leading historians from universities in the English-speaking world and beyond. It constitutes a forum for original scholarship from the United Kingdom, continental Europe, the USA, the Commonwealth and the Developing World. The books are the fruit of original research and thinking and they contribute to the most advanced historiographical debate and are exhaustively assessed by the authors' academic peers. The library consists of a numbered series, covers a wide subject range and is truly international in its geographical scope. It provides a unique and authoritative resource for libraries and scholars and for student reference.

1	Between Mars and Mammon: Colonial Armies and the Garrison State in India 1819-1835 *Douglas Peters*	1 85043 954 0
2	Empires in Conflict: Armenia and the Great Powers, 1895-1920 *Manoug Somakian*	1 85043 912 5
3	The Military Revolution in Sixteenth-century Europe *David Eltis*	Pb 1 86064 352 3
4	Patrons and Defenders: The Saints in the Italian City-states *Diana Webb*	1 86064 029 X
5	Independence or Death: British Sailors and Brazilian Independence, 1822-1825 *Brian Vale*	1 86064 060 5
6	Workers Against Lenin: Labour Protest and the Bolshevik Dictatorship *Jonathan Aves*	1 86064 067 2
7	European Impact and Pacific Influence: British and German Colonial Policy in the Pacific Islands and the Indigenous Response edited by *Hermann Hiery & John MacKenzie*	1 86064 059 1
8	Conditions of Surrender: Britons and Germans Witness the End of the War *Ulrike Jordan*	1 86064 100 8
9	Gentlemen Capitalists: British Imperialism in Southeast Asia 1770-1890 *Anthony Webster*	1 86064 171 7
10	Governed by Opinion: Politics, Religion and the Dynamics of Communication in Stuart London, 1637-1645 *Dagmar Freist*	1 86064 110 5
11	The New British History: Founding a Modern State, 1500-1707 *Glenn Burgess*	1 86064 190 3
12	Pilgrims and Pilgrimage in Medieval Europe *Diana Webb*	1 86064 191 1
13	The Politics of Diplomacy: Britain, France and the Balkans in the First World War *David Dutton*	1 86064 112 1
15	The Right in France, 1789-1997 *Nicholas Atkin and Frank Tallett*	1 86064 197 0
16	Retreat from Empire: Sir Robert Armitage in Africa and Cyprus *Colin Baker*	1 86064 223 3
17	Gentleman Radical: A Life of John Horne Tooke, 1736-1812 *Christina & David Bewley*	1 86064 344 2

GENTLEMAN RADICAL

A Life of John Horne Tooke 1736-1812

Christina and
David Bewley

Tauris Academic Studies
London • New York

Published in 1998 by Tauris Academic Studies
an imprint of I.B.Tauris & Co Ltd
Victoria House, Bloomsbury Square
London WC1B 4DZ
175 Fifth Avenue, New York NY 10010

In the United States and Canada
distributed by St. Martin's Press
175 Fifth Avenue, New York NY 10010

ISBN 1 86064 344 2

A full CIP record for this book is available from the British Library
A full CIP record for this book is available from the Library of Congress

Library of Congress catalog card: available

Typeset in Caslon by Dexter Haven, London
Printed in Great Britain by Creative Print & Design Group, Ebbw Vale

To all who labour in the cause of individual liberty

Contents

Preface

At the time of her death in January 1992, my wife had completed her manuscript of the life of John Horne Tooke and had begun the process of reducing it to a manageable length. Subsequently it fell to my lot to complete the editing and reduction of the original manuscript. I have checked almost every statement made and all the references. In the main, the writing remains in the form in which my wife left it, but here and there I have altered the text where I thought she had not clearly expressed the meaning that she had intended to convey, particularly where the content of a reference was not clearly explained. In a few places I have altered the order or added a few lines to make matters clearer.

Chapter 13 on the *Diversions of Purley* presented a particular difficulty as it is not biographical. It is the chapter that my wife was least sure about. Fortunately Dr Marcus Wood of Worcester College, Oxford was so kind as to make a number of very useful suggestions, following which I largely recast the chapter.

I am particularly grateful to Drs Mark Philp and Iain McCallman for their helpful advice about the rest of the book. Without it, I doubt if I would have completed the work. I would also like to record my thanks to the many people who have given helpful advice, and particularly to Dr Alice Prochaska, Professor T.J. Taylor, John Seed, Ann Bedell, Professor H.T. Dickinson, Jenny Graham, James Aldridge, Richard Milward and Alan Elliot of the Wimbledon Society, Alison Pearn of St John's College Library, and finally Ellen Hills, without whose secretarial help the book would not have been ready for another year or two. I apologise to those who helped my wife but of whose names I have no record.

Staff at a number of libraries have been unfailingly helpful, in particular the British Library and manuscript room, the Bodleian Library, Oxford, St John's College, Cambridge, University College, London and the Public Record Office.

INTRODUCTION

> Speak roughly to your little Boy,
> And beat him when he sneezes:
> He only does it to annoy,
> Because he knows it teases.
>
> Lewis Carroll

During his lifetime, John Horne Tooke was famous or, in most people's opinions, infamous, on account of his advanced and idiosyncratic views and the violence of his writing. Today he has been forgotten except by specialists in the history of the period and by priests of the Church of England wishing to be elected to the House of Commons. He was born John Horne, and was persuaded by his father to be ordained in the established church. But his interests were political, legal and linguistic, and he quickly renounced his clerical life in favour of radical political agitation. He was the only person in Britain to be sentenced to prison for supporting the Americans during the War of Independence, and was tried for treason but acquitted during the French Revolutionary wars. In 1801 he was elected to parliament for the rotten borough of Old Sarum, but was excluded by a special declaratory act, still in force today, forbidding priests of the established church from standing for election. William Tooke, a Norfolk landowner, was one of those who admired his actions, and he persuaded Horne in 1782 to take the additional name Tooke while promising to give him financial support. In this biography he is referred to as Horne until his change of name.

Horne Tooke was an important figure in the radical politics of the period from the Wilkite campaigns of the 1760s through the French Revolution to Westminster politics at the turn of the century. He had personal contact with major figures ranging from Prime Ministers to Wilkes and Paine. His friends included Chantrey, Hoppner, Humphry Davy and Godwin. Later his fame declined, because his ordination, at that time considered indelible, prevented him from making a career in politics or the law, because his philological work, the *Diversions of Purley*, which brought him widespread acclaim, was superseded by the work of German scholars, and because he was unlucky in his biographers.

Shortly after his death in 1812 W. Hamilton Reid published a brief life, rightly condemned at the time as beneath contempt.[1] A year later Alexander Stephens – a young Scottish lawyer and member of the Clapham sect who met Tooke when he was over sixty – produced a painstaking biography of variable accuracy. Stephens was no sycophantic admirer. He disagreed with many of Tooke's opinions; he detested Napoleon and was an ardent supporter of Mary Queen of Scots, whereas Tooke thought her foolish and believed Elizabeth to have shown courage and sense in ordering her execution. Stephens, whose style is bland and pedestrian, skims over many episodes and aspects of Tooke's life. Hazlitt wrote a brilliant description of Tooke in old age,[2] John Foster an excellent essay in the *Eclectic Review*.[3] Sir Leslie Stephen himself wrote Tooke's entry in the *Dictionary of National Biography*. In 1926, Minnie Yarborough published a brief competent biography. Its emphasis is literary and its political coverage limited. Tooke's *Tower Diary*, written while on remand in the Tower of London before his trial for treason, was published in 1995 with copious notes.[4]

Whenever possible we have sought our information in the original documents. Papers in the Public Record Office throw light on the activities of Horne Tooke and other reformers during the period of the French Revolution. We have found many useful letters in the British Library, in municipal archives and university libraries up and down the country and in the USA. Many of Tooke's speeches and remarks can be found in contemporary newspapers. Unfortunately Tooke burnt his papers before his death, and few of his own letters survive. In the circumstances, we have had to rely on Stephens's biography for much of the information on his early life.

Tooke was a man of great wit and charm. His Sunday dinners at Wimbledon were famous for their conversation and conviviality, and were considered by government spies as hotbeds of sedition. Tooke was one of the most fascinating conversationalists of his day, but Stephens is no Boswell. He fails to give an adequate impression of Tooke's wide-ranging interests and fund of anecdote. He says little about Tooke's illegitemate son and daughters, not even when they were born, and does not mention their mother Mrs Hart at all. We have been unable to find out anything about her.

Tooke was an enigma to his contemporaries and has remained so to posterity. Some historians regard him as a sinister revolutionary figure who got others to do the dangerous jobs. Personally we think he has been appropriately labelled gentleman *frondeur*, a term defined as 'a critic of the authorities, irreverent, insubordinate'. He was a man of diverse talents who deserves to be remembered. After all, who else has been tried for treason and then elected MP?

Our treatment of Tooke's contribution to the history of linguistics is limited. More information can be found in the excellent chapters by Hans Aasleff and Olivia Smith listed in the bibliography.

To avoid repetition we have used both the terms 'patriot' and 'radical'. In the mid-eighteenth century a patriot considered himself a defender of the liberties of ordinary people against abritrary power. He feared the corruption of MPs, the distribution of patronage and the power of rich, aristocratic boroughmongers. He therefore advocated parliamentary reform. By the mid-nineteenth century the word 'patriot' had lost this special meaning and had been replaced by 'radical'. This latter word was first used in a political context in 1797-8 when Fox, Tooke and their followers made a brief effort to combine in a demand for radical reform, radical meaning a return to roots. The word did not come into common circulation until about 20 years later. We have also used the terms 'working class' and 'middle class' anchronistically. Class antagonism and perception of the 'working class' as a separate entity was a later phenomenon, but they are useful descriptive labels. 'Reform' is another word which has had different connotations. Most men who were dubbed reformers in Tooke's time wanted to make the political system more democratic. Not all reformers had as advanced views as radicals, though all radicals were reformers.

Notes on Introduction

1 *Quarterly Review* VII, 1812, pp 313-28
2 Hazlitt, *The Spirit of the Age* (Works II, p 46)
3 Foster, J., *Critical Essays* II, pp 156-92 and in *Eclectic Review*, 1844
4 Horne Tooke, J., *Tower Diary*, ed. Harvey Beedell, 1995

Chronology

1736 Birth of John Horne
43 Begins school in Soho Square
46 Goes to Eton College
54 Admitted as sizar to St John's College, Cambridge
56 Enrols as member of Inner Temple
58 Obtains BA
59 Ordained deacon
60 Ordained priest, perpetual curate St Lawrence, Brentford
63 Accompanies Elwes's son to France
65 Writes 'Petition of an Englishman'
65-7 In France and Italy with Taylor's son; meets Wilkes
68 Helps Wilkes in Middlesex election
69 Wilkes re-elected with Tooke's help; founds SSBR; quarrels with Wilkes
70 Sued for libel by Onslow: £400 damages
71 Judgement overturned on appeal; affair of printers – freedom of the press. Obtains MA at Cambridge; correspondence with Junius
73 Resigns benefice at Brentford
74 Meets William Tooke and successfully libels the Speaker of the House of Commons
75 Publishes seditious advertisement
77 Prosecuted for criminal libel, sentenced to 12 months' imprisonment
78 Publishes 'A Letter to Dunning on the English Particle'
79 Rejected by benchers of Inner Temple
80-5 Works for Bernard, living partly at Witton, later in William Tooke's chambers
80 Publishes pamphlet with Price on American War
81 Joins Society for Constitutional Information
82 Publishes pamphlet on a proposed new system of representation
82 Becomes John Horne Tooke
86 Publishes *Diversions of Purley* Part I
88 Publishes *Two Pair of Portraits*
90 Stands for Westminster against Hood and Fox

90-2 Petitions Parliament on grounds of malpractice at election
92 Moves to Wimbledon
94 Imprisoned in Tower; tried for treason; acquitted
96 Stands for Westminster against Fox and Gardner; meets Burdett
1801 Elected for parliament to represent Old Sarum; bill passed to disqualify ordained priests of the Church of England
2 Ceases to be MP at dissolution of Parliament; death of William Tooke
4 Chancery case over William Tooke's will
12 Death and burial at Ealing

Chapter One

Early Life

John Horne, who later took the additional name of Tooke, was born on 25 June 1736 in Newport Street which adjoins Leicester Square, in an area inhabited by a mixture of county families, artists and craftsmen. His mother Elizabeth, of whom he was extremely fond, was affectionate, kind and popular with the neighbours. A generous woman, she persuaded her husband to give money to the Middlesex Hospital, founded in 1745, and he became one of its first treasurers. Horne's father, also called John, was a prosperous poulterer much respected in the trade. He was a courageous man of independent spirit, characteristics inherited by his son. A typical example of his determination to fight official despotism involved him in legal action against the royal family. Frederick Prince of Wales lived in Leicester House next door to Horne. Certain of his officials wanted to make an opening through a wall belonging to Horne, giving them access to Newport market. They cut a door without asking Horne's permission, and began to use his premises as a thoroughfare. Horne remonstrated without effect, so he took the case to court and won. He then wrote to the Prince saying that, having taught his servants to respect private property, he would be happy for the doorway to be reopened. The Prince was so pleased with Horne's behaviour that he gave him a warrant to supply his household with poultry. Alas Horne paid dearly for the honour, as the Prince of Wales died suddenly owing him several thousand pounds which George II never paid.

John was the youngest and favourite son. The eldest, Benjamin, was a highly successful market gardener at Brentford. He specialised in fruit and introduced the Saratoga strawberry plant to Britain, obtained for him by Lord Shelburne. Shelburne, besides being a leading Whig politician, was a keen horticulturist and sometimes passed the night with him. The second son Thomas, who started out as a fishmonger, succeeded his father in his business. He was a forceful personality, but had extravagant tastes, mismanaged his affairs and ended his days in an almshouse run by the Fishmongers Company.

There were four daughters who all married well. Mary, the eldest and considered a beauty, married Tom Wildman, a wine merchant and friend of Wilkes (see chapter 2 *et seq.*). The next daughter Sarah became the second wife of Dr Demainbray, an astronomer who was tutor to the future George III. Through his brother-in-law's introduction John, as a child, went once or twice a week to Leicester House to play with George. Elizabeth, the third daughter, was said to have the same wit and vivacity as her brother John, and married Clarke, a haberdasher. The youngest, Anne, married Dickers, a dealer in paints who left her a rich widow.[1]

In 1743, aged seven, John was sent to school in Soho Square. A year later he went to Westminster, then in 1746 to Eton, where he spent six years. There were about 250 boys. Although the majority belonged to the upper classes, quite a few were tradesmen's sons. John was elected a King's scholar, so lived in College where life was extremely spartan. College boys, who came from less affluent and distinguished families, were looked down on by the Oppidans, children of richer parents, who lived in houses in the town. John was teased about his humble origins, but was perfectly capable of defending himself. On one occasion he was in a group who were cross-questioning each other about their parents. One boy said he was the son of a baronet, another of an earl, a third that his grandmother was a duchess. John said he could not boast of any titles in his family and, when pressed, said with reluctance that his father was an eminent Turkey merchant. John's sensitivity to slights and dislike of the aristocracy may well have originated in his schooldays, but he never complained that he was unhappy at Eton, and he approved of the great schools as a microcosm in which boys performed that part in miniature which they would enact later. When they entered society their manners were in some measure formed, whereas those who were brought up at home became giddy at so much seeming delight.[2]

Although clever, he does not appear to have distinguished himself scholastically. As an adult he cheerfully admitted that he had employed other boys to do his homework, and maintained that it never augured well if a 'schoolboy… was willing to plod in the drudgery of learning and was not active in playful exertion'. One possible reason for his laziness was that at Eton he lost the sight of his right eye in a struggle with a boy who had a knife in his hand.[3]

A school anecdote, which John's friends considered a good illustration of his grammatical precision, concerned an Eton master who asked why he put a word in some case or mood. John said he did not know, so was beaten. Another boy repeated the grammatical rule and took his place in the class. John burst into tears. When asked why he replied, 'I knew the rule as well as he did. You did not ask for the rule, but the reason… and I do not know that now.' As recompense, the master gave him a copy of Virgil of which he was very proud.[4]

When Stephens was writing Horne's biography, he asked an old lady if she remembered him as a boy. 'No,' she said. 'He never was a boy, with him there was no interval between childhood and age; he became a man all at once.'

After John left Eton he was coached for Cambridge by tutors at Sevenoaks and at Ravenstone in Northamptonshire. He was admitted as a sizar* to St John's on 12 January 1754, and took up residence in 1755. He worked hard during his three years there, and as senior optime (equivalent to the modern Class II) graduated in 1758 with a BA honours degree in mathematics, the only tripos then in existence. The intellectual climate of Cambridge, which was then more progressive than Oxford, must have helped form his political views. A number of the men who worked with him in radical politics were there at about the same time. Some, who took holy orders, later became Unitarians and had to resign their Cambridge fellowships or livings. One undergraduate who remained a close friend all John's life was Richard Beadon,

* A sizar received an allowance from his college to pay for his studies, and in return undertook duties now performed by college servants.

who tutored the future Duke of Gloucester at Cambridge, became Master of Jesus, Bishop of Gloucester and finally Bishop of Bath and Wells. When Beadon met Horne in St Paul's churchyard and said he was to be Bishop of Gloucester, Horne replied, 'I suppose I must never call you Dick again'. 'Why,' responded Beadon, 'I don't exactly see the necessity of that.'[5]

John's parents were very keen that, like Beadon, he should enter the Church, a sure way to rise in the world in the eighteenth century. Horne senior was a devout member of the Church of England and there were good prospects of preferment through Demainbray. John, however, had already decided that he would far rather embark on a legal career so on 9 November 1756, while an undergraduate, he enrolled as a member of the Inner Temple. His parents refused to support him while he read for the bar. Their misjudgement of their son's character and insistence on his ordination was to have disastrous results. The fact that John's creed was remarkably vague – Wilkes said it was 'non credo' – did not matter much at a time when only respect for outward forms of religion was expected, but he was unable to reconcile himself, as Swift did, to paying lip service to the Church. His ordination was used by his political opponents to prevent him from becoming either a lawyer or an MP, and to a large extent soured his life.

After graduation, possibly hoping that his parents might relent, Horne took a job as usher at a school in Blackheath. Although this was an unpleasant change after Cambridge, he enjoyed instructing the young and had a benevolent attitude towards children. He had a forceful, magnetic personality and kept order with ease. One man told Stephens that, as a boy, he never stood as much in awe of anyone as Horne: 'There was something inexpressibly significant in his voice, manner and gestures, that made it impossible to approach him with the same ease as an ordinary mortal'. Horne advocated public education, but believed parents were the best guardians of their children's morals. He thought learning accurate English was the most important training children could have: it helped them to think and to distinguish between truth and falsehood. The greatest benefit of education was to give confidence. An uneducated man believes there is magic in it and stands in awe of those who have received its benefit.[6]

Horne had a love affair with a young woman living in the same house. Due to some formidable obstacle it was broken off and he departed. As he sardonically remarked, 'I luckily escaped from two evils – matrimony and misery – at the same time'. He gave way to his father, was ordained deacon on 23 Sepember 1759 and became a curate in Kent. Within a few months he had a bout of ague which he made the excuse to give up his post.[7]

When Horne recovered he determined to follow his inclination, so took commons daily at his inn of court, 'to eat his way to the bar'. His closest companions were two men who became famous lawyers. One, John Dunning, would later defend him, the other, Kenyon, would become his judge. Horne had had a better and broader education than the other two, who had not been to university. They had been called to the bar in 1756, but were still struggling students. All three were penurious. In the vacation they dined together in Chancery Lane. Horne remained a friend of Dunning's till the latter's death in 1783. Dunning, the son of a tradesman, was four years older than Horne. He had a brilliant career at the bar, was brought into Parliament by Lord Shelburne, and created Lord Ashburnham by Rockingham, leader of one of the Whig factions in Parliament. Kenyon, a Welshman, became Chief Justice of the King's Bench and Master of the Rolls.

It would have taken Horne several years to establish himself at the bar. When the money Horne had saved ran out, he was unwillingly persuaded to abandon his legal studies and on 23 November 1760 was ordained a priest. His father purchased him a living at New Brentford worth £200-300 a year, and offered further financial inducements if he would enter the church.[8] Horne did his best, within his natural limitations, to fulfil his duties to his parishioners in accordance with the standards of the age.

Horne's God, if he existed, was very impersonal. Horne believed in a first cause 'because every other supposition is more absurd'. His entry for 'Church' in the *The Diversions of Purley*, a book he wrote in later life, was 'An adjective and formerly a most wicked one, whose misinterpretation caused more slaughter and pillage of mankind than all the other cheats together.' Like many of his contemporaries he was violently opposed to the Church of Rome. He considered many of its observances rank superstition, its religion, in particular confession, 'destructive of the civil rights of mankind' and hated the foreign jurisdiction of the 'wretched Mummery of Popery'.[9]

Theological controversies bored him. Though a passionate supporter of individual freedom, he was not interested in alleviating dissenters' disabilities. He was anti-schism and admired the hierarchy of the Church. He told William Shepherd, a Unitarian friend, that since a Church establishment was necessary to the British constitution, he should be thankful the established church was the Church of England. It was a quiet, sleepy church. Give its ministers honours and emoluments and they would not disturb anyone on the score of doctrine. But if it were overthrown, methodism or popery would be established, 'and then you rational gentlemen will be persecuted with a vengeance'. He often cited Machiavelli's dictum that princes should uphold their countries' religion, making it easy to keep the people religious, orderly and united. Horne greatly admired Machiavelli. When asked if he was really a friend to liberty, he retorted, 'What did he undergo torture for then?'[10]

As he could summon up little interest in the spiritual comfort of his parishioners, he tried to improve their physical well-being by studying medical books. Having learnt how to compound a few medicines, he opened a dispensary at his parsonage and claimed that his medical labours were far more efficacious than his spiritual ones. Horne was lively and gregarious. Besides enjoying the fashionable games of ombre and quadrille, he shocked some of his parishioners by spending Sunday afternoons seated at a window overlooking the street playing whist at which he excelled.[11]

Horne himself had a pleasant, interesting, but not particularly handsome face with regular features and a high forehead. His hair was brown, he was sturdy, of medium height and athletic build. He enjoyed the company of women and knew how to make himself agreeable to them. He considered they had more feeling than men, so it was almost always possible to discover the degree of regard or aversion they had for a man. He had the least to say when with pretty women, for it was then that he was most anxious to recommend himself. He wished that women would purr when pleased.[12]

In February 1763, just after the Seven Years War with France ended, Horne jumped at a chance to abandon his tedious parochial duties and become what he termed 'a bear leader'. He went to France for a year as travelling companion to the illegitimate son of a celebrated eccentric miser John Elwes, MP for Berkshire. On crossing the Channel Horne abandoned his clerical garb, wore fashionable suits and had his hair trimmed in Parisian style. Although he worked hard, it took him nine months before he could speak French tolerably well. As an obscure young man with no contacts he saw little of Parisian society. He did, however, have an introduction to d'Alembert, one of the *philosophes* and a founder of *l'encyclopédie*, who received him very civilly and chatted about operas, comedies and parties. Horne withdrew disappointed, for he realised that d'Alembert thought little of him. A Scotsman in a plain suit, who had noticed his chagrin, followed him and explained that his gay garments had made d'Alembert think him a dandy. Horne returned soberly dressed and had a far more interesting conversation. He was delighted to discover that his benefactor was David Hume. Horne read and reread Hume's essays with delight, but disapproved of his history, 'written as witches say their prayers, backwards,' first a false account of the Stuarts, then volumes on earlier periods to justify it, an opinion fostered by Tory Hume's detestation of 'those insolent rascals in London and Middlesex,' in particular Horne's hero Wilkes who had savagely attacked the Scots.[13]

On his return, if Horne had been able to reconcile himself to the clerical life, he would almost certainly have gained promotion. Through Demainbray and his influential patron Elwes he had been promised an appointment as King's chaplain.[14] His heart, however, was not in his work. He was swept up into the far more congenial and heady world of politics. Brentford was on the fringes of London, the centre of power, where exciting developments were taking place.

When George III became King in 1760, William Pitt (later Lord Chatham) and the Duke of Newcastle were in charge of government. Pitt wanted to wage war against the French more vigorously. Newcastle was not convinced that the country could afford it. Pitt failed to get his way, so resigned in October 1761. Newcastle then failed to persuade his colleagues Lord Bute and George Grenville to continue support of Frederick of Prussia, so seven months later he too resigned. Bute, who became first Lord of the Treasury, was widely hated as a Scottish interloper. He in turn was driven out in April 1763 and replaced by Grenville. The

City, which had close contact with Pitt, resented its loss of power when he went out. Londoners considered he had been wronged and, encouraged by Pitt and Lord Temple, opposed the new leaders. George Grenville and Lord Temple were brothers. They supported Wilkes, and the family, which later included the dukes of Buckingham, became the greatest sinecurists of the time, thereby earning the hatred of Horne. Newspapers continued to abuse Bute, claiming that he owed his position of influence not only to George's affection but to the intimate favours of the Dowager Princess of Wales. Temple's most effective aide was John Wilkes, who attacked the Government in his journal the *North Briton* which had a large circulation of over 1,000.

Soon after Horne went abroad, Wilkes had produced number 45 of the *North Briton* which became notorious for its criticism of the King's speech approving the peace of Paris which concluded the seven-years war. A general warrant was issued to arrest all connected with the *North Briton* on a charge of seditious libel, a total of 48 printers and booksellers. A writ of Habeas Corpus for Wilkes was avoided by holding him incommunicado in the Tower. Sir Charles Pratt, later Lord Camden and a judge of great probity, ruled that since Wilkes was privileged as an MP, he should be set at liberty and, in a later judgement, that general warrants were illegal. The Government then brought an ordinary suit against Wilkes who, before his trial came up, retired to the Continent where he remained for four years.

Horne came back from France proud to be English, impressed by the nation's remarkable victories under her idol Pitt, appreciative of the benefits of the British constitution compared with Continental autocracy. Throughout his life he retained a fear that, through corruption, despotism might recur. In addition, his friends belonged to the urban professional classes which were increasingly frustrated by the oligarchical political and social system. He therefore gravitated to opposition circles.

Horne joined in persecution of Lord Bute and criticism of the administration, writing squibs and paragraphs in the popular papers. He followed the lead of his hero Pitt who greatly disliked Lord Mansfield, for 28 years Lord Chief Justice of the King's Bench. Mansfield, like Bute a Scotsman, was an outstanding lawyer but irresolute politician 'who hated the popular party'. Authoritarian in his views, a dictator on the Bench, he had passed severe, unpopular sentences on some of Wilkes's supporters and, like Lord Bute, was unjustifiably suspected of machinations to destroy the rule of law.

Horne's chief contribution was a pamphlet of 23 very large pages entitled 'The Petition of an Englishman', directed against Bute and Mansfield. The author's name was to remain secret unless prosecution threatened. Crude and virulent, lacking the polish of Horne's later efforts, it was a typical example of the vitriolic satire common at the time and contained several grossly offensive passages. Horne had difficulty finding a printer willing to publish it. He introduced a theme which he would reiterate throughout his life, his love of liberty and willingness to make sacrifices in its cause: 'Liberty… is twisted with my Heart-strings… They… cannot be untwisted by the subtle fingers of corruption, nor loosened by the touch of Fear'. One paragraph was only too prophetic: 'I, who am at present blessed with peace, happiness and independence, a fair character, and an easy fortune, am… forfeiting them all. Soon must I be beggared, vilified, imprisoned.'

For the time being he escaped prosecution due to the insertion of a large two-page plan of Kew Gardens which showed the path by which Lord Bute could quickly and discreetly walk from his house to that of the Dowager Princess of Wales. Allusions to this could have caused embarrassment if brought out in court. Family and friends, in particular Demainbray, remonstrated, predicting that he would lose all chance of preferment if he carried on like this, but Horne remained resolute.[15]

Horne was still well thought of by the neighbouring gentry and in the autumn of 1765 he went abroad again as companion to the son of Mr Taylor, a rich man who lived near Brentford. Neither young Elwes nor Taylor was told by their fathers that Horne had been asked to keep an eye on them. Both said afterwards that they had much enjoyed having him as a travelling companion. Horne and Taylor made their leisurely way through France to Italy.[16]

In Paris, Horne had a more amusing time than before, especially as he carried an introduction to Wilkes from Humphrey Cotes, a Westminster wine merchant. Wilkes was 40, eleven years older than Horne, dashing, irresponsible, spendthrift, ugly, yet a man of infinite charm. Wilkes and Horne had many similar qualities, though the differences in their characters and attitudes would grow increasingly important. Both were brilliant journalists – gay, quick, clever, companionable – and enjoyed shocking the establishment. Both had many amorous adventures and thrived on the rougher side of politics.[17] Wilkes was a staunch supporter of Pitt but had luxurious tastes and was unscrupulous over financial affairs. Horne, who never had much money, did not run up debts, had no extravagant tastes, nor any ambition to enter smart society. He was more of an intellectual, preferring the company of writers, artists and scholars. Wilkes was far more skilled at managing men. He took up the popular cause partly from inclination, partly love of mischief, mostly from ambition. Horne had a genuine desire to combat what he believed were political malpractices.

Wilkes had obtained a verdict with damages against the two secretaries of state, the Earls of Egremont and Halifax, who had authorised his arrest, but the House of Commons had expelled him for writing and publishing number 45 of the *North Briton*. He had been found guilty in the Court of King's Bench of publishing an obscene 'Essay on Women' and as he did not return to stand trial was outlawed. Having run through his own money and his wife's, he was heavily in debt and in addition was accused of embezzling the funds of a foundling hospital. He was widely considered to be a victim of political injustice, a champion who had raised the important question of the executive's use of general warrants.

Wilkes, who received Horne affably, wrote to Cotes on 7 October thanking him 'heartily for so valuable an acquaintance'. A week later Horne was still in Paris, and they were 'much together'. Horne, like so many others, succumbed to Wilkes's fascination. When he left for Geneva they agreed to write to each other.[18]

Horne paid a call on Voltaire at Ferney, which cannot have been a success for he never talked about it and had few good words to say for the great man, though when he was in the Tower he made copious notes on Voltaire's *Pensées sur l'Administration Publique*. Horne considered Dryden, whose 'practical knowledge of English was exquisite and wonderful', a more universal writer and believed that Voltaire was 'inferior in everything… as a poet, a biographer and an historian'. Although Horne was well-read in

French literature he did not have a high opinion of it. He read the *Arabian Nights* in French almost every year only because there was no comparable English translation.[19]

Horne and Taylor went south to Lyons where they stayed a week, dining every day with ten or twelve other Englishmen including Sterne. Horne spent much of his time with Sterne who was 'accompanied by two ladies of most vulgar manners'. Sterne found him a likeable young man, but was bored by his eulogies of Wilkes.[20]

Horne and Taylor spent some time at Montpelier, then a fashionable winter resort, where they moved in rather grand Franco-British society. Among the visitors was the young Duke of Buccleuch, accompanied by his tutor Adam Smith. Horne did not take to Smith as he had to Sterne. He maintained that Smith was inferior to his teacher Hume, that his theory of moral sentiments was nonsense and that the *Wealth of Nations*, though 'full of important facts, was written with a wicked view'.[21]

From Montpelier, Horne wrote to Wilkes on 3 January 1766. His adulation was sincere but obtrusive. He wanted both to disarm Wilkes and impress him as a man of the world. His letter was amusing but indiscreet and contained some impertinent advice. It was ultimately to have most unfortunate consequences. 'You are entering into a correspondence with a parson, and I am a little apprehensive lest that title should disgust you; but give me leave to assure you, I am not ordained a hypocrite. It is true I have suffered the infectious hand of a bishop to be waved over me; whose imposition… is only a signal for the devil to enter… I hope I have escaped the contagion; and if I have not, if you should at any time discover the black spot under the tongue, assist me kindly to conquer the prejudices of education and profession.'[22]

Horne and Taylor stayed nine months in Genoa, where they made the acquaintance of a distinguished Italian family who introduced them into Genoese society. A Marquis took them to a ball of the nobility and asked Horne his opinion of each lady as she entered. He expatiated on the great beauty of one, Signora Durazzo. When the Marquis told her how much Horne had admired her, she appointed him her cavaliere servente. Horne, who thought love at first sight should be acted on, became her devoted attendant. One evening several weeks later, when he called to accompany her to a party, she had already gone. He followed and found her playing cards. She greeted him coolly as did the rest of the company of about two hundred. It transpired that they had discovered he was a Protestant clergyman. Horne resolved not to be browbeaten. He walked calmly about, took snuff, pretended nothing was wrong. He was so entertaining that they were all on the best of terms again before the evening was out. Not all of the signora's relations approved of Horne's attentions. When he finally left Genoa, her brother warned him to stop at a villetta on the first day of his journey to avoid meeting members of the family, who had sworn to take vengeance. On the road, Horne heard shots and found an Englishman, who had been mistaken for him, wounded in his chaise.[23]

Horne had one alarming problem to contend with. Young Taylor was subject to fits of insanity and would sometimes cause disturbances at inns in the middle of the night. At a dinner-party many years later discussion turned on the acquittal of Hadfield, who had just been tried for shooting at the king. Horne wished he had been hanged. Shepherd expostulated that he was a madman. 'What matters is what becomes of a madman. Hanging one might deter others and save the king's life. I speak warmly, but my warmth is selfish. I was private tutor to a young man.... In the South of France… one day, after dinner, in a fit of frenzy he drew his sword and ran me through the body. When I recovered I resumed charge of my pupil and conducted him back to England, but since that period I have entertained a rooted dislike of madmen.' Horne told Godwin that on the coach journey back he put Taylor at the bottom of the chaise and sat on a seat holding pistols. He would not allow Taylor to handle a knife or fork.[24]

When they reached Paris again in spring 1767, nettled by his hero's neglect, Horne contrived to meet Wilkes without the humiliation of a formal call. Wilkes tried to turn Horne's queries about the lack of an answer to his letter into a joke over a bottle of burgundy. When Horne persisted, he denied having received it. Horne discovered that Wilkes had shown it to friends and threatened publication. He sensibly dropped the matter, and they parted on such good terms that when he left on 25 May Wilkes took charge of his five fashionable suits decorated with gold, silver and embroidery. This time Horne's accompanying note was brief, witty and complimentary: 'If you have any fellow-feeling, you cannot but be kind to them; since they too, as well as yourself, are outlawed in England; and on the same account – their superior worth'.[25]

Notes on Chapter 1

Full details of each reference are given in the bibliography. *DOP* means *Diversions of Purley* by Horne.

1 Stephens I, pp 6-14
2 Stephens I, pp 13-16, 21; Rogers *Recollections*, p 144
3 Stephens I, p 17; Shepherd MSS X f21, p 1
4 Robinson, *Diary* II, p 62
5 Rogers, *Recollections*, p 138; Stephens I, pp 22, 23.
6 Stephens I, p 23; Rogers, *Recollections* p 146
7 Stephens I, p 28
8 Stephens I, pp 30-4
9 *DOP*, pp 309, 314
10 Shepherd MSS X f21, p 4
11 Stephens I, pp 39-40
12 Rogers *Recollections*, pp 129, 131
13 *Ibid.* pp 136, 147; Stephens I, p 35; Rogers, *Table Talk*, p 123
14 Stephens I, p 36
15 Horne, John, 'Petition of an Englishman'; Stephens I, pp 57-67
16 Stephens I, pp 67-8
17 Bleackley, pp 6, 445-6; Stephens I, p 69
18 Wilkes, John, *Correspondence* II, p 209
19 *DOP*, p 604; Stephens II, p 435; Rogers, *Recollections*, p 140
20 Wilkes, John, Add MSS 30877 f51-2; Shepherd MSS X f21, p 4
21 Rogers, *Recollections*, p 136
22 Stephens I, pp 76-80
23 Rogers, *Table Talk*, pp 124-5; Clayden, *Rogers and his Contemporaries* I, pp 76-9
24 Shepherd, MSS X f21, p 2; Paul I, p 148; NB Godwin confused young Elwes with Taylor
25 Stephens I, p 83

CHAPTER TWO

WILKES AND LIBERTY

On his return Horne, who was popular with his parishioners, made one final effort to come to terms with clerical life. He gained a reputation for preconfirmation talks. When one young lady brought her doubts to him he boasted that he found her 'an infidel and left her a good member of the Church of England'.[1] He preached charity sermons which attracted large audiences in City churches – one at Whitechapel received wide coverage in the press – and he often officiated at St Paul's Covent Garden, near his birthplace. A fluent, lively speaker – although his heart was not in it – he was in a fair way to becoming a successful preacher when Wilkes, unwilling to be left to moulder abroad, reappeared in time for the general election of spring 1768.

By now Pitt (ennobled as Earl of Chatham) had retreated into mental depression, and the Duke of Grafton was left in charge, propped up by the Duke of Bedford and his followers. Wilkes first stood for the City but failed to be elected, so instead offered himself as candidate for Middlesex. Here was Horne's lucky chance. With his church and rectory close to the Brentford hustings, where polling would take place, he was able to offer Wilkes enormous assistance.

Horne was inspired by hatred of injustice and a desire for greater equality of opportunity. Wilkes was to him a symbol of resistance to an administration which had acted contrary to the public interest. Now aged thirty-two, he considered that he could do no greater service than espouse Wilkes's cause 'which the weakness and wickedness of our Court had made… the cause of every Englishman'.[2]

Wilkes was a cynical, able demagogue. His commitment to reform was equivocal. He exploited every opportunity to further his career, but in the process engineered disputes with the authorities which involved fundamental constitutional principles. Englishmen were suspicious of any concentration of power. The legislature must have the power to prevent the executive from suppressing liberty. The Wilkites advocated a free press and an uncorrupted legislature which would be accountable to the people it was supposed to represent.

Wilkes had chosen the right moment to return, a catalyst for discontent. Until the second half of the eighteenth century land had been the main source of the country's wealth, and it was the landed interests which were primarily represented in Parliament. In England and Wales there were 92 county and 417 borough members. The nomination of most borough members was controlled by landowners or Treasury managers. A few men had the disposal of many seats while ministers used patronage to obtain a majority. The 'knights of the shires', chosen by the gentry and large farmers, tended to be more independent, but they too represented country areas. This system was becoming progressively unsatisfactory due to shifts in population and growing urbanisation. The expanding middle classes, the City in particular, which now contributed so much to the wealth of the country, lacked power. Its citizens were proud of their bourgeois virtues and traditions, their autonomous, democratic municipal government, the important City privileges. They were resentful and suspicious of aristocrats and rich magnates with their arrogant assumption of superiority. Although the great merchants supported the Ministry, smaller men were traditionally hostile to the Court and ruling elite with whom they had no profitable financial connections. There was strong resentment that the metropolitan area, now spreading into Middlesex and Surrey, and containing about a tenth of the population of the country, only had ten MPs and paid a far higher proportion of the land tax than the northern and western counties with 216 MPs. The development of urban radicalism was encouraged by the comparatively wide electoral franchises in the City, with four MPs, and Middlesex, Westminster and Southwark, each represented by two. In addition, a belief was spreading, based on very little evidence, that the constitution and liberties of the subject were in serious danger because Parliament had been corrupted by a Court clique which wanted to impose autocratic rule.

Wilkes had no programme or party. He posed as a martyr, persecuted by an inefficient and extravagant government. He drew support from the discontented minor trading and manufacturing elements, and from the labouring classes suffering economic hardship, recently exacerbated by the Government's quarrel with America.

Horne realised that he must not presume too much on Wilkes's friendship. He did not get in touch 'till it was very evident you had lost your election in the city', six days before polling would open in Middlesex.[2] He threw himself heart and soul into the campaign. The next day, 23 March, he inserted advertisements in the newspapers attacking the sitting members, George Cooke, an old and gouty Tory, and Sir William Beauchamp Proctor, a prosperous bad-tempered Whig barrister. Both had held their seats unopposed for many years, and expected automatic re-election. On the twenty-fourth, Wilkes and Horne set out to canvas. In no other county could numbers have succeeded so well against influence. Middlesex being relatively urbanised there were few great landowners, and a large proportion of the freeholders were small commercial people, less subject to intimidation than tenant farmers. The majority of the gentry and clergy supported Proctor and Cooke.

Wilkes and Horne were joined by Serjeant John Glynn, aged forty-six, a total contrast to them, a distinguished lawyer, pedantic, antiquarian. He had defended Wilkes over general warrants in 1763 and fallen foul of Mansfield through challenging his legal opinion on contempt. He became an intimate friend of Horne, but was never close to Wilkes. He fought skilled battles in the law courts and brought sober commonsense to the triumvirate of 'The Three Johns', after whom four pubs were named (one still exists in Baron St., Islington). Every type of propaganda was used – newspapers, pamphlets, ballads – to bring politics to a mass audience. With the rousing slogan 'Wilkes and Liberty' the poor and uneducated were encouraged to demonstrate in favour of liberty as well as against high bread prices. Wilkes was a past master at manipulating the press and his pupil soon learnt how to discredit opponents. Puns and letters flowed from Horne's pen. He was indefatigable, covering the whole of the constituency on foot or horseback. Sometimes with Wilkes, sometimes on his own, he addressed large meetings and proved to have a flair for rousing oratory. Forty thousand handbills were issued. Horne pledged himself for all he was worth to keep the taps of the two best inns in Brentford flowing. His own family was divided. One brother-in-law, Wildman, supported Wilkes, another, Demainbray, canvassed for Proctor.[3]

The election on 28 March was electrifying. Crowds escorted the electors 19 miles from London to Brentford. Popular backing was skilfully organised. Every passenger in 250 coachloads of Wilkes's supporters was given a blue cockade and badge. Voters had to pass the gauntlet of Wilkites at strategic points. The Spitalfield weavers, normally a tumultuous lot who were suffering from high unemployment, took possession of Piccadilly and the Oxford Road and helped to keep order. Thousands of spectators occupied the entrance to the polls. At the end of polling, Wilkes had 1292 votes, Cooke 827, Proctor 807. There were grand celebrations. London was illuminated, the crowd insisting that everyone light up their windows.

So far the Government had avoided tangling with Wilkes who still had to face trial. After the Easter recess, Wilkes insisted on being arrested. He set off to await prosecution in prison accompanied by Horne. At Westminster Bridge a mob took charge and dragged their carriage in triumph to the Three Tuns in Spitalfields;* a heady time for Horne, basking in reflected glory. After dark, Wilkes slipped away in disguise to the King's Bench prison in St George's Fields, which became the headquarters from which Horne, Glynn, Cotes and other patriots planned future strategy.

When Parliament opened on 10 May an unfortunate incident provided fuel for the Wilkite cause. About 300 people assembled round the prison thinking Wilkes would be allowed to take his seat. After unpopular Scottish soldiers had been sent to relieve

* Talking about these events many years later Horne said such demonstrations were not entirely spontaneous. The men who unharnessed the horses and pulled the carriages were hired in advance and paid according to the distance covered.

troops already there, more people came in from the fields to see what was going on. There were protests when a magistrate, Gillam, sent constables to disperse the crowd. When they seized several inoffensive bystanders and handed them to the soldiers, the crowd became enraged. Gillam was struck with a brickbat. A captain and two private soldiers pursued his assailant, but in the confusion chased an innocent bystander into his father's cowshed and shot him dead. Stones were again thrown at Gillam who ordered the troops to fire into the crowd. Five men and one woman died, two women and three men were wounded.[4]

Due to Horne's persistence Gillam was charged with the murder of the six bystanders. He was acquitted, but a Coroner's jury found one Private guilty of abetting him.[4] Subsequently, in the face of conflicting evidence, a grand jury at Guildford threw out the charges.[5] Still, Wilkes and Horne, who gave evidence, ensured that the 'massacre of St George's Fields', which had captured the popular imagination, should go down in radical mythology. With a propaganda campaign accusing Scottish butchers of intimidating Englishmen, the minister's action was made to appear the deliberate policy of a tyrannical executive trampling on Englishmen's liberties.

The Government wanted to avoid making Wilkes more of a martyr than need be. Lord Mansfield contrived the cancellation of his sentence of outlawry on a legal quibble. On 18 June 1768 he was sentenced to a total of 22 months' imprisonment and fined £1,000 for the *Essay on Women* and republishing number 45 (see page 8).[6]

In the autumn, Horne helped Wilkes draw up a petition to Parliament recapitulating his grievances and asking for an enquiry and redress. Meanwhile Cooke had died. Proctor hoped to replace him as member for Middlesex. Glynn was chosen as the Wilkite candidate. He was supported by two MPs, John Sawbridge and James Townsend, who espoused the popular cause and were to become friends of Horne. Still in their early thirties, they were coming men in the City. Both were friends of Lord Shelburne. Townsend, whose father had been attached to the Court, had inherited a large fortune and, in addition, had married an heiress. He was courageous, with a fiery temper. When the House of Commons decided to expel Wilkes so that, lacking parliamentary privilege, he could be kept indefinitely in the King's Bench prison for debt, Townsend agreed that Horne should introduce them to one another.[7] The Sawbridge family bore a grudge against the Government because their father had been a director of the South Sea Company, and his estates in Kent had been sequestered with no possibility of appeal. Sawbridge was honest but not brilliant, coarse in manner, and had married two heiresses.

Both factions fought a protracted, strenuous election contest. Once more Horne's vicarage was campaign headquarters. Proctor was said to have spent £6,000 on the election, Glynn nothing. His expenses were paid with money Horne collected from sympathisers. In a series of bitterly sarcastic letters in the *Oxford Magazine* Horne defended Wilkes, praised Glynn and hounded Proctor, who 'never went near his constituency till Wilkes loomed up as candidate'.[8] Proctor retorted that Glynn had hired a band of writers – in fact Horne masquerading under different pseudonyms – to assassinate his reputation with gross falsehoods and malicious innuendos. Horne's style was simple and to the point – 'he was dextrous in the employment of short, strong arguments' – with the ability to dissect and demolish his opponents' case.[9]

Rioting at elections was a national prerogative and sport for the plebs. At the previous election there had been accusations that Court supporters were intimidated. This time there was more rowdyism than usual. Proctor hired his own bravos, Irish chairmen, at a guinea a day. Armed with bludgeons, 'Proctor and Liberty' in their hats, they manned the narrow lanes to Brentford Butts. Weavers and butchers with cleavers backed Glynn. Rival gangs prowled the town. In an affray round the hustings, the chairmen attacked Glynn's supporters, and a young lawyer, George Clarke, was hit over the head. Friends helped him escape into Horne's vicarage nearby. At two o'clock in the morning Horne tracked down the culprits, Balfe and McQuirk, to an alehouse. He persuaded the night constable to arrest them and helped get them to Covent Garden roundhouse. Clarke died of his wounds a few days later. Matters got so badly out of hand that polling was suspended, Sawbridge and Townsend arriving dramatically in the House from Brentford to describe the scene. Six days later, when the poll recommenced, Glynn won a convincing victory with a majority of 264.[8]

Glynn offered a 20-guinea reward for information about Clarke's murder. Balfe and McQuirk were arraigned for assaulting a constable, and tried for murder at the Old Bailey. Although the jury found them guilty, they were given a royal pardon which increased anti-Government feeling. A pamphlet, 'An Appeal to the Public Touching the Death of George Clarke', was published under the name of the surgeon who had examined Clarke and reported that he died from a blow to the head. Except for the surgical evidence, it was written by Horne. It was a powerful indictment, culminating with the protest that people were reduced to slavery, living 'under laws which punish but do not protect'.[10]

1769 was a triumphant year for Wilkes's supporters and one of enormous activity for Horne. The first success was the election of Wilkes while in prison as alderman for the ward of Faringdon Without on 2 January. Wilkes now had official standing in the City, whose democratic elective system could be used to organise political agitation. Horne and his associates, keen to exploit the possibilities of the Middlesex victory, now formed Wilkes's supporters into a coherent party with a definite creed. Their weapon was public meetings – used as a method of expressing opinion and influencing the Government – at which petitions were drafted and signed. At a meeting of Middlesex electors on 12 January 1769, an important innovation was introduced: Wilkes and Glynn were given instructions by their constituents, the first attempt at drafting a political programme. Horne moved that they should endeavour to maintain the constitution and ensure trial by jury. Serjeant Adair, another Wilkite lawyer, moved that they must try to obtain justice for the murders at St George's Fields and Brentford. The third instruction asked for an enquiry into the Justices, to ensure that only firm, impartial men were elected. The fourth affirmed the right of the public to the revenue of the East India Company.[11]

The previous December, Wilkes had published a letter from Lord Weymouth, Secretary of State, to the Chairman of Lambeth quarter sessions, written before the affray of St George's Fields, which authorised the magistrates to use troops if necessary. Although Wilkes had not yet been condemned by any court, the House voted his action libellous and expelled him. On 16 February another election was held. No Government candidate appeared, but 2,000 freeholders went to Brentford in pouring rain to ensure that Wilkes should be returned. The House once more voted to expel him and declared that Wilkes was incapable of being elected. This raised a constitutional issue of considerable importance. The Government had played into Wilkes's hands. Men of standing, who thought Wilkes an unscrupulous adventurer, now felt they must oppose Parliament's questionable action.

Society of Supporters of the Bill of Rights

Wilkes's threatened bankruptcy endangered his position. Temple had helped Wilkes financially for many years, but after Wilkes, in spite of Temple's objections, insisted on sending a highly critical letter to Grenville about Lord Weymouth's actions, Temple never spoke to him again.[12] On 20 and 25 February, under Horne's auspices, meetings were held at the London Tavern at which the Society of Supporters of the Bill of Rights (SSBR) was founded by 20 of Wilkes's wealthier supporters. They thought he had suffered persecution on behalf of the public, so the public should rescue him from encumbrances, but some of them had a poor opinion of Wilkes and did not intend, as Wilkes later claimed, that their activity should be solely for his personal assistance. Horne was asked to draw up an advertisement for the newspapers stating that the society had been formed by 'Many gentlemen… unconnected with any party… to defend the legal and constitutional liberty of the subject. They mean to support Mr Wilkes and his cause, as far as it is a public cause.'[13] The SSBR was one of the first real political clubs. It placed the Wilkite movement on a solid basis and made it less dependent on the personality of Wilkes than it might otherwise have been. Its immediate purpose was to retrieve his finances, but in a few months it took up broader objectives.

Wilkes had incurred legitimate election expenses, but the members had no conception of the magnitude of his private liabilities. At the first meeting £3,023 was raised. Horne and Glynn then patiently sifted his creditors' innumerable claims. Although patrons had supported MPs before, it was Horne's original idea to support Wilkes through subscriptions. Funds came chiefly from SSBR members and their connections. When Wilkes left prison in April 1770, the society had discharged £12,000 debts, paid fines of £1,000, settled nearly £3,000 election expenses and given Wilkes £1,000 for personal expenditure. His remaining debts of nearly £7,000 were then compounded. In all, the society paid out about £20,000.[14]

By July the club had about 50 members. Some were MPs, others, like Horne, members of the rising professional classes. They included Sawbridge, Townsend, Glynn, Sir Joseph Mawbey Bt MP, a rich distiller and Dr Thomas Wilson, Rector of St Stephens Walbrooke. Robert Morris was one of several lawyers. There were City magnates: Sir William Stephenson, Townsend's father-in-law, Watkin Lewes, and Samuel Vaughan, a Unitarian friend of Horne's brother Benjamin, Frederick Bull and Richard Oliver. There were also a few country gentlemen whom Horne brought in: Sir Francis Delaval, Sir Cecil Wray MP and Sir Robert Bernard. Aged twenty-five, Bernard had been put in as MP for Huntingdon by the Duke of Manchester, but had quarrelled with the Duke and lost the seat in 1768. Bernard then adhered to Shelburne. The first treasurer was William Tooke, a Norfolk squire, later Horne's patron. Most of these men were still in their thirties, educated and independent-minded, many were to become Horne's friends and be connected with him in political agitation for years to come. Their aim was to release Parliament from what they saw as excessive Government control, their motives a combination of idealism and grievance which had crystallised round the Middlesex election. Some had American or other overseas interests, so disliked the Government's foreign policy. They knew that, however unsuitable, Wilkes was at the moment essential to their cause. Without his charisma it would founder.[15]

The Government now found someone foolhardy enough to oppose Wilkes, Colonel Henry Luttrell. Charles James Fox, at this time a vociferous supporter of the Ministry, canvassed for Luttrell, which may be one reason for his and Horne's lifelong antipathy. Once more the freeholders rode out to Brentford. In spite of a mounted escort, Luttrell only reached the hustings with the assistance of Townsend and Horne who rescued him from menacing crowds. Luttrell received 296 votes, Wilkes 1,143, but on 16 April the House resolved that, as Wilkes was ineligible, Luttrell was elected. The country was in an uproar; many independent MPs could not stomach the Luttrell affair.[14]

Horne became embroiled in a longstanding, shifting struggle between rival groups trying to control the City. This was complicated by Wilkes's intrusion. There was a faction adhering to the Court, one led by Rockingham and Burke who were only interested in forcing a dissolution of Parliament, and one by Chatham, since his illness directed by Shelburne, as well as Temple and the Grenvillites. They all disapproved of Wilkes. Chatham's chief ally in the City was Alderman William Beckford MP, a parvenu West Indian sugar-planter, who spoke with a broad cockney accent and enjoyed quoting Latin. Good-humoured, lacking judgement, he was a contradictory character, a passionate devotee of liberty, though owning many slave-run plantations. He disliked Wilkes and never joined the SSBR, but appreciated the need to back him. He dominated the popular party in the City. Under his leadership, the Wilkites worked in rough liaison with Chatham and Shelburne.

On 17 April, at a meeting of several thousand Middlesex freeholders, Townsend introduced a proposal from Horne for a committee to draw up a remonstrance to Parliament. Horne made a stirring speech, which was much applauded. He used a phrase frequently quoted against him by his opponents: he 'would rather see [his] black coat dyed red with blood than live to see slavery introduced'.[16]

The SSBR wanted to make Wilkes's disqualification the occasion for an onslaught on Government policies, but the Rockinghams insisted that protest must be limited to the single issue of the Middlesex election, so a cautious petition was presented to Parliament by the much-respected Yorkshire MP Sir George Savile. This did not satisfy the Middlesex freeholders who appointed a committee of Townsend, Sawbridge, Bellas (a City attorney) and Horne to consider the best means to obtain redress of grievances. They drafted a petition, a long catalogue of complaints skilfully worked up to paint a fearful picture of widespread injustice, ranging from general warrants, the murder of peaceful citizens, squandering of public funds, mismanagement of the American colonies, and the avoidance of habeas corpus and trial by jury. This was signed by 1,565. A month later the London livery elected Townsend and Sawbridge aldermen and sheriffs for the year, then adopted an even more strongly-worded petition. Both were presented to the King and received a chilly response.[17]

Horne and Sir Joseph Mawbey tried to get a similar petition adopted in Surrey, where Mawbey had an estate and Horne a small freehold farm, so they qualified as freeholders. Horne and Dr Joseph Allen, Master of Dulwich College, addressed a meeting at Epsom of nearly 2,000 freeholders, but as many country gentlemen, adherents of Rockingham, were present, the petition was rejected. Shelburne was in constant touch with Townsend and, on his instructions, Townsend and Shelburne's protégé Colonel Isaac Barré MP helped Horne tone it down, and a revised version was adopted. Although Horne was one of the ablest members of the SSBR, the Rockinghams found him too flamboyant and outspoken, a liability rather than an asset. After the Surrey meeting there were complaints of 'the warm proceedings of Messrs Horne, Bellas and others of the London Tavern... the generality of whose opinions and ideas I could not agree or subscribe to'. Rockingham wrote to Burke, 'I wish the zeal of Rev. Mr Horne may not have gone too far, and that the petition which will be presented will [not] be too much in the general vague and wild manner of the other two.'[18]

At this meeting Mawbey, whom Horace Walpole considered 'vain, noisy and foolish',[19] criticised the absent George Onslow, MP for Surrey. Onslow, a former friend of Wilkes, had accepted a Government post in 1765, been appointed Privy Councillor and granted a pension of £3,000. As he had carried Parliament's resolution for Luttrell's election he was anathema to the Wilkites. Horne, always on the look-out for a specific enemy to attack, taunted Onslow in his customary defiant style: he had hoped to see Onslow at the meeting, when he would have told him to his face that he was a man incapable of keeping his word. If Onslow would lay aside his privilege he (Horne) would lay aside his gown. 'Onslow never spake a word of truth but for his interest.'[20]

In a letter signed 'Another freeholder of Surrey' published in the *Public Advertiser* on 11 July 1769, Horne insinuated that Onslow had accepted a £1,000 bribe for obtaining a lucrative post in America for a Mr Burns. This was the culmination of a venomous press campaign against Onslow which stung him to reply. He disclaimed any knowledge of the transaction, said his name had been used to hoodwink a foolish man into paying out money, and threatened a libel action. On 24 August, Onslow started a civil action which came up the following year.[20,21]

Horne led a foray to Bedford which alarmed the Rockinghams almost as much as it annoyed the Ministry. The Duke of Bedford, as hereditary Recorder, controlled the Corporation and the election of its officials. His negotiation of the peace treaty and his alliance with Grafton had made him extremely unpopular. The Corporation wanted to break its dependence on the Duke and chose Sir Robert Bernard, who had large estates in Huntingdonshire, to be their patron. At Bedford, where householders, burgesses and freemen had the vote, burgesses and freemen did not need to be residents. Furthermore, the Corporation could by ancient right make honorary freemen. Bernard and Horne seized their opportunity. They hoped to establish a precedent for a general revolt against borough patrons. On 4 September 1769, at a meeting in the Town Hall, the Corporation voted in as freemen a number of Bernard's Huntingdon tenants and London associates, including Townsend and Horne. The Duke tried to prevent this as he would lose control of the borough. When the names of the popular candidates were read he restrained himself until it came to Horne, then could contain himself no longer: if they admitted such a man as that, all was over. Horne was a man that would let no-one be quiet either in his country or his borough; he was 'the cause of all the disturbances in Middlesex, London, Surrey and the whole kingdom, stirrer of sedition, a restless turbulent spirit'. Horne was elected by 17-11. Popular candidates defeated the Duke's nominees for Mayor and other officers. Junius, who had recently begun his famous series of letters attacking the Government, observed that the Duke 'tried his whole strength against Mr Horne and was beat upon his own ground'.[22]

Wilkes was not at all pleased with the activities of his supporters, whose energy he considered should be concentrated on himself. Horne's advertisement for the SSBR, emphasising that their cause was a public one, had annoyed him. In May there were hints in the newspapers that some of Wilkes's supporters, 'having ascended by his popularity', did not want to be connected any longer 'with the irregularities and follies of his life'.[23]

During the first year of Wilkes's imprisonment he and Horne appear to have worked harmoniously together on public and private affairs. Wilkes rebuked Garrick when he pointedly referred on stage to a 'meddling priest who kindles up confusion'. Political friendships are often ephemeral. Wilkes and Horne never became intimate. Wilkes was intolerant and self-absorbed, preferring to be surrounded by docile satellites rather than anyone as demanding as Horne. By now Horne had got to know sincere reformers such as Sawbridge far better than he had ever known Wilkes. As Wilkes's charm wore thin, Horne began to view his egocentricity with contempt. Wilkes was understandably annoyed by Horne's constant reminders that his most generous supporters disapproved of his 'lace, liveries and French servants'. He complained that whenever Horne appeared he cast a gloom over his jolly parties, and ridiculed Horne's 'lack-laughter sangfroid'. Horne himself admitted that 'the sincerity with which I always spoke disagreeable truths to Mr Wilkes has entitled me to a considerable share of his resentment. I… warmly combated those… of his partisans who endeavoured to narrow the society (SSBR) to a sponge which should suck up the generosity of the public to be squeezed into his pocket.'[24] Horne had imagined him to be more altruistic than he had ever pretended to be. Wilkes was a remarkable character, an opportunist who gained great popularity among plebeian Londoners for his effrontery and skill in putting down the authorities. They were unaffected by his habit of running up debts he had no intention of paying. He was indifferent to most of the issues which concerned Horne and his comrades and not, as he himself said, a 'Wilkite'. He was neither the stuff political leaders are made of, nor willing to be a docile figurehead.

In 1769 Horne published one of his sermons, entitled 'The Faithless Desertion of Friends, the Insensibility shown to the Misfortune of Others'. It had a personal bearing on Wilkes, and was so understood by him. Horne's text was taken from Psalm LV: 'It was not an open enemy that hath done me this dishonour, for then I could have born it. But it was even thou, my companion, my guide and my own familiar friend.' He gloomily advised men to put no confidence in man, whose friendship fails; God alone is faithful. Well written in plain, clear English, it was a typical example of the conventional religious writings of the day. It received tepid reviews yet went into many editions.[25]

Horne was accused of trying to climb to fame on Wilkes's back. There were satirical references to the Bishopric of Brentford, cartoons of 'Parson Horne' in gown and bands with a defective eye, receiving inspiration from the devil. Junius referred to 'the solitary vindictive malice of a monk'.[26] When Wilkes made public Horne's incautious comments on his ordination in his letter from Montpelier, Horne's reply revealed his feelings: 'I thought it proper to inform you that I was only a poor country clergyman, whose situation, notwithstanding his zeal, would never enable him to perform any considerable service to you or the public. I disclaimed in a joking manner those views which, from the dependent situation of its professors, are too frequently attendant on it... hypocrisy, servility, and an abject attention to private interest.'[27]

During the winter Chatham emerged from retirement and attacked the Government. Grafton and his colleagues, who had taken office as Chatham's friends in 1766, resigned. Lord North took over; he was to remain in power for the next 12 years. Chatham renewed his alliance with Shelburne, but as he and his followers were a small group he made peace with Rockingham whose support he needed. Horne continued to work closely with Beckford, Sawbridge and Townsend. They evolved a moderate reform programme, approved by Shelburne. Retaining the connection between representation and property, it had three main points: shorter parliaments, a Place and Pensions Bill and more equal representation of the people. There were frequent meetings over dinner in Mawbey's house or at Shelburne's in Berkeley Square. Through his brother, Horne had a long-standing acquaintance with Shelburne whom at this time he greatly admired.

It is difficult to assess how much of the policy of the City patriots and Middlesex freeholders was initiated by Horne. He certainly wrote, or knocked into shape, most of their official utterances. He voiced his opinions forcefully, was more intelligent than the majority of his colleagues and had considerable influence over them. According to Wilkes, Sawbridge's 'Sherifallty passed in a continued secret cabal of Beckford, Townsend and Horne', which told Sawbridge nothing 'till the moment of execution'. All the same, Horne considered himself a very junior partner. When attacked by Junius, he said he knew of no reason but his 'zeal and industry in the same cause' which would entitle him 'to the honour of being ranked with persons of the fortune and station of Sawbridge, Townsend, Oliver etc'.[28]

They embarked on a campaign against the King's refusal to dissolve Parliament. In consultation with Shelburne, they produced an Address, Remonstrance and Petition. The City had the right to approach the King in person with petitions, so on 14 March

1770 the Lord Mayor, sheriffs and City officers went in procession from Guildhall to St James accompanied by a huge crowd. The remonstrance claimed that the Ministry was affected by a secret malign influence, and demanded a new parliament. The King angrily replied that this was disrespectful to him, injurious to Parliament and irreconcilable to the principles of the constitution.

Next, Beckford organised a Mansion House banquet at which he hoped to persuade Chatham, Rockingham and Grenville to subscribe to his reform programme. He asked Horne to draw up a draft 'couched in cautious and precise terms which would leave no room for evasion'. When the Rockinghams heard of this, they objected. Beckford then said 'they should eat none of his broth', but was persuaded to change his mind. It was extremely difficult for the popular party to secure the co-operation of the opposition groups inside Parliament. Chatham would not commit himself because it would limit his power to manoeuvre with the Rockinghams. The Whigs were unwilling to support any demand for parliamentary reform. Burke hated the SSBR, 'a mere club of tradesmen', and referred to the 'infinite mischief of that rotten subdivision of a faction among ourselves... The Bill of Rights People'.[29]

On 30 March 1770 Horne made a speech to the Middlesex freeholders, later published as a pamphlet, which was a remarkable *tour de force*. On arrival, Horne and Sawbridge had been greeted with cheers by a huge crowd outside and in the Mile End Assembly rooms. Adair was late. When Sawbridge, who took the chair, asked if anyone had a proposal, there was dead silence, so Horne stepped into the breach and spoke off the cuff with his usual energy. He said that after the City representatives had been insulted by the King and Court, sullen resentment had taken possession of his mind. He had intended to take leave of the freeholders. Indeed why should they meet? 'For it is a mockery to call us freeholders... the people of this country... cease to have any share in government. Rights and power which the constitution has placed in their hands are either forgotten or denied... Parliament is notoriously at the disposal of the Minister, the Minister at the mercy and pleasure of the Crown.' Horne contrasted the treatment in the courts of those protected with those attacked by the Government. 'The two most effectual engines of government are punishment and reward.' Ministers had pushed corruption combined with violence beyond all bounds. 'The power of reward... is more fatal than that of punishment, and it has become as necessary to curb... the exercise of the one as it was formerly of the other.' Horne had the audience roaring with laughter at his amusing account of his forthcoming legal battle with Onslow. He pointed out that 'The true friends of liberty are not lawless and disorderly, as they are represented to be; but they are the best friends to the laws; for they know the laws are the people's strong weapons in which they trust'.[30]

Legal Actions

The Wilkites wanted to ensure that those who administered the laws were answerable through the law for their actions, and that the law worked for the benefit of all sections of society. They were able to attract considerable support from middling people discontented with British justice which appeared to favour the powerful and affluent; in Horne's oft-quoted phrase, 'The hand of the law is on the poor, its shadow on the rich'.[31] The Wilkites believed that strict adherence to the common law preserved the subject's rights. Their lawyer allies Camden, Dunning and Glynn were worried by its current interpretation, particularly by Mansfield. 'Happy for us,' declared Horne, 'if the common law he despises had known as little of Lord Mansfield as he does of the common law'. For, since he presided in the Court of King's Bench, 'those extraordinary discretionary powers which the equity of former judges had rarely ventured to exercise... he has brought into common use... bailing murderers, granting new trials, setting jurymen aside'.[30]

'The Law,' said Judge Ashhurst, 'is open to all men,' to which Horne retorted, 'And so is the London Tavern, but they will give you a very sorry welcome, unless you come with money sufficient to pay for your entertainment'. He would take up any case where the law had been, in his opinion, unfairly administered. He became renowned as 'a walking depository of grievances', the champion of those unjustly punished, the assailant of those who escaped due punishment.[32]

Although Horne was unable to use the platform of the courts as lawyer members of SSBR did, he used his legal skills. He initiated an attempt to help two Spitalfield weavers. The master weavers had reduced rates of pay, so the journeymen formed a combination to oppose this and to collect strike funds. At night they damaged looms of men and masters who resisted. On 30 September 1769 troops invested a public house where contributions were being collected. According to the official account, weavers attacked the soldiers. Be that as it may, the result was one soldier and two weavers dead, and more weavers wounded. Many weavers were arrested and two of their leaders, Doyle and Valline, condemned to death. The prisoners had been sentenced to be taken 'to the usual place of execution'. The order was varied by the Recorder, to be read 'in the most convenient place near Bethnal Green Church'. This was to intimidate the weavers by holding the execution in the centre of their quarter. Horne discovered that an alteration in the wording of the death sentence was illegal. He claimed it would therefore be murder if the warrant were adhered to.

Horne persuaded Sawbridge and Townsend, in their capacity as sheriffs, to write to Lord Weymouth who postponed execution. Lord Camden referred the case to 12 judges. Horne produced notes citing Coke and previous cases, but his efforts were unsuccessful. On 6 December, Doyle and Valline, protesting their innocence to the last, were hanged before a huge crowd. Still, due to the questions raised, executions were in future limited to the authorised place. The letters Horne composed show his extensive knowledge of legal theory and practice.[33]

Wilkes now achieved a great triumph. In the long-postponed action arising from the use of general warrants, on 11 November 1769 he was awarded £4,000 damages against the two secretaries of state, the Earls of Egremont and Halifax, who had authorised his arrest. In addition, the Assembly of South Carolina sent the SSBR £1,500 from its public treasury 'for the support of the constitutional rights and liberties of the people of Great Britain and America'. The King was furious, and the Royal Governor had a bitter argument with the Carolina legislature. The SSBR's letter of thanks, agreed after objections by Wilkes, included the provocative statement 'our cause is one, our enemies are the same'.[34] These large sums of money increased friction between Wilkes and some members of the SSBR, including Horne. Wilkes thought the money should be for his personal use, they thought it should be put into the Society's coffers. The Society kept the

American donation. Wilkes paid off his debt to the Buckingham militia, then stuck firmly to the rest of Lord Halifax's £4,000.

Onslow's suit against Horne came on at Kingston on 6 April 1770. Onslow complained about two letters. Glynn, who defended Horne, raised certain legal technicalities. The original of one letter was missing. The printed version of the other did not tally exactly with the original. The case was therefore nonsuited. The inhabitants of Kingston rang the church bells all day in celebration. A new trial was brought in the King's Bench on 1 August before Lord Mansfield, on the grounds of misdirection on the part of the judge. This time Horne was also charged with using defamatory words before the freeholders at the meeting in Surrey. Horne did not plead his own cause, but worked out strategy in consultation with Glynn. Glynn maintained that it was improper to prosecute a constituent at a political meeting for making a charge openly, to which Onslow could reply if innocent; that the words were not actionable unless specific damages were proved, and that the evidence respecting the letters was insufficient. Mansfield overplayed his hand. In a very strong charge to the jury he emphasised the great impropriety of the various accusations, and declared that a defamatory libel had been uttered by the defendant. He reiterated his opinion, strongly opposed by the popular party, that in libel cases it was for the judge not the jury to decide whether the matter complained of was libellous or not. The jury acquitted Horne over the letters, but for his words at Epsom gave a verdict for the plaintiff with £400 damages.

Horne appealed to a superior tribunal. On 26 November the case was argued before 12 judges. Glynn claimed that Mansfield had misdirected the jury. This was a very important legal point, so judgement was deferred. On 17 April 1771, in the Court of Common Pleas, the judges unanimously declared in favour of Horne, a great triumph, as he had superintended the proceedings. Horne's statement 'Should Mr Onslow promise his assistance I will not believe him' was judged to be not libellous as it was only a statement of opinion. Onslow's costs came to £1,500, Horne's to £200, a large sum for a poor man to find in those days. Exceptionally heavy wagers were laid in the London clubs on the outcome of the trial. Junius had prophesied correctly to Woodfall, the printer of much radical literature, that 'Onslow would get nothing but shame by contending with Mr Horne'.[35,21] This case gave Horne confidence and a reputation, the first of several fencing matches with the distinguished lawyer as judge and Horne as defendant, at which Horne took every opportunity to oppose Mansfield and denigrate his talents. In future, he adopted an intrepid attitude of equality with judges whenever he appeared in court.

Notes on Chapter 2

1 Stephens I, pp 85-7
2 *Controversial Letters of John Wilkes and Rev. John Horne*, pp 34-5
3 Stephens I, pp 94-9
4 Hickey, p 57; *English Liberty* I, pp 289-348
5 Wilkes, *English Liberty* I, pp 358-72
6 *Annual Register* II, p 127, 1768
7 Wilkes-Horne, *Letters*, p 149
8 *Oxford Magazine* 1, pp 238-41, 1768; *Political Register* IV, pp 36, 62-4, 1769; Stephens I, p 106; *English Liberty* II, pp 12-37
9 Brougham, *Historical Sketches* III, p 138
10 Yarborough, p 39; *Political Register* IV, pp 105-8, 1769
11 *Political Register* IV, p 73, 1769
12 *English Liberty* II, pp 303-16
13 Wilkes-Horne, *Letters*, pp 150, 156-60
14 Watson, p 136; Wilkes, *Correspondence* IV, pp 7-9
15 Christie p 33; Stephens I, p 163; Bleakley, p 243
16 *London Chronicle* XXV, p 366, 1769.
17 *Oxford Magazine* II, pp 197, 265, 1769
18 Sir A. Abdy to Sir G. Colebrook, *Rockingham Papers* R1/1204, 1.7.69; Burke, *Correspondence* II, p 36; *Public Advertiser* 28.6.69
19 Walpole, *Memoirs* III, p 175
20 Stephens I, pp 121-37
21 The whole proceedings in the cause on the action brought by G. Onslow against the Rev. Mr Horne. J. Gurney, 1770
22 Stephens I, p 107; *Oxford Magazine* III, p 101, 1769; Junius XXIII 119n; *Public Advertiser* Sept. 6, 8, 12, 19, 27, 1769; *Annual Register* 1769, p 128
23 *Gazetteer* 15.5.69
24 Wilkes-Horne, *Letters*, p 153
25 Horne, Sermon; Stephens I, pp 116-20
26 Junius L, p 253; George M.D., IV 4225, 6, 4863 etc.

27 Wilkes-Horne, *Letters*, p 32
28 Junius 415, Wilkes to Junius; LIII p 268, Horne to Junius
29 Portland MSS Burke to Portland 22.4.70. Burke, *Correspondence* II, p 150
30 Horne J., Middlesex Oration, March 30 1770
31 Rogers *Recollections*, p 148
32 Blackwoods XXXIII, p 969, 1833; Walker, *Review*, p 88
33 Stephens I, pp 108-14; Genuine copies of all letters... relative to the execution of Doyle and Valine., ed. J. Horne, 1770, *Annual Register* XII, pp 136, 154, 159-60, 1769
34 *Annual Register* XIII p 225, 1770
35 *London Chronicle* XXVIII, pp 113, 141, 516, 1770; XXIX, p 378; *Blackwoods* XXXIII, p 970, 1833; Junius, p 352

Chapter Three

Quarrels with Wilkes and Junius

Horne says that Wilkes, a vile blasphemer
Has ridiculed his dear Redeemer
John Wilkes affirms that Parson Horne
Treats e'en the name of God with scorn
Strange that such bickerings there should be
Twixt atheism and blasphemy.[1]

In April 1770 Wilkes was released from prison to a jubilant welcome from his many admirers. Thanks to the SSBR, who had met every day for the previous week to ensure that his outstanding debts were settled, he was for the time being financially solvent. As he was still excluded from Parliament, he decided to concentrate on gaining control of the City's political machinery.

At the end of April the popular party had an important success, when Bernard was elected MP for Westminster. The Rockinghams supported him in an attempt to bolster their influence in London which had diminished with the return of Wilkes, the people's hero.

Beckford and Horne drew up a more moderate remonstrance which Beckford presented to the King on 23 May. The petitioners complained that Middlesex had been deprived of one of its representatives. Again they implored the King to dissolve Parliament and remove his evil ministers. George III had decided on his reply in advance: he would not deserve to be considered the father of his people if he granted a dissolution which would be an improper exercise of his prerogative. Beckford then took the unprecedented step of answering the startled King. The City officers retired delighted with his bold action which created a nationwide sensation. Beckford died three weeks later, and the City voted unanimously to erect a statue with his speech engraved in gold on the pedestal; this still stands in the Guildhall. The inscription is identical to the version circulated by Horne to the press, according to which Beckford had assured the King of the City's loyalty and begged him not to dismiss them without some comfort or prospect of redress.[2] Dunning, Glynn, Horne and Barré waited anxiously at a tavern for Beckford's return: Beckford was honest, blunt, ignorant, a bold man much given to swearing. When Beckford came in, he confessed he had spoken to the King but was so damnably confused he could not remember the details. Horne said this would not do, took a pen and produced a polished version of Beckford's halting recollection. He read it aloud and asked if Beckford had any objection to it. 'None at all,' he replied.[3]

Beckford's sudden death left the City without a strong unifying leader. It deprived Chatham of his chief liaison officer and gave Wilkes more power. For a time Sawbridge, Townsend and Horne continued to co-operate with Wilkes, often dining together to discuss tactics. Trecothick, a follower of Rockingham, temporarily replaced Beckford as Mayor; Oliver, a dark, lively little man, son of a Leeward Island judge, protégé of Sawbridge and friend of Horne, was elected to both Beckford's aldermanship and his parliamentary seat.

There were ominous signs of a split among the Wilkites. Wilkes was trying to place his relations and followers in lucrative City posts. An uneasy truce continued over his finances. Some SSBR members thought enough had been done for him and talked of quitting. On 4 September Morris, the secretary, resigned. Oliver was reputed to be jealous of Wilkes for trying to buy power with donations. Horne's relationship with Wilkes was deteriorating fast. The dominant personality of the SSBR, since Wilkes's release he had been relegated from virtual leadership. Wilkes, as intelligent as Horne and more astute, had been delighted for Horne to promote his cause, but did not want him to remodel it. In the *Public Advertiser*'s words, 'There cannot be two Kings at Brentford'. Neither would brook contradiction. Both wanted fame, though by different means. Horne, who had expected too much of Wilkes, was bitterly disillusioned, embittered by his financial irresponsibility and lack of interest in anything but his own career. 'We seldom did concur in any measure, except in those which tended to his private advantage.' On public matters 'our opinions have been… as different as our aims'.[4]

The open breach between Wilkes and Horne began after a mass meeting of the Westminster electors on 31 October 1770, chaired by Wilkes, who proposed that their MPs should be given instructions to impeach Lord North. Unlike Horne, Wilkes was a poor public speaker. He was totally inaudible, handled the meeting ineptly, and invited onto the platform a heckler who got the better of him. Sawbridge pointed out that it would be ridiculous to impeach North as he had a majority in both Houses and there were no grounds for doing so. He proposed yet another remonstrance. Wilkes made several attempts to get a vote for instructions, but in the end the remonstrance was carried by a large majority, a blow to his prestige. Horne sent a mildly derogatory account of Wilkes's performance to the newspapers. Wilkes then published his version, denying that he had attempted, as Horne implied, to dictate to the electors. Horne was always ready to rush into battle with his pen; this time he had taken on an adversary more experienced and skilful than himself.[5]

On 12 November Horne published an unsigned letter beginning, 'I find myself in a situation which most of your friends have at some time or other experienced. It is painful to me, but not surprising. I have long foreseen it, and most earnestly endeavoured to avoid it.' Wilkes took up the challenge, complaining of the 'baseness and treachery of subtle, designing and insidious friends'. He insinuated that Horne had misappropriated funds he had assiduously collected for Glynn's election, the Spitalfield weavers and other causes, plus profits from the pamphlet about Clarke's death. There was no justification for these accusations, but Wilkes astutely infuriated Horne by turning the tables and denouncing him for financial dishonesty.[6]

After Christmas, Horne defended himself in a long letter: he had never been a candidate for honour or profit, he had canvassed many votes for others, none for himself. Wilkes then accused

Horne of belonging to the SSBR though contributing not a penny. Horne was bound to make a case against Wilkes's jibes or forfeit credit with the public. He refuted Wilkes's charges, contriving to sound resentful and self-righteous: 'I have been… the drudge of almost every popular election and prosecution… For three years past my time has been entirely and my income almost wholly applied to public measures.' The profits of all the pieces he had written amounted to £66 4s 1d, not sufficient to furnish Wilkes with two months' supply of claret. Many of Horne's colleagues, including Glynn and the printer of the pamphlet, published testimonies vindicating him. Wilkes replied briefly, then the controversy lay dormant.[7]

Townsend and Horne had meetings with Shelburne at Townsend's home. Wilkes dubbed them Shelburne's banditti, his creatures who hoped he would give them places. Shelburne had a difficult personality. He was arrogant, unable to communicate satisfactorily with others, and widely believed to be devious, hypocritical and untrustworthy, hence his nickname 'Malagrida', said to have been coined by Wilkes (Malagrida was a Portuguese Jesuit who had been executed for suspected treason in 1761). Shelburne's unpopularity rubbed off on Horne.

Meanwhile there had been ructions at the fortnightly meetings of the SSBR. Wilkes pressed for a lump sum, but the society was only willing to give him an annuity. Some members were exasperated that Wilkes accepted their generosity as his due and never produced a satisfactory explanation for all his debts. No sooner had one bill been settled than another was produced. Wilkes asked why Horne belonged to a society whose aim was to settle his debts. Words ran high. Horne declared that the Society had not been formed to enable Wilkes to live as a charge on the prudent and industrious.

At a meeting on 1 December Wilkes's brother Heaton had been so rude to Townsend that Sawbridge said he would move for his expulsion if he did not apologise. After Wilkes left, Horne was reported to have abused him for an hour and a half. Wilkes worked hard to pack the next neeting. As a result, 16 of Wilkes's followers came who had hardly ever attended before. Wilkes declared he would lay down his life in the public cause, Horne that his principles were as disinterested as Wilkes's, and that he had never received sixpence for being a patriot. A motion that the society should approve Wilkes's conduct was carried by a small majority. At this Horne said they might as well expel him and suggested Wilkes himself should draw up the resolution. This stroke of humour was little appreciated.[8] To test Wilkes's supporters Horne then moved that, as this was what they wanted, a subscription should immediately be opened for Wilkes's outstanding debts. The motion was carried but none subscribed.

On 12 February 1771 Horne raised the question of financial help for a printer, William Bingley, who had been prosecuted for publishing in the *North Briton* a letter from Wilkes criticising the courts of justice. As there was insufficient evidence to obtain a conviction, Lord Mansfield, who resented libellous attacks on his judicial career, had adopted a novel procedure. He had tried to get Bingley's confession of guilt by appointing a day on which he was to answer questions tending to incriminate him, or be committed for contempt. Encouraged by Horne, who took up this means of opposing Mansfield with alacrity, Bingley refused to answer questions, and was imprisoned by arbitrary mandate of 'attachment' on 7 November 1768. Having studied legal precedents, Horne was confident he could prove Mansfield's action illegal. He encouraged Bingley to resist and drew attention in the press to a potentially iniquitous practice.

Some of the most generous subscribers to the SSBR were keen to help Bingley and other printers who had suffered harassment and heavy fines for publishing the *North Briton* and articles by Wilkes. In spite of opposition from Wilkes's supporters (Wilkes himself was not present) a motion was passed that a subscription should be opened to raise £500 for Bingley, now in his third year of imprisonment, and half the money was immediately subscribed. Mansfield eventually gave way and instructed the Attorney General to discharge Bingley. Due largely to the publicity Horne obtained for the case, a law was later passed putting an end to interrogations by which men could be obliged to incriminate themselves.[9]

Horne's victory was short-lived. Wilkes rallied his supporters, and at the next meeting a motion was carried that no new subscriptions should be undertaken until all his debts had been paid. Horne protested that, leaving aside the fact that Bingley had suffered as much for the cause as Wilkes, it was essential that the printers should know they had the Society's backing.

Trouble was brewing over press reports of parliamentary debates, and he had devised a scheme by which, with the printers' help, they could outwit the Ministry and bring this struggle over freedom of the press into the open.[10] By standing order of the Commons proceedings could not be published, but this was tacitly ignored, and most newspapers now carried accounts. The audacious scheme involved a conflict between the privileges of Parliament and the City, the latter maintaining the right under its charters to all jurisdiction, and therefore responsibility for keeping law and order within its boundaries. Horne hoped that Parliament could be enticed by the printers' defiance to order their arrest. If the printers took refuge in the City it would be illegal to arrest them, and anyone attempting to do so could be charged by the City magistrates. Because the co-operation of aldermen sitting as magistrates was needed, differences in the SSBR were temporarily papered over.

On 5 February Colonel George Onslow, supported by his cousin the George Onslow who had sued Horne, drew the Commons' attention to misleading reports of their debates and raised a motion to enforce prohibition of their publication. Some editors desisted, others continued. Horne placed an offensive piece in the *Gazetteer* and *Middlesex Journal* which criticised Colonel Onslow's action and referred to him as 'little cocking George'.[11] On 8 February the offending printers were ordered to attend the House. Wheble of the *Middlesex Journal*, primed by Horne, ignored the order, and went into hiding. Thompson of the *Gazetteer* did go to Parliament, but when the matter was postponed, he then disappeared. Messengers were sent daily into the City to find the two men without success, so finally on 9 March a royal proclamation was issued offering £50 reward for their arrest. The Government had fallen into the carefully-prepared trap.

Horne told Wheble that he must be patient. They had already gained greatly by the delay, for the House had now issued an illegal proclamation. Wheble, however, became apprehensive. Taking advantage of this, Wilkes called on him every day, made out that he had been abandoned by Horne, and threatened that if Wheble did not co-operate now Wilkes would do nothing for him later. Finally, without telling Horne, Wheble agreed to work with Wilkes.

On 15 March, Wheble was arrested by his own compositor, Carpenter, and taken to the Guildhall, where Wilkes was conveniently officiating as sitting magistrate. Wilkes denied the legal authority of the proclamation. Carpenter was charged with assault, but granted a certificate of arrest so that he could claim the reward from the Treasury. The enraged Commons sent messengers to seize the other missing printers and bring them before the bar of the House. Thompson was arrested and dealt with by Oliver in the same way as Wheble. The comedy was completed when a Commons messenger, trying to arrest another of the printers, was given in charge for assault and only released by Lord Mayor Crosby after bail had been provided by the Deputy Serjeant at Arms.[12]

Crosby, Oliver and Wilkes were summoned to Parliament to answer for their conduct. Wilkes declined to attend unless summoned as MP for Middlesex. Lord North avoided trouble by ordering him to attend on a day when Parliament would not be sitting. Oliver and Crosby were accompanied by huge crowds to Westminster, then committed to the Tower for the rest of the session. Many outside the patriot faction supported them, angry at the flouting of ancient City rights. On 8 May, when Parliament was prorogued, they were released with a salute of 21 guns and conducted to the City in triumph.

Technically, Parliament did not give way, but the House tacitly abandoned claims to control reporting, a process helped when MPs, who became increasingly keen to gain public support, began to give the text of their speeches to the press. This was an important victory, for which Wilkes received nearly all the credit. The plan, which Horne claimed and others corroborated was his, certainly bears the hallmarks of his inventive mind.[13]

On 9 April the largest SSBR meeting ever held took place, a trial of strength between Wilkes and Horne and their supporters. There were fierce altercations. Horne dubbed Wilkes selfish, malignant, fraudulent. Wilkes said Horne's conduct was not consistent with the truth of a clergyman or the faith and honour of a gentleman. Horne complained that public interest was absorbed in the petty faction of one individual. He moved that the society be dissolved. Both parties, sure of victory, put dissolution to the vote. There were 24 for, 26 against; two absentees had authorised Townsend to remove their names from the society. Horne, accompanied by Sir Francis Delaval, Sir Robert Bernard, William Tooke and other dissidents, retired to another room and formed a new society, the Constitutional, to exist only on the public ground. Those who remained were Wilkes's faithful henchmen, few of whom were men of note.[14]

Someone less intransigent than Horne might have avoided the split, but the fact that he was supported by the most influential members is proof that his criticism was largely justified. Failure to achieve the Society's dissolution was a defeat for Horne and his colleagues. The two societies coexisted for a few years, one dominated by Wilkes, the other by Horne; Wilkes was favoured by the Rockinghams, while Horne and his friends liaised with Chatham and Shelburne. Wilkes had more *panache*, his rivals more disinterested zeal.

In May 1771 Horne published two articles on electoral reform in the *North Briton*. His ideas were sensible, moderate and concisely set out. They were extended in a later pamphlet in 1782 (see pp 77-79). His starting-point was the arbitrary action of parliamentary committees in settling disputed elections, particularly the replacement of Wilkes by Luttrell, tantamount to disenfranchisement of the constituency. Most disputes were on grounds of bribery and what was the use of such committees when many of their members had entered the House through corrupt means? 'Disputes should be decided by the interpreters of the law, the Courts of Justice.' Liberty could only be preserved if the constitution were re-established on first principles, this entailing more equitable representation and the removal of temptations to bribery. The number of qualified residents in a district was the best basis on which to determine the number of their representatives. This could be adjusted according to population changes.

Horne did not advocate universal suffrage, though he thought that the labouring poor, who carried a heavy burden of taxes, should have more say in government. The apparent reason for a property qualification was that it presupposed the owner had some education and regard for the country in which he had a stake. On this basis, electoral rights should not be confined to the landed interest, since other 'personal property lays the possessor under as great an obligation to be a good citizen. Not all the... wealthy traders, as such, have one representative in Parliament.' There was also a new factor, stockholders. A revolution might not affect a landholder but would probably ruin stockholders. In spite of its drawbacks, Horne thought property the best qualification, provided personal property was included. As it would be odious and difficult to go into a person's precise circumstances, he proposed that the voter should have rented a house or land of a certain value for a certain time and paid scot and lot (local poor rate and church taxes levied on householders). Qualification for a member should be real estate of a certain value, and disqualification any place or pension from the Crown.

Horne suggested the admirable innovation of simultaneous voting at different places in each constituency as a deterrent to electoral rioting. Parliaments should be annual, so that bribery on a large scale would not be worthwhile. There would be no need to dread troublesome contested elections, for with so many voters and such frequent elections people would lose interest. They might 'fall into the opposite extreme and leave elections to be managed by a… busy few', who might think it best to return the sitting member. He shrewdly foresaw that democratic representation can breed inertia, but did not go into the question being debated by the City radicals: should a member vote as he saw fit, or must he follow his constituents' wishes and, if he refused, lose their support? Extension of the vote to a much larger section of the population was the main goal of his scheme. He was not sanguine that it would be adopted, but it was practicable. He left 'others to improve on the hints and carry it into execution or consign it', like other 'well-intended Utopian schemes… into the limbo large and broad far distant, call'd the Paradise of Fools'.[15]

Correspondence with Wilkes

Meanwhile Wilkes and Horne and their supporters spent much energy warring with each other for City places. Wilkes announced his intention to stand for Sheriff. He tried to detach Oliver from Horne and Townsend, suggesting he should run in tandem with him as Under-Sheriff. Oliver, who disliked Wilkes, sent a curt refusal: Wilkes's political aims were incompatible with his own. Horne determined to put Oliver up as rival candidate. The two tribunes of the plebs therefore fought a campaign not only against the Court party but against each other.

Goaded by further accusations of theft and stinging references to his clerical poverty, Horne reopened his correspondence with Wilkes. This proved a fatal mistake. Besides vindicating himself, Horne wanted to put a stop to Wilkes's misuse of the popular party's cause. 'You are a public man; and it is necessary… that the public should be told, since nothing can restrain you… into what destruction and disgrace… you would plunge them.' For the next two months the reading public was diverted and shocked by their virulent exchanges. As Horace Walpole remarked, 'Wilkes and Parson Horne have a civil war between themselves and no one insists upon one's lighting up candles for either'.[16]

For the only time in his career, Horne lost control of his temper. By employing indignation rather than mockery, he appeared a rancorous curmudgeon while Wilkes, though proved to have adopted dubious shifts to avoid duns, emerged the more attractive personality. Instead of concentrating on a few important matters where Wilkes had been in the wrong, such as his hypocrisy over Bingley and his applications for pensions from successive governments, Horne launched into petty grievances and old charges, for example that he had embezzled the funds of the Foundling Hospital, committed a breach of trust with the Bucks Militia, cheated the Jew Da Silva and swindled French jewellers. In the surprising guise of a righteous puritan he enumerated Wilkes's expensive tastes in laced liveries, French servants and watering places. In Junius's words, 'What a pitiful detail, some old clothes, a Welch pony, a French footman and a hamper of claret.'[17]

In return, Wilkes raked up Horne's philandering in Genoa, harped on his clerical profession: 'the parson's dull, monotonous disapproval'; or conversely the whist-playing priest. He mocked Horne's penchant for retailing his sacrifices for the cause, 'the tedious Brentford preacher's… fulsome accounts of his meritorious actions'.

Wilkes insinuated – deadly blow – that through Demainbray Horne was being bribed by the Court.[18] Horne's response reveals how hurtful this jibe was: 'Without having received the slightest favour from any party or great man in administration or opposition, I could not foresee that, by all my labour… and expense, I should gain the contradictory imputation of being… the hireling of the one, and the tool of the other: and that Mr Wilkes, the only private gainer in the struggle, should, of all men in the world, be the person to bring the charge against me'.

Long ago Wilkes had threatened to publish Horne's letter from Montpelier. Now he cruelly doled it out in instalments. The derogatory remarks about bishops, coupled with Horne's notorious statement about dyeing his black coat red, ensured that he was labelled a licentious renegade cleric who had disgraced his cloth. Wilkes could jeer that Horne had been injured by his own letter: 'Scorpionlike you have stung yourself to death'. Horne objected that 'The extracts you have meanly made from my letter had not the least relation to anything in discussion; you gave them merely to injure me in my profession: it was needless'. Though he had determined 'to be as prudent as I could… I gave up all hopes of preferment from the moment I… embarked in the public cause'.[19]

The correspondence dragged on for weeks. With a puff for his sufferings in exile, Wilkes reminded Horne that it must end on midsummer day when he expected to be elected Sheriff. The election came on. Wilkes had found a docile running-mate in Frederick Bull, now an alderman. They easily defeated the Court candidates. Oliver was nowhere. That evening Horne's effigy in canonical habit was carried round the City and burnt before the Mansion House.[20] Horne wrote his last letter on 7 July. He attempted gaiety, but anguish breaks through, 'Give you joy, Sir,* the parson of Brentford is at length defeated. He no longer rules with an absolute sway over the City of London… the poor parson has been buffeted on the hustings where he did not appear, hissed out of playhouses which he never entered; he has been sung down in the streets, and exalted to a conspicuous corner with the pope and the devil in the print shops.'[21]

This controversy did Horne's moral and political reputation enormous damage. Others were disillusioned with Wilkes, but no-one else burst into print. Horne's vituperative accusations did not endear him to sober men. Though it should have been a great point in his favour that many distinguished men of integrity took his side and that most of Wilkes's erstwhile backers turned against him, popular opinion was for Wilkes. As the *Public Advertiser* pointed out, 'The numbers were on Wilkes's side, the men of sense, always fewest, with the Parson'. Wilkes's accusations stuck, and many believed that Horne was deserting the

* 'Give you joy', a hit at Wilkes's City ambitions. This was the form in which the Chamberlain addressed a recipient of the honorary freedom of the City.

patriot cause. Ironically, Horne was not only condemned for criticising Wilkes, but his image tarnished by his association with him. He later acknowledged to Junius, who thought Horne's mode of attack showed that he either lacked judgement or was blinded by resentment, that Wilkes was wiser, his political sensibilities sharper, 'I am sometimes inclined to suspect he formed a truer judgement of mankind than I have'.[22] Wilkes never divulged what he really thought about Horne.

Although they did not achieve many short-term tangible results, while working together they had an extraordinary impact, challenging judicial authority, forcing the Government onto the defensive. Most Englishmen experienced government through dealings with the law. The Wilkites drew attention to important questions: the use of general warrants, the right of individuals to protection by the law, the imposition of excessive legal fees, the law of libel. Through agitation which Hume dubbed a 'frenzy of liberty' Wilkes and Horne helped forge popular opinion into an effective political weapon and lay the seeds of radicalism.

Cambridge MA; Junius

To add a little lustre to his tattered reputation, Horne now applied for his MA at Cambridge. It would also provide a useful additional qualification as he hoped to abandon the Church for the more congenial legal profession. This was the first of several occasions when Horne attempted to advance his career and encountered abnormal opposition. His blasphemous remarks proved a great obstacle. At election time, clergymen were considered first-rate canvassers; there were many hunting parsons and pluralists, but to the more conservative elements in an irreligious but outwardly conforming age, Horne symbolised hateful politics and disgusting morals. He was a cleric who danced on tables, caroused with Wilkes and carried on with loose women.

When reports circulated that Horne was coming to take his MA at the beginning of July 1771, an opposition party was formed consisting of Lord Sandwich and his religious friends, including William Paley, Lord Montford and Henry Hubbard of Emmanuel. Horne was supported by his friend Dr Beadon, then Public Orator, and Dr Jebb of Peterhouse, both men of influence in the University, who pointed out that Horne had been the senior optime of his year and that his residence at the university had been distinguished by hard work, academic distinction and correct behaviour. The only pretext found against him was his letter to Wilkes which had been reproduced in the newspapers. Although Horne shocked the Commons many years later by claiming that the degree 'would tomorrow be conferred upon a great dog if he could pay the fees and call out 'Pro Domine Rege',[23] an MA was not conferred as a matter of course.

As it was known the election was to be contested, the theatre was crowded not only by members of the university but also neighbouring gentry. When it came to the point, Lord Montford's heart failed him and he would not read the obnoxious extract aloud. Hubbard was hissed, Paley laughed at. Horne said this was the first time a candidate for an academic degree was examined out of a newspaper; that a university had nothing to do with party. If these gentlemen did not scruple to be mean and illiberal they should take care not to be unjust. Cambridge maintained its liberal tradition. The Vice Chancellor and all heads of houses bar Goddard, Master of Clare, voted for Horne, as did the two proctors, the moderators and all the professors except the Professor of Anatomy. The voting was 60 for Horne, 20 against, a large majority: so Horne was admitted by the Vice Chancellor to loud clapping in the Senate and cheers from the undergraduates in the gallery.[24]

Horne returned victorious, only to be attacked from another quarter: Junius, the dread unknown who had been mauling the Government in the press. The most formidable libeller of his day, he wrote with vicious brilliance for a sophisticated audience, producing in three years 60 letters which were published in the *Public Advertiser*. He had a personal antipathy to Grafton, and his immediate objective was the overthrow of his ministry which he considered too subservient to the King. In a letter of 9 July 1771 to Grafton, Junius mentioned Horne's 'new zeal in support of administration' and, whether knowing it was false or misled by inaccuracy in the newspapers, accused him of working secretly for the Court candidate in the election for City sheriff. He condemned Horne for turning on Wilkes, and told him to 'go back to his cloister'.[25]

This led to a brisk correspondence. Horne replied on 13 July: 'Farce, Comedy and Tragedy, Wilkes, Foote* and Junius united... against one poor Parson, are fearful odds'. In a concise letter, he denied having any connection with the administration, and challenged Junius to produce proofs of his accusations. Junius responded abusively on 24 July: 'to gratify your personal hatred of Mr Wilkes you sacrificed, as far as depended on your interest and abilities, the cause of the country'. Wilkes, whatever his faults, should be forgiven 'so long as he is a thorn in the King's side'. Junius sent this letter privately via his printer, Woodfall, telling Horne to publish it if he wished. As the letter contained violent criticism of the King this might have involved Horne in a prosecution for libel. Undeterred, he directed Woodfall to publish.

In a long reply Horne pointed out Junius's failure to produce proof for his accusations; his illogicality in attributing Horne's motives at one moment to 'sordid desire of gain', at the next to the 'solitary vindictive malice of a monk'. He made skilful use of Junius's incautious revelation of his bitter hatred of the King and lack of interest in constitutional change: 'The cause of the country, it seems, in the opinion of Junius, is merely to vex the King'.[26]

Horne, whose own aim seems to have been to detach George III from his aristocratic entourage, explained his concept of sovereignty: 'The right divine and sacredness of kings is to me a senseless jargon.' 'The King, whose actions justify rebellion... deserves death from the hand of every subject, and should such a time arrive I shall be as free to act as to say. But till then my attachment to the person and family of the Sovereign' would be 'zealous and sincere'. 'Whoever or whatever is Sovereign, demands the respect and support of the people.'

At first Junius, who realised Horne had proved his charges of bribery and corruption ill-founded, did not reply. Then, taunted by jeering comments in the press, he wrote a long final letter addressed not to Horne, but to the printer. He cleverly mocked Horne's bombastic assertion of his courage, and defended Chatham and Rockingham; otherwise he only produced further petty jibes. Horne's short parting letter appeared on 17 August. He admitted that Junius's style was more polished than his own, but it gave the impression of long labour. 'Let me communicate to you the secret of my fluency. Truth needs no ornament.' Junius

* Samuel Foote, playwright and comedian, had satirised Horne and the smart clothes he left in Paris.

had said that Horne had not the power to do 'some signal mischief to the community'. Horne was well satisfied with Junius's panegyric, 'Monument I shall have none; but over my grave it will be said, in your own words, Horne's situation did not correspond with his intentions,' an equivocal epitaph which was to prove most apt.[27]

The general consensus of opinion was – and is – that Junius, who had worsted so many adversaries, had met his match in Horne. Junius had attacked from a weak position and was relieved to retire leaving Horne victor of the field. After the Wilkes débâcle this controversy gave a much-needed fillip to Horne's reputation. According to Godwin, who considered Horne the victor, Horne thought he had 'sunk Junius at last by law arguments, a science in which he was uninformed, and City politics, which he did not understand'. Coleridge, who thought Junius's style was often slovenly, later said 'Tooke and a long sentence seemed the only two antagonists that were too much for him'.[28]

Speculation as to Junius's identity has continued to the present day. Based on available evidence the most popular candidate is Sir Philip Francis. It is a tribute to Horne's skill as an antiministerial journalist that he was one of the candidates put forward at the time. Four men wrote short books attempting to prove that he was Junius. Philip Thicknesse in 1789, J.B. Blakeway in 1813 and two Americans who had met Horne when they were in London, John Graham and John Fellows in 1828/9. None of their arguments are very convincing. The fact that Junius attacked Horne so violently and was goaded into such a rage by his last reply, coupled with Junius's intense antipathy to Horne revealed in his private letters to Woodfall, makes it seem unlikely, in spite of ingenious arguments, that Horne deliberately attacked himself to put people off the scent.[29]

Horne, who delighted in paradoxical insinuations, made various pronouncements about the identity of Junius, some of which implied that he knew who he was, some that he himself was Junius. Wilkes was put forward as a candidate, but Horne, who detected Wilkes under many pseudonyms, never made that suggestion. It seems unlikely that Horne suspected Francis, as his name was not seriously suggested until the publication of Junius's private letters to Woodfall after Horne's death. Horne, who knew his father, had a slight acquaintance with Philip Francis, but they were never friendly.

Mayoral elections were pending, and Junius thought Sawbridge should be Lord Mayor. Wilkes considered that Sawbridge was mulish and stupid, the dupe of Malagrida's gang. He proposed to support Crosby for a second term as Mayor: Crosby had helped keep the SSBR going since the split. On 5 October Junius sent a letter to the *Public Advertiser* saying that he had too much respect for the abilities of Horne to expect a reconciliation, but that the various opposition factions should work, if not together, then in tandem to prevent the Court being victorious. In the event, both Crosby and Sawbridge ran against Nash, a moderate Court supporter. There were angry exchanges on the hustings. The Rockinghams peversely supported Nash, so it was not surprising, with the patriots split, that he was elected. Junius told Wilkes they must persevere: 'management and determined good humour will set everything right and, in the end, break the heart of Mr Horne'.[30]

1771 had not been a good year for Horne. The Court, the Rockinghams, Junius and Wilkes were now ranged against him, most of the general public despised him and did not consider him a man of integrity. He had received a great blow to his self-confidence and *amour propre*. One result was that he never again clearly revealed himself. In future he would raise a smokescreen to ensure that if he were wounded by his opponents they should not know.

The futile quarrels between Wilkes and Horne continued in 1772. Wilkes embarked on a campaign to become Lord Mayor while Horne promoted Townsend. There were violent scenes at the October election. At these elections the liverymen chose two candidates, from whom the Court of Aldermen then chose one as Lord Mayor. Wilkes topped the poll, but the aldermen chose Townsend. Wilkes harassed and insulted Townsend throughout his mayoralty.

Horne caused an uproar at a meeting of the Middlesex freeholders held on 30 April 1773 chaired by Wilkes. First Horne was indignant that Watkin Lewes, a vain, boorish alderman, had been knighted. Lewes, although a butt for Wilkes's humour, had remained faithful to him. Lewes rambled on at the meeting with complaints about the number of placemen and pensioners 'and knights,' cried Horne, confounding Lewes, who broke off in midstream. Horne continued to hound Lewes in the newspapers with rude comic rhymes and jingles which illustrate Horne's passionate disapproval of the purchase of honours. He then inveighed against politicians: they treated the public as they treated their girls, called them angels and goddesses to debauch them, then, when they had gained their ends, turned them over. He next attacked the chairman as being a pensioner, and the argument became so heated that his friends tried unsuccessfully to restrain him.[31]

The next autumn Wilkes and Bull stood as running partners for Lord Mayor. Wilkes headed the poll, but after a very bitter contest, due to Townsend's casting vote Bull was elected. The following year, Horne and Oliver decided they had better be done with their opposition to Wilkes, and Sawbridge came to an understanding with him: he would not contest the mayoral election in return for Wilkes's support for his candidature as City MP.

At the general election in the autumn of 1774, although the rival factions were not on speaking terms, they worked for the same ends and supported a similar reform programme which included the restoration of American rights and liberties. Sawbridge and Wilkes captured all four City seats. Bull, Sawbridge, Oliver and Hayley, Wilkes's brother-in-law, were elected. Horne worked hard for Oliver who beat Wilkes's other candidate Crosby. Wilkes and Glynn, whose health was deteriorating, were again elected for Middlesex, Wilkes being finally allowed to take his seat. In Westminster, however, the two Court candidates were elected, and Horne's friend Bernard, having turned against Wilkes, lost his support and was out.

Flying squadrons under Horne and Bernard's command operated at Bedford. In 1771, on the fourth Duke's death, Bernard had become Recorder of Bedford and by now his electoral influence rivalled that of the new Duke. Largely due to Horne's efforts, two candidates who had agreed to subscribe to the reform programme were approved at a London meeting: Sir William Wake, a Northamptonshire squire, and Robert Sparrow, one of Bernard's brothers-in-law. They won, mainly on the vote of the non-resident freemen, after over 200 votes for their opponents had been disqualified on the new and dubious grounds, thought up by Horne, that participation in local bounty constituted acceptance of charity. Sparrow's election was set aside on petition, but Wake represented Bedford for the next ten years.

Altogether 12 patriots were elected, a very small fraction of the 558 MPs. The election was a victory for the King and Court party, with their non-conciliatory policy towards the colonies. There was no widespread desire for reform. Wilkes made little impact in the Commons. A poor speaker, he gained a reputation for levity and concern with his own popularity, and concentrated his energy on obtaining the lucrative post of City Chamberlain.

Social Life

Though Horne was much preoccupied with politics, he also led a busy social life. He dressed elegantly and had the bearing of a man of fashion. He numbered among his acquaintance able, cultivated men and women from all walks of life, many of whom, like himself, had risen by their abilities. Considered one of the most brilliant conversationalists of the day, Horne had a reputation for charming both sexes. He was in the habit of flattering women, but did not like to flatter men.[32] His political coterie met at Richard Oliver's house. He himself kept rooms in Frith Street near his friends Michael Moser, Keeper of the Royal Academy, and Thomas Sheridan, actor manager and father of Richard Brinsley. Horne played backgammon and whist with friends, including Sheridan and Domenico Angelo. Horne often visited the two Angelos, Domenico from Leghorn and his son Henry, doyen of fencing masters, who knew everybody. Henry claimed that the first open breach between Horne and Wilkes took place in his house. Two distinguished musicians, Johann Christian Bach and Karl Abel, pretended to take sides, Bach with Horne, Abel with Wilkes. Abel called it the squabbles of Pot and Kettle.[33]

Horne had achieved much for Wilkes but little for himself. His parents had died and he had given up all pretence at interest in his clerical career, so in 1773, aged thirty-seven, he resigned his living, intending once more to read for the bar. It would take him five years. His father had left him some money; in addition four friends offered a bond of £100 a year each until he was called. Although he accepted their offer, he never needed to take advantage of their generosity. He rented a cottage near Brentford and lived economically.[34]

From the little information available, Horne must by this time have fathered his son, Sidney Montagu(e), the eldest of his three children. Godwin, who was keenly interested in Horne, calculated that his son was about twenty-one in 1788. This would mean that he was born by 1768; but, in his oration to the Middlesex freeholders in March 1770, Horne declared that he had 'neither wife nor children, nor any connexion to which my life was of much consequence to others'.[35] Horne's two daughters Mary and Charlotte took their mother's surname, Hart(e). They were younger than their brother. Sidney may well have had a different mother called Montagu(e). The later career of Sidney appears on page 117.

Stephens unfortunately gives little information about Horne's children, neither their dates of birth, character nor physical appearance, and does not mention their mother(s) at all. It is an interesting sidelight on eighteenth-century mores that, although Horne was accused of many misdeeds, no-one criticised him for his mistresses or illegitimate children. He ensured that his daughters, to whom he was devoted, were well educated. When they were old enough he sent them to boarding school, and they made their home with him. In this he once more resembled Wilkes who, with an estranged wife, a mistress and second family, had his legitimate daughter Polly to keep house for him. In those days men spent much time at clubs and coffee houses. Wilkes and Horne preferred to have as resident companions daughters who could act as hostesses and secretaries, but who were easier to control and less demanding than a wife.

Nothing is known about Mrs Hart. There is no evidence as to whether Horne supported her from the start of their liaison. In 1794 he was paying her an allowance, and he organised an annuity for her in his old age. Her daughters appear to have had little contact with her, and she can have had no niche in Horne's Wimbledon life, for in 1804 Captain Harwood, who had known Horne well for many years, gave evidence in a lawsuit that he thought Mrs Hart was dead. 'Far from it,' replied Horne.

Horne could not have supported a family in comfort on the small income he received as Vicar of Brentford. On the other hand, he did not want to marry a rich wife – 'a wedding for the sake of a bargain' – though in his view, 'For mutual comfort the wealth ought to be on the side of the female'. On one occasion he proposed marriage to Miss Arabin in a letter, but thought better of it, went to the post office and reclaimed it. She died soon afterwards. When Horne was inveighing against matrimony, someone suggested that, if she had lived, he might have married her and been 'the slave of a woman'. 'No, no,' replied Horne, 'she was not a woman but an angel.'[36] Horne hung a portrait of her brother, a general in the horseguards, in the back parlour of his house at Wimbledon.

The playwright Fred Reynolds remembered Horne saying to his father, Wilkes's attorney, who 'according to his custom in the afternoon was pushing about the bottle', 'Reynolds, you will soon be able to boast that you have drunk as much wine as would float a 74.' Reynolds retorted that it was high time Horne reformed and took a wife. 'Whose wife?' he asked in his dry, cool manner. He did not care much about chastity, believing that infidelity was only a dishonour to a husband when he accepted it. Women, he said, value themselves on their chastity as men on their courage. Why? Because of the rarity and difficulty of these virtues. They are both contrary to nature.[37] In 1792 *The World* published a mock review of 'The Diary of Hildebrand Freeman' (i.e. Horne): 'He lived freely with women and made no scruple about declaring the connection'.[38]

At a political dinner in 1792 – the only occasion when, whether serious or not, he unequivocally expressed republican views – Horne declared, 'I am... persuaded that an individual may live more happy with a wife than without one and that a nation may be more happy with a king than without one, but I am afraid that individuals and nations are much more likely to be happy without them than with them. If it were my lot to choose either... I ought to be very cautious in my choice... and attentive to keep... them within the bounds of their duty... I should be very sorry to quarrel and be divorced from them. However extreme bad qualities and extreme bad conduct would overcome my reluctance to a separation and I have no religious or political... superstition which would prevent me... from... obtaining a divorce.' Horne, incidentally, approved of Queens, whose reigns had produced men such as the Cecils and Marlborough, whereas in France, where they were excluded, 'the country had been governed for nearly a century by pimps and prostitutes'.[39]

William Tooke

In February 1774 Horne achieved a notable triumph. He had known William Tooke, treasurer of the SSBR, for six years. Tooke, a Norfolk landowner, had made a great deal of money in trade, some of which he invested in a joint purchase with Oliver of a profitable West Indian plantation. This incurred Horne's mockery, 'that such sticklers for liberty should buy and sell their fellow creatures'. Tooke was involved in a dispute with a neighbour, Sir Thomas de Grey, lord of the manor of Tottington, over grazing rights. Fences were erected and demolished. Tooke learnt that de Grey was petitioning Parliament for permission to present an enclosure bill. He rushed to town and with Horne's help prepared a counter-petition for a delay of action on the grounds that customary notice had not been given to the inhabitants of Tottington, whose interests, as well as Tooke's own, would be seriously affected by the bill. Tooke approached Sir Edward Astley, the local MP, who was already engaged to present de Grey's petition. Astley, with the Speaker's permission, presented the two diametrically opposed petitions. De Grey, whose brother, formerly Attorney General, was now a Lord Chief Justice, had more powerful contacts than Tooke. In spite of Sawbridge's protests it was arranged that de Grey's bill should be read on 10 and 22 February, when he hoped it would slip through while Tooke's petition lay on the table. Here was an opportunity for Horne to champion the individual against venal authority. It was too late for ordinary means of delay, so Horne, with his bent for ingenious ploys, his delight in shocking public opinion and willingness to dare any hazard, published an enormously long anonymous letter in the *Public Advertiser*, a virulent attack on the Speaker, Sir Fletcher Norton, accusing him – unjustly – of partiality in handling the petitions, and implying that he accepted bribes. Fletcher Norton was not generally admired: Horace Walpole wrote, 'Nothing can exceed the badness of his character,' and Lord Eldon (the future Lord Chancellor) claimed that he was known as Sir Bull-Face Double Fee, taking money from both sides in private causes.[40]

'Thus with the connivance of such a speaker, may the rights and property of any private gentleman… be in a fortnight, transferred to another by the House of Commons, even without its own knowledge; whilst the lawful, unoffending Owner may be on a voyage to the continent, or even on a journey to Yorkshire, and find on his return his lands… transferred. De Grey would get near £1,000 a year profit which would save the Ministry the expense of a pension.' Whatever the punishment, Horne would think himself well rewarded if he could 'only awaken from their lethargy some few honest members of the… Commons to watch over the wickedness which you are daily perpetrating'. He ended with the arresting phrase 'Strike but Hear'.[41]

The Commons, sensitive after earlier attacks on its privileges, were enraged. On 11 February, in a full House of over 300, members pressed for Woodfall, printer of the *Public Advertiser*, to be interrogated. Lord North wisely reminded them what had happened over Wilkes, but this was no deterrent. There was momentary silence, astonishment and consternation when Woodfall, being summoned, revealed that Horne was the author. Horne was popular with Woodfall – who was always keen to knock the House – because his controversies with Wilkes and Junius had greatly increased his newspaper's circulation. Fox demanded that Woodfall should be sent to Newgate – another notch in his and Horne's enmity – but Lord North adroitly scotched that suggestion. A message was sent to William Tooke's rooms in Serjeants Inn, Fleet St, with an order for the Rev. John Horne to attend at the bar. Horne sent a polite reply saying that there must be some mistake, there were several John Hornes in London besides himself, but when the House desired his attendance, he would pay them all proper and prudent respect. Glynn explained to the Commons that Horne, who wished to enter a lay profession, did not want to be recorded as a clergyman on the journals of the House.

The next day, when correctly summoned, Horne appeared. This caused some embarrassment, because Lord North had prophesied that Horne would probably think it prudent to take refuge in the City 'imagining that the order of the House of Commons might be as infectious as the hand of a bishop'. According to Walpole, Horne, 'who seemed to be running a race with Wilkes for popularit', 'was pale, but well made, and had a sensible countenance. He was neatly and decently dressed in grey. He spoke with affected respect, much deliberation and firmness.' Horne argued that he could not be guilty of contempt as he had sent a polite answer to the first summons and obeyed the second with alacrity. 'He had been urged beyond the usual bound of discretion by hatred to oppression and zeal for his friend.'[42]

However, the House ruled that he must answer the libel. Horne pleaded not guilty; the only evidence against him was the unsupported testimony of Woodfall, who had accused him to clear himself. Dunning ably defended Horne in a heated debate. When Townsend produced a panegyric of Horne's virtues there was general laughter. Finally the House adjourned for further evidence to be collected against Horne, who was sent to join Woodfall in custody.

The following morning, Woodfall's three journeymen printers stated that they knew Horne by sight but had never spoken to him and did not know his handwriting. Told by the Speaker to make his defence, Horne replied that he had only his thanks to return for the indulgence and personal favours shown him. A wise man (Lord Bacon) had said that 'truth, however strong of itself, was never strong enough to oppose a vote'. He trusted, however, that in this instance, the maxim had failed. To general relief, Horne was discharged as there was no legal proof of his identity. When he was made to pay the jailor's fees, he maintained that no fees should be demanded from a prisoner detained on an accusation that could not be substantiated. His audacious plan succeeded. Not only were the objectionable clauses in de Grey's bill removed, but a measure was passed to prevent such bills being so swiftly pushed through in future.[42]

Though Horne had run the risk of attracting further disapproval while studying for the bar, his modest appearance and polite behaviour disappointed but conciliated MPs: he was not the raffish renegade parson they had expected. Walpole considered it did 'great credit to Horne's address and parts'. Even George III wrote to Lord North 'It is rather surprising to me that Mr Horne has been so decent and submissive'. In cartoons Horne, who had formerly appeared as a scheming priest in the pay of the devil, is far more sympathetically portrayed, standing with a jaunty air declaiming at the bar of the House. Horne told Tooke he had long been waiting for an occasion to write a libel whose intention was indubitably libellous.[43]

Tooke was delighted with Horne's success, showered him with presents and promised to make him one of his heirs. Horne often stayed in Tooke's house in Purley for a month or six weeks at a time, walking, riding on the downs, playing piquet or chess and mixing with other clever, amusing people. Politics and compliments, according to Horne, were strangers at Purley. 'We always put them off when we put on our boots and leave them behind in their proper atmosphere, the smoke of London.'[44]

Tooke encouraged Horne to continue his legal studies and, though Horne later complained that Tooke made many financial promises which he did not fulfil, he did provide him with the much-needed support of a wealthy, established patron and friend. Horne's finances had also improved with the death of his eldest brother Benjamin, who had made a great financial success of his market garden and left him £200 a year. He was a rather pompous man to whom John once remarked, 'You, my dear brother, have inverted one of the laws of Nature; for you have risen by your gravity, while I have fallen by my levity'.[45]

Notes on Chapter 3

1 *General Evening Post* 22.5.71
2 *Public Advertiser* 24.5.70
3 Chatham III, p 458; Conway, M., letter from Thomas Cooper, *Athanaeum* p 503, 16.4.1898; *London Chronicle* 24.5.70; Rogers, *Table Talk*, pp 129-130
4 Wilkes-Horne, *Letters*, pp 181, 182
5 *London Chronicle* XXVIII, pp 424-8, 455-6, 470, 1770
6 *London Chronicle* XXVIII, pp 468, 476, 1770; Wilkes-Horne, *Letters*, pp 8-12
7 Wilkes-Horne, *Letters*, pp 13-24
8 *Gazetteer* 28.1.71
9 Watson, p 140; Foster, J., *Critical Essays* II, p 172; *Middlesex Journal* 12.2.71; Stephens I, pp 170-5
10 Wilkes-Horne, *Letters*, p 263
11 *Middlesex Journal* 5.2.71
12 *Annual Register* 62 *et seq.*, 1771
13 *Middlesex Journal* 24.10.71; Bleackley, pp 260-3; Wilkes, *Letters* I, p 117
14 *Annual Register* 9.4.71
15 *North Briton* May 1771, pp 731-41
16 Walpole, *Correspondence* XXXI, p 151, 27.1.71
17 Junius LII, p 258

18 Wilkes-Horne, *Letters*, pp 308-11
19 Wilkes-Horne, *Letters*, pp 106, 178
20 *Annual Register* 1771, p 121
21 Wilkes-Horne, *Letters*, p 314
22 Junius LIII, p 260
23 *Parliamentary History* XXXV, p 1380, 1801
24 *London Chronicle* 9.7.71
25 Junius, pp 252-3
26 Junius, p 259
27 Junius, pp 254-82
28 Godwin in Abinger MSS 74 supp. to Journal, Dep.e. 273.f.3; Coleridge, *Table Talk* II, p 213
29 *Athenaeum*, p 503, 16.4.1898
30 Junius, pp 294, 398-9, 415, 427
31 *Public Advertiser* 3.5.73
32 *State Trials* XXV, p 395
33 Angelo I, p 58
34 Stephens I, pp 418-9
35 Horne, Middlesex Oration, 30.3.70, p 14
36 Stephens II, p 486
37 Reynolds I, p 42; Rogers, *Table Talk*, pp 129-135
38 *The World* 22.6.92
39 SCI Anniversary dinner, 1792, TS 11/951/3495 Exhibit 3
40 Stephens I, pp 423-6; Walpole, *Correspondence* XXIII, p 176; Eldon, p 34
41 *Public Advertiser* 11.2.74; Horne's original letter Add MSS 27784, pp 17-21
42 Walpole, *Last Journals* I, pp 289-98; Walpole, *Correspondence* XXIII, p 555; *Parliamentary History* XVII, pp 1003-50, 1774
43 George III, *Correspondence* III, 17.2.74
44 Stephens II, p 29
45 Rogers, *Recollections*, p 148

Chapter Four

Trial for Libel: Support of American Revolution

While proceeding against Horne, Parliament had dropped important debates on the American crisis. London merchants, who had many personal bonds with the colonies and a large stake in trade with the New World, feared that an American embargo on imports from Britain would greatly reduce their business. They were keen to defend the colonists in their demand to be free from taxes imposed by the British Parliament. In 1774 the City patriots and Wilkites insisted that their parliamentary candidates should pledge support to a bill giving colonists the right to elect their own parliament and tax themselves. Horne maintained that Wilkes's American sympathies were bogus, that he only wanted presents and money. Wilkes hotly denied this. Horne and other members of the SSBR had had arguments on the subject with Wilkes when he was incarcerated in prison, and this was one reason for the split.[1]

Horne himself, who like Wilkes never visited the New World, said in 1804 that he had met and respected Jefferson, but 'in general Americans were of a very inferior cast; a prodigious number of pigmies, and but few giants... a man who knew little, thought himself an extraordinary character there, and was actually so, when compared with the common herd'. Bentham, who disliked Horne and thought his zeal was 'not prompted by the highest motives', was present at dinner when Horne teased two Americans with derogatory comments on their country, conveyed 'not so broadly as to justify their showing any resentment, but obviously giving them pain'. On the other hand, Horne strongly supported America's constitutional demands. He had told the Middlesex freeholders that they 'must not forget the important truth that the security of the freedom and rights' of their American brethren was 'essential to the enjoyment of our own. When the people of America are enslaved we cannot be free. We are stones of one arch and must stand or fall together.'[2]

The Boston tea-party occurred at the end of 1773. It was not until the beginning of 1775 that the seriousness of the situation was realised in England. Franklin, at that time agent for Pennsylvania in England, now left for America. In April, the Lord Mayor and Common Council addressed a remonstrance to the King against the anti-colonist measures. The Constitutional Society voted £100 for the Bostonians in February and March which was sent by Oliver to Franklin via his bankers, and for which he returned thanks. Their third donation caused a sensation. When news of the affray at Lexington reached London, a special meeting of the society was convened by Oliver at Horne's suggestion on 7 June, at which a further subscription was proposed and immediately subscribed. Horne was to pay the money into Franklin's account. Horne drew up the minutes of the proceedings, which it was agreed should be published in the newspapers. The notice said that the sum was 'to be applied to the relief of the widows, orphans and aged parents, of our beloved American fellow-subjects, who, faithful to the character of Englishmen, preferring death to slavery, were... inhumanly murdered by the King's troops at or near Lexington and Concord...'. On 15 July Horne put a second notice in the newspapers, thanking an unknown contributor who had sent £50.[3] Though Horne had followed the general radical line which denounced the stamp act and tea duty, this advertisement was particularly challenging. Notice of prosecution for libel was served on some of the printers whose newspapers had carried it, but no further action was taken.

Protests continued. One American, Sayre, was sent to the Tower on a flimsy charge of plotting to kill the King. Quickly released, he joined his fellow-countrymen in France. In September the liverymen issued an 'Address to the Electors of Great Britain' which attacked the impending war and criticised the use of foreign troops and illegal claims to taxation. In November, Oliver and Sawbridge introduced a motion in Parliament against the Government's policy, which failed to make any impact. Although Shelburne's followers and the Wilkites were more or less in accord over colonial policy, the Rockingham faction still supported the Declaratory Act which gave Parliament the right to tax the colonies. Burke laboured to keep the City 'now and for ever out of the hands of the Wilkeses, Olivers and Hornes'.[4]

Anti-American feeling in the country increased in 1776, particularly after the Declaration of Independence in July. Those who continued to support the colonists became objects of suspicion. On 27 June an *ex officio* information was lodged by the Attorney General Thurlow against the printers of the Constitutional Club advertisement and Horne as author. The cases which ensued were concerned with two very important points of law which the radicals fought hard to resolve. The first was the practice by which, at his personal discretion, if the Attorney General considered a piece libellous, he could issue an information against the printer and distributors, who had to defend themselves before a petty jury. This avoided the need for a grand jury to consider first whether there was sufficient evidence for a case to be brought. Even if acquitted, the accused could not recover their costs. A feature of this method, about which Horne complained at his trial, was that the Attorney General could delay bringing a case for months. A threat of prosecution was thus kept hanging over the accused, which effectively silenced many journalists and put printers to inconvenience and expense. In this case a printer who lived in Middlesex was the first to be tried, in December 1776, because it was easier to get a jury to convict there. Altogether eight printers were found guilty, and two months later four of them were fined £100 each. There were objections in the press on the grounds that the proceedings were based on *ex post facto* law, as the statements had not been illegal at the time: the Americans had not then been declared rebels.

The prosecution of Horne for criminal libel in 1777 was one of the principal cases in the controversy over the second legal point: the jury's right to give a general verdict in seditious libel cases. Wilkes, Horne and their printer colleagues were major combatants in the struggle which was fought out in the second half of the eighteenth century to ensure the right to liberty of discussion. One reason for Mansfield's unpopularity with the Wilkites was that, in opposition to Lord Camden but supported by nearly all members of the bench, he upheld the doctrine that the jury's function was limited to deciding if the evidence proved who had published a piece. Though they did not always obey his instructions, he would tell the jury to find for the Crown, as it was for the court to decide whether the words constituted an offence. This meant that in the printers' trials the prosecution had only to prove that the defendants had published the advertisements.* When Horne addressed the jury at his trial he emphasised that there could be no guilt without intention, and that it was the duty and right of the jury to determine what his intention had been.

Horne, who was engrossed in his legal studies and knew that the prosecution might affect his intention to be called to the bar, claimed that it was initiated when it was learnt that he had begun eating his commons in the Inner Temple. Having gained notoriety and unpopularity through the Wilkes fracas and not being a member of the upper classes, he was a suitable scapegoat for the Government, who wanted to make an example of someone and had waited until opinion hardened against America as the war intensified.

Horne appeared at the Guildhall on 4 July 1777 in the Court of King's Bench, with a special jury, before his old adversary Lord Mansfield, now aged seventy-two.[5] He was prosecuted by Thurlow, a blunt, overbearing, intolerant, self-confident man with quick wits, who glowered from under bushy eyebrows. Though not a great lawyer, he was a successful politician, a King's man. He had first encountered Horne in the Fletcher Norton Case. Horne was dressed in a black suit with ruffles, and had his hair tied. Although up against two of the most formidable men on the bench, Horne, who enjoyed the scent of combat, was undeterred and vigorously attacked them both. Mansfield, equally unperturbed by Horne's impertinence, treated him with the consideration usually shown to the man who chooses to be his own lawyer. Horne had not yet much experience in the courts. All

* Horne was for once fully in support of Fox when Fox introduced his Libel Act which settled the matter. By it jurors were empowered to bring in a general verdict of libel or no libel, i.e. to deal with the question of the meaning and scope of the publication. Pitt strongly supported the bill which was passed on 21 May 1792.

contemporary accounts of the trial agree that he defended himself with pertinacity and lively repartee. One journalist said that he proved himself a man of extraordinary abilities but, if he had sacrificed less to private resentments and personal invective, he would have acquitted himself better before the dispassionate part of his audience, and his arguments would have carried more weight stripped of digressions.[6]

Horne made waspishly amusing comments on the selection of special juries, which in his view told unfairly against the defendant. They were supposed to be chosen from men with sufficient education to understand difficult points. The jury's names had been taken from a book in the presence of the Treasury solicitor, the sheriff's officer and himself. When Horne asked how he selected jurymen, the Master of the Crown Office explained that he took those personally known to him. If a name occurred which the sheriff's officer did not like, he would say, 'That man has retired, that man is too old, this man has become bankrupt, this man will not attend. It seemed very extraordinary to me... I begged him not to kill men off because he understood them to be friends to liberty... we shall see them alive again next week.' But Horne wanted them alive then. One name Horne noticed was Mr Sainsbury, a tobacconist on Ludgate Hill. The sheriff's officer said he had been dead seven months. Horne, who bought snuff at his shop, knew this could not be true. He could only have died within a day or so, 'for I saw in the newspapers that he was appointed to receive the toll of the Thames navigation, and the City of London does not often appoint dead men for these purposes'. The sheriff reinstated his name, but the Treasury solicitor later contrived to strike it out.[7]

At the recent printers' trials, contrary to normal practice, the Attorney General had made a speech after the defendant's. Horne wanted to object to the possibility of his doing this now. Mansfield said he should object when Thurlow rose to reply. That, said Horne, was what he expected, for the Attorney General probably imagined it his duty 'to baffle me in any manner, and to take all advantages which he can whether fair or unfair against me'. Thurlow's agreement to announce his intentions in advance did not satisfy Horne: 'My Lord, I had rather that this had come as a matter of justice than a favour.' Horne wanted to ensure that future defendants had the same right. He took a rather childish delight in taunting Mansfield and Thurlow. He contrived to bring in a reference to his former trial, where he had worsted Mansfield, and to Mansfield's recent earldom. 'However impatient I may be thought to be, I am very patient under personal injuries. I have never complained of the practice used against me... nor of the mistake which your lordship made.'

When Horne began his defence, he accused the Crown of deliberately trying the printers first, as the jury were likely to be influenced by their conviction. 'Murder and sodomy... have in these days often found successful solicitors.' Treason had been pardoned but, 'whilst mercy and forgiveness... have been thus flowing unnaturally in a full stream over the highest mountains of iniquity, has anyone of you ever spied the smallest rivulet descending towards the valley of the libeller?' He raised a great laugh when he expressed his pleasure at seeing Wilkes, who had also once charged the King's troops with murder, sitting chatting happily to Lord Mansfield. Burke, whom Horne referred to as a 'most distinguished member of the House of Commons', also sat on the bench throughout the trial.[8]

Horne's witticisms at Thurlow's expense caused amusement. He compared the Attorney and Solicitor Generals to the two brazen pillars of Solomon, Jachin and Boaz, sitting in the House on each side of Lord North. Whatever was contrary to the interests or even the vices of a minister had always been and always would be charged as a libel. Whether a bad minister by mistake chose a good Attorney General, or a good minister chose a bad Attorney General, it made no difference: 'Under a good minister there are no prosecutions for libel, under a bad minister you meet with little else'. Horne reminded Thurlow, who firmly rebutted Horne's wilder statements, that Thurlow had asked Dunning to introduce them, and that they had spent an evening together. The Attorney General, Horne said, represented him as a 'scurrilous, ribald, balderdash, Billingsgate, impudent fellow'. But the boldness with which he defended the rights of the subject was not impudence. The Government knew that men who acted as he had always done would not be deterred by imprisonment and fine.

The charge against Horne was a tendency to excite sedition. 'What, come two years and a quarter afterwards to prosecute... not actual mischief, but a tendency to mischief... A man might have had a wife and children since the publication of his libel...

and then comes a vindictive Attorney General and drags him away from his peaceful family and fireside.' If the advertisement was libellous, it should have been prosecuted as soon as published to prevent its mischievous tendency. What might be deemed a libel in 1777 could not be in 1775, in a time of peace. When Horne wanted to read the advertisement, Mansfield said the jury must have read it long ago. 'My Lord,' said Horne, 'that is my misfortune that it is so long ago'.

The trial revealed Horne's merits and demerits. He argued several points of law with eloquence and proficiency, but talked for four hours so that the weary jury and spectators were relieved when he finished. Mansfield complained about the extraneous facts he introduced for which no witnesses were called. Horne was reluctant to admit that he might sometimes misjudge the best course of action. A tone of bitterness, of self-denigration coupled with self-pity, creeps in. 'I know nothing of the law,' he announced with false modesty. He compared himself to Thurlow, a gentleman in great office: '... myself an obscure man, who never did enjoy any office of trust or of consequence; who never was a candidate either for honour or for profit... I have had the honour to be burnt in effigy... I have been sung about the streets in ballads, and I saw a little pert person cocked up on a stick in the singer's hands. As for caricature, I have myself bought enough of them to furnish a room – my rooms are but small as you may easily suppose.' The Attorney General had now relieved him of one imputation – that he was a corrupt pensioner of the crown. But then 'in a nation of lepers like this, who can expect to be thought clean?'

When Horne finished speaking, Thurlow rose to address the jury. Horne interrupted, claiming that due to the shame he felt for making any defence to such a charge he had forgotten to examine his witnesses. Some attributed his omission to inexperience and enthusiasm, Thurlow suggested that he 'had cast about to be stopped in a great variety of parts for the sake of making it a topic of complaint'. Mansfield told him he had better hear Horne's witnesses. Then came the most comical moment in the trial: Horne insisted on calling the Attorney General. When Mansfield asked what questions he wished to put to Thurlow, Horne said that he wanted to examine him about the duty and integrity of his motives; it would be ludicrous if he would not answer to his reasons for bringing his accusations; but Thurlow refused to be examined. The jury took one-and-a-half hours to decide that Horne was guilty.[5]

Horne moved for an arrest of judgement. The trial was reopened on 19 November, the court packed 'as if Garrick were to perform'. People stood on stools, on each others' shoulders to get a look at Horne. Counsel had to get in through the judges' door, and silence was obtained with great difficulty. Joseph Cradock, who had never seen Horne before and had recently produced an anti-Wilkite pamphlet, stood for four hours. He said the audience was filled with admiration and astonishment at Horne's legal knowledge and firmness before such adversaries.[9]

This time Horne modified his conduct. He kept to the point and did not 'use asperity or unbecoming warmth of language'. Dunning, who had refused a Crown brief because he disapproved of the prosecution, may have given him useful advice on how to conduct himself. Dunning, incidentally, thought Horne's arguments among the most ingenious he had ever heard. Horne maintained that he had merely been charged with accusing the troops of murder which was not necessarily criminal, that the written information contained no statement that Massachusetts was in a state of rebellion and the legal position of the King's American subjects who had fought his soldiers was not defined. Thurlow replied that the written information averred 'seditious libel of and concerning His Majesty's Government and the employment of his troops'. Horne retorted that there was no crime in 'of and concerning' which could be of and concerning good as well as bad; besides this form of words made no difference to lack of facts in the indictment. He personally did not know what libel meant. It was not a technical term. Perhaps if it had been the Attorney General would not have had so much trouble in producing a satisfactory indictment. Mansfield asked them to look for precedents, at which Horne complained that he was not likely to find any. Mansfield then ordered Horne to be committed. 'What!' cried Horne. 'Will your lordship commit me before it appears whether I am even accused of any crime?' Mansfield agreed that he could come up voluntarily.[10]

An enormous crowd gathered when the court reconvened on 24 November. Mansfield, who emphasised that five juries had already found the advertisement actionable, produced two precedents. As they had been supplied by the judge, not the Attorney General, Horne had no legal right to challenge them, so 'on the strength of these two precedents alone, he decided against me'.[11] One result was that in future informations of the crown in seditious libel, prosecutions were drafted with strictest attention to detail.

Thurlow condemned Horne's arrogant conceit. He had abused judge, jury, himself and government officials. 'Woodfall's rabble of authors stand forth in the face of the country and say, "Punish me if you dare". Horne's crime was really High Treason.' He claimed 'that imprisonment would be no inconvenience, for he had employment which would keep him to his room longer than they dare confine him, [so] the pillory would be the best punishment'. This suggestion, however, was not taken up. Thurlow's contemptuous criticism evoked further illuminating remarks from Horne. After qualifying statements he had made on other occasions, he added, 'I was not made to be a martyr... I have opinions of my own; but I never intended to suffer for them at the stake... The mob have conferred no greater favours on me than upon Mr Attorney General. I have been repeatedly followed by very numerous mobs... two or three thousand at my heels. If popularity should offer itself to me, I would speedily take care to kick it away... There is no man from whom I expect help... or friendship... beyond that which my principles or services may deserve from them individually. When first I began my life, I was encouraged to... virtuous actions by the temptation of praise. I have learned... to be able to do those actions which I think virtuous, in despite of shame.' He wanted to impress on himself and others that he could not temper his actions without compromising his honour. Some of his audience found this tiresome.

Horne was sentenced to 12 months and a fine of £200, then to find sureties of his good behaviour for three years, of which £400 was to be assured by himself and £200 each by two others. The sentence, which was generally considered severe, was attributed to Mansfield's desire for revenge. Horne brought a writ of error in Parliament to reverse the judgement which was argued by Dunning. Dunning was the only barrister in the King's Bench capable of arguing points of constitutional law with Mansfield, whom he used to tease in court. As Horne unkindly reminded Mansfield, Dunning had written a pamphlet after the

Onslow trial criticising Mansfield's conduct. Dunning proved the non-existence of the main precedent, but failed to convince the House of Lords who affirmed Horne's sentence on 11 May 1778.[5]

Prison

The King's Bench prison was extremely unhealthy. Built on swampy ground, its basement was several feet below the level of the Thames at spring tide. It was grossly overcrowded, and prisoners had to pay for decent quarters. On arrival, Horne was offered a room on down-payment of ten guineas, only to discover that it already contained four debtors. He was finally accommodated in a small house outside the prison walls but within the 'rules' for £10 a week. He estimated when he left prison that the total cost of his trial, fine, appeal, lawyers' fees and imprisonment came to £1,200, an enormous sum for a man of slender means at that time.[12]

There was no public outcry over Horne, who was not fêted in prison as Wilkes had been, though shortly after his trial a pamphlet on libels with particular reference to his case was issued by men who hoped to 'rescue his reputation from the jaws of envy and calumny'.[13] Horne's friends visited him, one sent him a bottle of wine a day. Till now he had been very abstemious, but when he contracted jail fever he took to drinking claret, considered the best remedy for the illness in those days. Soon after he was released he had a severe attack of gout which was to plague him for the rest of his life; he attributed it to claret. He was treated with considerable leniency. When summoned as witness to a trial at Reading he was allowed to travel with his servant, spent a few days *en route* with his former parishioners at Brentford and returned in an equally leisurely manner. Every Wednesday he dined at the Dog and Duck in St George's Fields with Bernard, Oliver, Sawbridge, Townsend and William Tooke.[14] In 1778 Oliver went to the West Indies to supervise his estates; he died on his way back to England six years later, a sad loss for Horne, who hung Oliver's portrait in his sitting room and spoke affectionately of him.

Enforced leisure in gaol spurred Horne to write 'A Letter to Mr Dunning on the English Particle', a 72-page critical examination of the precedent which had been quoted against him. This was incorporated into his book *The Diversions of Purley*, and is described in detail in chapter 13. Horne said that notes on the ideas he had formed on language had lain among his loose papers since he left Cambridge, and would probably have been consigned with himself to oblivion if he had not been made the miserable victim of 'two prepositions and a conjunction'. That the prepositions 'of' and 'concerning' and the conjunction 'that' should be made the instruments of his civil extinction appeared to him as degrading as if he 'had been brained by a lady's fan'. He decided to write the Letter because his case afforded 'a very striking instance of the importance of the meaning of words; not only to metaphysicians... but to the rights and happiness of mankind in their dearest concerns – the decisions of the Courts of Justice... Mankind in general are not sufficiently aware that words without meaning, or of equivocal meaning, are the everlasting engines of fraud and injustice.'[11] The *Quarterly Review* tartly commented that he 'went hot from the Court of King's Bench to discuss the nature of particles, of which, it seems, a shameful ignorance on the part of the judges had just been manifested in a verdict against him'.[15] Boswell mentions a conversation which arose after Johnson read the letter. Johnson and Horne had diametrically opposed views and heartily disliked each other. Johnson had severely condemned Horne's support of the colonists. Horne accused Johnson of being a Government hack. However, Johnson said that if he were to make a new edition of his dictionary he would adopt several of Horne's etymologies. 'I hope they did not put the dog in the pillory for his libel; he has too much literature for that.'[16]

Horne, whose enemies were more powerful than his friends, was the only man imprisoned for his criticism of the Government's treatment of the colonists. Though the City of London drew up an address and petition censuring the war, the majority of the nation was not pro-American, but supported the King and thought the war would soon be over. When France and Spain joined in, radicals were faced with charges of disloyalty. By the time Horne was released, after serving eight months of his sentence, reform, inevitably connected with the American Revolution, was temporarily discredited.

Horne came out of prison physically impaired – he no longer kept up the incessant activity he had shown when young – shocked but untamed by his misfortunes. He took a room in Vine

Street and continued his legal studies, on which all told he spent six years. The following year, when he had kept the required number of terms, he applied to be called to the bar. He had been a member of an inn of court since 1756, and foresaw no difficulty. Several eminent attornies had promised him briefs. At last, aged forty-three, he would be able to embark on the career he had always wanted. By eight to three the benchers of the Inner Temple voted that he was ineligible on the grounds that he was a clergyman. They consulted the benchers of Lincoln's Inn who reported unanimously that it was not proper to call anyone in holy orders. The benchers could use their discretion, but it was extremely unusual to refuse admission. Although they had recently refused to admit an actor, this decision had been reversed as ludicrous by Mansfield. Some thought other lawyers were jealous of Horne's ability and afraid he would outstrip them, others that Mansfield could not endure the prospect of Horne appearing regularly to torment him. In November, Horne wrote to Bernard of the patience he was forced to employ to watch himself 'completely and silently undone', notwithstanding he was 'perfectly happy'.[17] The decision was not final. Horne consulted Dunning, who advised him to wait, so in Trinity term 1782 he presented a second application, supported by Dunning, now Lord Ashburton and a Privy Councillor. This time six voted for and six against, with a casting vote against him. Believing it would be futile to appeal to the judges or Parliament, Horne abandoned the law. In 1794, in a gesture of defiance, his name appeared once more on the list of applicants, but no bencher moved for his call.[18]

This was the nadir of Horne's life. Later he drew up a brief résumé of his career. His entry for 1779 contains two items: Gout; Rejected at Inner Temple.[19] The cruel disappointment embittered him, marred his character, hardened his heart, and increased his cynicism and antagonism to authority. There was no other opening now left where such an ambitious, clever man without money or connections could find compensation. His talents, his shrewd, incisive mind, were ideally suited to the legal profession. He would have learnt with experience to curb his pugnacious temperament and use it to the best advantage. Instead of challenging the judges as an amateur, he would have appeared on an equal footing. His powers of ridicule, his delight in teasing authority, would have been kept in bounds by the restraints of professionalism. For the rest of his life Horne was to pass from one conflict to another, the means by which he tried to avenge himself on society. He continued his interest in the law, often advising those in difficulties, but only on rare occasions was he able to seize the opportunity to appear in court himself.

Notes on Chapter 4

1 Wilkes-Horne, *Letters*, p 158
2 Stephens II, p 337; Prentice, p 384; Horne, Oration Middlesex Freeholders, p 36
3 *London Chronicle* 10.6.75; *Public Advertiser* 15.7.75 and many other papers
4 Burke, *Correspondence* III, p 224, to Rockingham 1.10.75
5 *State Trials* XX, pp 651-802, 1389-1400
6 *London Evening Post* 3-5.7.77
7 *State Trials* XX, pp 690-1
8 *Gazetteer* 7.7.77
9 Cradock I, p 98
10 *Public Advertiser* 20.11.77
11 *DOP* I, pp 38-40
12 Stephens II, pp 1-6
13 Anon., 'An interesting address to the independent part of the People of England on Libels... with a view of the case of John Horne...', 1777
14 Michigan MSS, Horne to J. Lee, 13.5.78
15 *Quarterly Review* VII, 1812, p 324
16 Boswell III, p 354
17 Manchester MSS. 12/2/25, 11.11.79
18 Stephens II, pp 12-18
19 Stephens, appendix

Chapter Five

Life Renewed: Parliamentary Reform; William Tooke

Stephens is vague about Horne's movements over the next few years. Horne probably did not reminisce about a period which ended painfully; his notes on his life include nothing for 1780-4. According to Stephens, as the American war drew to a close Horne gave up his cottage near Brentford and, with money from the sale of his living and legacies from his father and brother, purchased a small estate at Witton, near Huntingdon, and spent money on its improvement.[1]

Horne bought Witton because it was near Sir Robert Bernard's house at Brampton. He needed to earn a steady income. He had incurred heavy expenses on political campaigns and legal actions; in addition he was always a generous subscriber to radical causes. As a result, he was for many years short of money. Bernard, who was four years younger, had extensive estates in three counties besides financial interests in London. Although Bernard could have attached himself to the Rockinghams, he preferred to work with more advanced reformers. He gave them large sums and was casual about business matters, so his affairs were in a terrible tangle. In September 1778, just after Horne left prison, Bernard wrote to say that he wanted an accountant. Horne replied that he would look for one and, if no proper person could be found, would 'with great pleasure and diligence undertake it myself, having no wish in the world greater than to catch some opportunity of being in the smallest manner useful... to you'.[2] Bernard promptly appointed Horne his agent. Although he may have offered employment out of kindness, he had worked closely with Horne and much admired his organisational powers and intelligent approach to radical politics.

A sketchy indication of Horne's movements can be gleaned from his few extant letters. In 1779 he went to live at 12 Paper Buildings, The Temple, where he stayed at least until September 1780. He does not refer to the Gordon riots. By 1784 his London address was William Tooke's chambers, Serjeants Inn, Rathbone Place. Horne later stated that he had lived mainly with Tooke for sixteen years, from 1771 until 1787. Presumably he spent what time was left with Tooke after supervising his estate and travelling about on Bernard's business.

Horne also renewed his connection with Shelburne who encouraged him to collaborate with Dr Richard Price, a member of the Bowood circle, on a statistical study of the costs of the war. They proposed to reveal how North's corrupt ministry wasted public money.

Their pamphlet appeared in 1780: 'Facts Addressed to Landholders, Stockholders... and all the Subjects of Great Britain and Ireland'. Though anonymous, the authors' identities were generally known. Chapters 2 and 8, concerned with finance, were written by Price, the rest by Horne.[3] Price produced the fiscal calculations, Horne exploited them as anti-war propaganda. The tract was in tune with widespread criticism of the Government's performance and the growing demand for economic reform such as Burke's measure, first introduced in 1780. Unfortunately Shelburne did not like its tone. He thought it would affect his manoeuvres in Parliament where he commanded little support, and feared it would antagonise county members who would object to interference with the King's household: the chapter on the civil list dismissed the King's empty promises of economy made on his accession. Still, few specific names were mentioned and its arguments had all been stated in stronger terms in Parliament by Barré and Dunning.

The pamphlet castigated Parliament for lacking the courage and competence needed to settle the war and emphasised the corrupt influence of the Crown. It attempted to expose a scandal over the purchase of rum at extortionate prices. The governors of the West Indies were said to have received enormous special payments, ostensibly for defence, for which no account had been given to Parliament; now, to the indignation and shame of the English, 'the standard of America or France is flying in each of those plantations...' 'Improper practices and impositions... have been gradually increasing in the administration of the executive branch of the legislature... if HM should now chose to promote his postilion or... his horse to the office of First Lord of the Treasury, his neigh would be attended by as great a majority as that which now follows the heels of the present noble lord in possession.' Sold at two shillings, 'Facts', as it was popularly known, was an immediate success. It had a wide circulation and went into eight editions. Contrary to Shelburne's predictions, it roused the country to protest at the profligate waste of resources, increased disillusion with the Government's war policy and contributed to its fall.

Price's nephew, William Morgan, the actuary, pioneer of life insurance and an intimate friend of Horne, said that Shelburne and Horne quarrelled irrevocably over the pamphlet.[4] If never truly reconciled, they must have remained on passable terms, for Horne continued to work with Townsend and Bernard promoting Shelburne's policies for the next four years. By July 1784, however, Horne was thoroughly disillusioned. He wrote to Bernard 'I despise Lord Shelburne... His Lordship has been worse than a murderer to me. He has destroyed everything but my character and the independence of my mind; and I will be bold to say they are both out of his reach, or the reach of any man.' Horne seems to have suspected that Shelburne had been responsible for his rejection for the bar. In the Commons in 1801, recalling his rejection, Horne said that a noble marquis, 'now a member of the House, interfered and, his influence being great, my application was rejected,' presumably a reference to Shelburne, then Marquis of Lansdowne.[5] In 1794, Horne summoned many witnesses in his defence to his treason trial, but not Shelburne. This distressed Shelburne, who asked Lord Stanhope, radical politician and scientist, to write to Horne expressing his regret, so perhaps Horne had been misinformed.

Parliamentary Reform

Loss of national prestige led to a revival of interest in reform which embraced a much larger section of the population than the Wilkite movement. It was initiated in 1779 by Christopher Wyvill, a Yorkshire clergyman and landowner of integrity, high ideals and organisational ability, who was backed by an influential group of Yorkshire gentry. He began by supporting Burke's 'economical reform', disenfranchisement of electors holding paid posts (often sinecures) under the Crown, and abolition of a number of similar posts held by members of Parliament. This would reduce the power of the Crown and administration to control elections in small boroughs and to control the votes of MPs. He set up the Yorkshire Association to apply pressure in Parliament, and encouraged other counties and boroughs to do the same.

In 1780 committees were formed in several constituencies, the first being Middlesex where the membership included Thomas Erskine, the future Lord Chancellor who was to defend Horne at his trial for treason, George Byng, since Glynn's death MP for Middlesex and parliamentary whip for Rockingham, Horne and Samuel Vaughan. The movement soon developed into a call for constitutional reform: annual parliaments and a more equal representation by the addition of more county members. In Westminster, Fox made a rousing speech and emerged as a popular leader, espousing parliamentary reform as a useful ploy to gain power. The committee there was dominated by two idealistic extremists, Thomas Brand Hollis and his mentor Dr John Jebb.

Following the example of the SSBR, Wyvill launched a petitioning movement. He initiated a scheme for county committees to send three deputies each to London to discuss the formation of a nationwide reform association. In March 1780 the Westminster committee took the initiative in calling a general assembly of deputies. More petitions were produced, but the movement ran out of steam due to differences between the various opposition factions and to the failure of Burke's motion in Parliament for economical reform. Shelburne was genuinely keen on constitutional reform, but uncertain of his strength in Parliament. The Yorkshire associators disliked the aristocratic Rockinghams, and mistrusted the radicals. In April Dunning's famous motion was passed that the influence of the Crown had increased, was increasing, and ought to be diminished. In June the Duke of Richmond, Fox's uncle, introduced a motion in the Lords for manhood suffrage. Though divided upon what form peace should take, all sections of the opposition wanted to end the war. Then on 2 June the Gordon riots occurred, causing a deep seated and long-lasting fear of mob rule. The riots frightened away many moderate advocates of reform and caused an upsurge of support for Lord North.

The Government called an autumn general election. It was very quiet and few constituencies changed hands. Fox was elected for Westminster as 'the man of the people', and held the seat till his death. Temporarily he went along with Jebb's proposals, adopted by the Westminster Committee, for annual parliaments and equal electoral districts. At Bedford the Government put up a placeman, but Samuel Whitbread (senior) 'an uncertain man for either side' kept his seat and, due to Bernard and Horne's efforts, Sir William Wake, staunch supporter of Shelburne, retained his.

In December the radicals reasserted themselves. Delegates from the five metropolitan constituencies, the City, Middlesex, Westminster, Southwark and Surrey, gathered under Townsend's chairmanship. Meetings of these committee members, among whom Horne was one of the most prominent, became known as the Quintuple Alliance. It was designed as an extension of the Westminster Committee, a parliamentary pressure group. Wyvill naturally disliked the rival body which he feared would be too extreme, while its large size and energetic activity alarmed more conservative MPs.

After news of Cornwallis's surrender reached London, the war drew to an ignominious close. In March 1782 Lord North resigned. Rockingham took over, with Shelburne, Fox and Dunning in his administration. In the new climate, Burke's bill for economic reform was successfully passed. Wyvill then agreed to a conference with the leaders of the alliance, Jebb, Townsend, Price and Horne. Wyvill tried to convince them that it was essential to have a moderate reform programme which would be widely acceptable. They agreed to co-operate in the coming parliamentary session. As reward, Wyvill included the abolition of rotten boroughs in the Yorkshire proposals. This was the only occasion on which Wyvill and Horne met privately.

On 7 May Pitt, in co-operation with Shelburne, moved for a committee of enquiry into electoral representation, and was defeated by 20 votes. A few days later Horne called on Pitt at the head of the Westminster delegates to congratulate him on his efforts. Pitt was out, but wrote Horne a friendly letter which was to prove useful to him in very different circumstances.[6] On 18 May Horne was present at the Thatched House tavern where Pitt, the Duke of Richmond, Earl of Surrey and many MPs who had voted with Pitt held a conference with leading reformers. They decided to organise petitions in support of a renewal of Pitt's proposals in the next parliamentary session. This was an important occasion, the first time that an alliance was formed between campaigners in and outside Parliament.

A few days after the defeat of Pitt's motion Horne dashed off a pamphlet, 'A Letter to Lord Ashburton' (Dunning), containing a 'sketch of a plan' for a new system of representation, in which he elaborated the ideas on electoral reform which he had formulated eleven years before in the *North Briton* (see pp 41-2).[7] It contained the core of his political creed. The goal to which all other objectives were the means was the 'happiness of all beings capable of happiness... as universally extended as possible'. Although an individual's wishes should be unbounded, his endeavours must usually be limited: 'therefore national happiness, with the permanent security of that happiness, is the ultimate object of a patriot... Even freedom itself is valuable, only as a means indispensably to that end.' Though such ideas were in the air, Horne expressed them with more clarity and brevity than his fellow-reformers. That the aim of good government was the greatest possible happiness of the individual was a flexible proposition of vast importance as a framework for reform. It was taken up by Godwin, and in Bentham's hands became a central tenet of utilitarianism.

Like Locke, Horne believed that every man had an equal right to freedom and security and a voice in framing those laws by which he was to be governed. Those who advocated universal suffrage claimed that therefore every man had an equal right to an equal share in the representation. Horne thought this at present impracticable. There was 'a very great difference between having an equal right to a share and a right to an equal share'. He held the Aristotelean view that justice and policy required 'that the share of power and the share of contribution to that power' should be as nearly proportionate to the burden of responsibility as possible. General happiness, freedom and security might even be increased by the exclusion of some, not from freedom and security, but from a share in government. Extreme misery, dependence, ignorance, lack of a sense of responsibility, were just reasons for exclusion as well as criminality, for all these faults tended to end in crime.

He did not attempt to deal with Scotland, which must make its own decisions. Like Jebb he advocated equal electoral districts. England and Wales should be divided into 513 districts which would each choose one representative. Every male aged twenty-one who had paid rates of £2 for the preceding year should be entitled to vote. At least 4,000 votes must be cast in each constituency. Every elector must pay two guineas. This levy would bring in over £4,000,000. Votes should be taken at one place in each parish. Elections should be held annually at a fixed time of year. If voting fell short of 4,000, all persons in the district rated at £20 per annum or more could have a second vote, paying another two guineas. Then all rated at £50 a third vote, then £100 and so on. Each representative should receive £400 from the election levy, the rest to be paid to the exchequer. Election revenue would provide useful government funds. Taxes could be cut, in particular the tax burden of the poorest. He was 'still sanguine enough to believe' that Britain was on 'the eve of a peaceful revolution more important than any… since the settlement of our Saxon ancestors' which would 'convey to endless posterity all the blessings of which political society is capable'. He ended with an attack on the Rockingham faction who, carrying all for themselves, had done nothing for the people. If administration had been 'half as unanimous for national rights as for honours and emoluments' Pitt's motion would have been carried.

The pamphlet created considerable interest, went into several editions and was reprinted in 1793. Horne's suggestions formed a useful basis for discussion for many years. In 1818 the *Edinburgh Review*, in an article on Bentham's schemes for reform, commented favourably on Horne's plan, which would make elections more truly popular, and praised 'his ingenious stratagem for augmenting the power of wealth though bestowing almost universal suffrage'.[8]

Horne showed little interest in ending discrimination against dissenters. He thought the Church of England admirably suited to the English temperament and, lacking any religious fervour, saw no point in agitating for the right not to subscribe to the 39 articles. He had many dissenting friends, but preferred to leave the battle of the Test Acts, which disqualified dissenters from most public offices, to those who were personally involved, though he said of a sect whose principles he found abhorrent, 'persecute them tomorrow and I will declare myself of that sect the next day'. He knew Henry Grattan and John Curran the Irish MPs well and sympathised with Irish aspirations but, possibly through dislike of Catholicism, never campaigned on Ireland's behalf. He also paid little attention to abolition of the slave trade. Though he never put private connection before principles, his close friendship with Oliver and other slave-owners could have had a deterrent effect; also he had little affinity with some of the devout, high-minded abolitionists. When Godwin first met Horne dining at Brand Hollis's, he noted in his diary, 'Horne is pro-slavery,' but Horne was probably pulling his leg.[9] In addition Horne may have decided not to dissipate his energies. He was a Londoner who had grown up at the centre of patriot politics, the cause nearest to his heart.

With a few personal variations he subscribed to many views current in the second half of the eighteenth century. He believed that before the Norman conquest there had been an excellent system of parliamentary representation which was later embodied in the principles of the Glorious Revolution of 1688. This had implicitly confirmed, as a principle of law, the subject's right to open, peaceful discussion of public affairs. Those outside the centre of politics thought the executive had won too much control of the legislature. They wanted to reorganise the distribution of seats and increase the number of electors, thus broadening the composition of the Commons at that time controlled by an aristocratic elite. Corruption was one of the most important political issues of the eighteenth century. Horne was in favour of specific measures introduced by Burke, Shelburne and Pitt to reorganise the customs, reduce the number of sinecures and reduce the burden of taxation on the poor.

Until the French Revolution the country gentlemen, City merchants and tradesmen seeking change were guided by patrician leadership. The Whigs were still fighting the old-fashioned duel between the King and the aristocracy. The Yorkshire Associators and City patriots wanted more power for the 'people', by which they meant the middling classes. Horne's views were always pungently expressed and they were roughly in line with those of Shelburne, more advanced than Wyvill's, less extreme and doctrinaire than those of Jebb. Horne was in some ways a Tory. He defended the hereditary principle in monarchy and Parliament, but deplored the fact that over 50 MPs were peers' sons. He preferred the old aristocracy to the *nouveau riche*, referring to the newly enobled Baron Hawkesbury as 'that skipjack Jenkinson'.[10]

On 1 July 1782 Rockingham unexpectedly died. His faction hoped their leader would be succeeded as Prime Minister by the Duke of Portland, but the King chose Shelburne. Fox, who disliked Shelburne immensely and had differed with him over the aims and methods of peace negotiations, resigned. There were now three main groups in Parliament: those who supported Shelburne as Chatham's heir or as a potential reformer or simply because he was the King's chosen minister, Fox's adherents, who had served under Rockingham, and Lord North's followers, who opposed constitutional change; there were also over 100 independent members. Horne was delighted when Pitt, aged twenty-three, was appointed Chancellor of the Exchequer. He defended him from charges of inexperience, saying that 'his youth was an involuntary defect... that mended daily'.[11]

Society for Constitutional Information; Westminster Election

For some time William Tooke, who wanted to make Horne one of his heirs, had been pressing him to take his name. When Horne's hopes of a legal career were dashed, Tooke finally persuaded him to do so, a token of support and encouragement. When there were legal ructions on Tooke's death, his nephew Captain Harwood claimed that Horne had implored Tooke to let him change his surname, as Horne wanted a Government place and feared his own name was too notorious. This seems totally out of character and there is absolutely no evidence for it. William later left property to Harwood and a great-nephew on condition that they took his name.[11,12]

John Horne Tooke, as he was now known (for brevity's sake he will be referred to as Tooke), had been put up on 6 July 1781 for the Society for Constitutional Information (in future referred to as the SCI) by his 'virtuous and inestimable friend' Major John Cartwright, the veteran campaigner for manhood suffrage. This society had been founded in April 1780 by Cartwright, Jebb and Capell Lofft, a barrister and rich Suffolk landowner, 'to revive in the commonality at large a knowledge of their lost rights respecting election and the duration of the representative body and to circulate this knowledge to every village and into the humble dwelling of the cottager'.[13] Its membership was originally 14 but quickly rose to over 100 and stabilised at about 130. Although most members were Londoners, some lived in other parts of the country. They included liberal-minded country gentlemen, JPs, eight Scottish and English peers, 15 MPs and a number of influential unitarian ministers. Sir Cecil Wray was first president. Several of Tooke's friends such as Sawbridge joined. Tooke nominated, among others, Townsend and William Tooke. Sir William Jones, elected an honorary member, wrote pamphlets and a song for the society. Election was by ballot, the minimum annual suscription one guinea, life membership 50. Extra contributions were intermittently solicited to pay for publications.[14]

Attendance at meetings was low, on average 20. The society was run by a devoted little band of intellectuals, professional men who manned its printing and correspondence committees. It printed and distributed free of charge standard political, historical and philosophical works, also articles and tracts written by members. The first tracts concentrated on means for obtaining sound economical government: Tooke and Price's pamphlet was widely distributed. Jebb wanted the lower classes instructed in the meaning of terms such as sovereignty, allegiance and prerogative, which Tooke was soon to promote with his book *The Diversions of Purley*. Considering its small size, the society had considerable influence in a limited sphere, at first among the middle classes, as time went on spreading lower down the social scale. Many people were worried that the society's emphasis on self-education and its efforts to extend literacy would lead the lower orders in the wrong direction.

In February 1783 Fox and North in combination brought down Shelburne's ministry with a vote of censure on the peace negotiations. Tooke's distrust of Fox was confirmed: he showed he cared more for power than for reform. In Tooke's opinion, 'the

Whigs added hypocrisy to a factious spirit' by constantly pledging 'themselves when out of office to what they never meant to perform when in power'.[15] George III was so horrified by the alliance that at first he refused to summon the Duke of Portland to take charge and only reluctantly gave way in April. Stunned by Fox's defection, nearly all the reformers turned to Pitt.

Pitt planned to bring in a motion for limited reform. He and Wyvill made concerted plans for massive public demonstrations, supported by petitions. Parliament was bombarded with resolutions, but outside the metropolis and Yorkshire there was little enthusiasm. Bernard and Tooke had no success in Huntingdonshire. Lack of support in the country may have been due in part to the activities of the SCI. The Gloucestershire committee wrote to Wyvill 'The publications of the Constitutional Society have… alarmed many and caused them to shrink from further zeal.'[16] Under the influence of North, Pitt's motion was lost on 7 May by 293 to 149. This led to a period of recrimination and disagreement. The Westminster committee became the tool of Fox's party. Jebb and other advanced reformers then concentrated on the Quintuple Alliance where they overcame the City moderates and gained control. At this time SCI was run by the same men as the Quintuple Alliance. It promoted the Duke of Richmond's pamphlet calling for universal suffrage, and under Jebb's guidance embarked on a comprehensive enquiry into electoral representation.

The coalition did not last long. Fox's unpopular India Bill was defeated in the Lords on 18 December, George III took the opportunity to dismiss the ministers he disliked and Pitt formed a new administration, popular with the public but faced with potentially hostile majorities in Parliament. After a period of manoevering, Parliament was dissolved on 25 March 1784.

In the ensuing election Tooke began by ensuring that Bernard's nominee, William Colhoun, was elected at Bedford together with Whitbread, one of the sitting members. However, Colhoun turned out to be an unfortunate choice. Although pledged to support Pitt, he promptly joined Fox and consistently voted with the opposition.

Tooke then plunged into the Westminster election, where polling lasted 40 days. In a determined attempt to drive Fox from Westminster, the Government candidate Admiral Hood joined forces with Sir Cecil Wray, Pitt's candidate, who was backed by

Jebb and most members of the SCI and Quintuple Alliance. Hood and Wray employed gangs of ruffians disguised as sailors, ostensibly to keep a way to the hustings clear, really to intimidate the pollsters. The Whigs employed Irish chairmen. In the end Hood came top of the poll, Fox second, 236 votes ahead of Wray.

The result of the election was decisive. Pitt gained a large majority and was to be Prime Minister for the rest of the century. The result was also a vote of confidence in the King. Even Tooke and most of his colleagues, who had been prepared to ally with the Rockinghams to put an end to the American war, had now decided that the monarchy was more trustworthy than Fox and his aristocratic friends.

The election had unpleasant repercussions for Tooke. His relationship with Bernard broke down, probably partly owing to his promotion of Colhoun. Bernard's family seems to have suspected Tooke of feathering his own nest at Bernard's expense. It seems unlikely that he swindled Bernard. Wilkes's hacks had accused him of embezzling subscriptions, but that was a retaliatory smear refuted by all Tooke's friends. In the words of a hostile journalist, 'His dealings with mankind were correct and regular. Indeed the contrary would too much check the independency of his spirit.'[17] Using illness as a pretext, he sold his estate at Witton to its former owner and returned to London where he soon regained 'his former health and gaiety'. Bernard, who spent an increasing amount of time taking the cure for gout at Bath, died in 1789.[18]

Social Life

Tooke now made William Tooke's rooms at Serjeants Inn his permanent base. He lived free of charge there, but received no money from William. In many ways he must have been delighted to be, for the first time, living permanently in the centre of London, within easy reach of his friends. Though he quarrelled with a few of them, the majority remained loyal for their lifetime. Stephens said that when he first surveyed a stranger, he seemed to take a peep into his heart. 'The quickness of his perceptions, his wonderful simplicity and clearness of expression, the polished keenness of his repartee, and his elegant manners, placed him very high indeed, even in the society of the first men of his time.' Though Tooke came from an unsophisticated background he was perfectly at home in society. He had, however, a lasting prejudice against Whig aristocrats. One summer evening Tooke and Arthur Murphy, playwright and biographer of Garrick, walked along Oxford Street, sat on a bench outside a small alehouse and ordered a pot of porter. 'This is the grandeur of human life,' said Tooke. 'Those scoundrels in their carriages have no taste of happiness.'[19]

He usually wore brown cloth with steel buttons and silk stockings, with his own hair tied and powdered. His face, interesting rather than handsome, had become more striking in middle-age. Women still found him 'extremely agreeable and attractive'. He disdained 'to handle any truth daintily... lest it should sting me'. He thought nothing of style as such: 'Truth is all I wish for'. He thought that no-one could have a good prose style unless he was accustomed to talk in company, but admitted that, like many fluent talkers, 'I converse better than I write, I write with labour.' His handwriting was vigorous and remarkably legible; it can be seen on many of the books he once owned in the British Library.[20]

A consummate retailer of jokes, Tooke was delighted when they were appreciated. Ridicule he considered no mean test of truth. 'If a thing to be made ridiculous must be ridiculed and distorted, then are we sure it is an object of respect?'[21] He had a large fund of stories which were retold long after his death. His friend Samuel Rogers, the poet and art connoisseur, published a selection in his *Recollections and Table Talk*. Tooke considered 'Do as you would be done by' a paltry precept: 'A generous man goes beyond it.' One of his favourite maxims was 'not to omit doing a small kindness on account of a man's insignificance, the odds are that every individual may have it in his power to help or hurt once in seven years'.[22]

Tooke often dined with John Elwes MP, where he met Major Edward Topham who founded *The World* in 1787, a fashionable newspaper to which Tooke became a contributor. Journalism was one means through which he could supplement his small income. He continued to make new political contacts. Price, for instance, introduced him to John Adams when he returned to London as American Ambassador. Tooke frequented two rendezvous for liberal-minded scholars, writers and politicians, the houses of

James Perry, a brilliant Scottish journalist who in 1790 became the owner and editor of the *Morning Chronicle*, and of Joseph Johnson, a Unitarian, founder of the *Analytical Review*, who had a bookshop in St Paul's churchyard. He was Tooke's publisher. Both men stood out firmly against the Government's attempts to intimidate them with libel prosecutions.[23]

In 1788 Tooke told William Tooke that he no longer wished to make his home with him. Due to lack of hard facts one can only speculate about much of Tooke's private life. He may have found living exclusively with William oppressive. He wanted a place where he could have his children to stay. When William complained that he would be lonely, Tooke suggested that he ask his sister's son, Captain William Harwood of the 19th Dragoons, to live with him. Harwood became as great a friend of Tooke's as his uncle was. He joined the SCI, where he became an assiduous, though unobtrusive, member. Later, Harwood also departed after marrying the daughter of Thomas Holcroft, a well-known playwright, a marriage which William disapproved of.

Tooke rented a furnished house in Richmond Buildings, Soho, to which his elder daughter Mary, now at a boarding school near London, came for the holidays. Later her younger sister Charlotte joined her. Tooke, though not well off, was now able to entertain his friends, and was a popular and expansive host. He was a member of the Speculative Society, a philosophical and literary debating club where he met many of the most interesting men of the day, *literati*, philosophers, scientists. He formed a close friendship with one member, Richard 'Conversation' Sharp, a brilliant critic who had made a fortune in hat manufacture. A kind and generous man, he shared Tooke's philological interests. James Mackintosh, Scottish philosopher, journalist and lawyer, who had just arrived in London aged twenty-three, was introduced to Tooke at the Speculative Society. After the debate Tooke took him back with other members and treated them to supper and champagne. Mackintosh, who immediately found himself at home in Tooke's circle, told Stephens that Tooke's parties at that time were superb.[24]

Tooke's fiftieth year at last brought him success. Since producing his 'Letter to Mr Dunning on the English Particle' he had been reading widely on the subject of etymology, which had fascinated him since his student days. In 1786 he published the first part of the *Diversions*, which was concerned with the origins and usage of language, a mixture of philosophy, philology and politics. It will be discussed in chapter 13. The book was greeted with enormous enthusiasm and extensive coverage in the press. Tooke was now recognised as a man of great intelligence and learning. Here was fame of a very different order, to counterbalance his dubious political reputation, and which gave him an honourable position in the world of scholars.

Quintuple Alliance; Westminster Election

After his return to London, Tooke played a vociferous part at the Quintuple Alliance, now purged of Foxites. In April 1785 Pitt introduced a bill to broaden the county franchise, buy out rotten boroughs and redistribute these seats among the counties, London and large unrepresented towns. He was defeated by 74 votes. On 24 May there was an acrimonious meeting of more than 100 friends of reform, including 27 MPs. Wyvill's motion that reform on the lines of Pitt's bill would be a substantial improvement of the constitution was defeated decisively 63 to 38. Jebb and other advanced reformers objected on principle to Pitt's plan of purchasing boroughs and doubted Pitt's sincerity. Fox had voted for it in Parliament, but he and his supporters now cast their votes against in party animosity. Tooke, who supported Pitt on grounds of expediency and practicability, debated the question with Fox and voted with Wyvill. After this débâcle the reform issue sank into abeyance. The Yorkshire Association ceased to meet. The SCI, which had backed the bill in spite of some members' opposition, became less active. Pitt decided it was not practical to continue with a policy which had so little support, so turned to economic reform. Only a minute fraction of the population was interested in Pitt's proposals, let alone the major changes advocated by the radicals.[25]

Tooke next turned his pen to the current national scandal, the Prince of Wales and Mrs Fitzherbert. In May 1787 he published an eight-page pamphlet, 'A Letter to A Friend on the Reported Marriage of HRH Prince of Wales'. 'After amusing himself with a number of critical discussions... on the subject of nouns, pronouns, adverbs and prepositions; in order to give a variety to his studies, he had taken a political, but very uncourtly view of the nature, the extent, and the true signification of the conjunctive copulative.' The assumed marriage, strongly denied by Fox, was widely considered improper and illegal because Mrs Fitzherbert was not descended from a sovereign house. Tooke argued that English kings had frequently married commoners; the degrading notion that a beautiful English woman was unworthy to be the companion of an English prince had been imported from Hanover. They must pray for offspring from the marriage, as then Hanover and Britain would be separated by differing laws of succession. George III's Royal Marriage Act transgressed the laws of God and nature. There was alarm that Mrs Fitzherbert was a papist. It was much safer to trust a sovereign to a papist wife than to a corrupt Parliament. In any case, Mrs Fitzherbert was willing to give proof of conformity to the established religion.

The pamphlet, published in London and Dublin, was widely reviewed and provoked a shoal of other pamphlets. The Attorney General had apparently given his sanction, as no action was taken against it, though it rapidly disappeared from the London shops, due to purchasing by Carlton House. Philip Francis, who said Fox positively could not endure Tooke and abused him as the greatest villain he had known, thought Tooke 'had wounded Fox in a vulnerable part', and it was to do with Mrs Fitzherbert.[26]

In July 1788, as Hood had been appointed to a seat on the Board of Admiralty, he had to submit himself for re-election. The key constituency in the metropolis was no longer Middlesex, as in the days of Wilkes, but Westminster, which had a tradition of distinguished members and, like Middlesex, a comparatively wide scot and lot (approximately householder) franchise. Bounded roughly by Oxford Street, Temple Bar and Kensington Palace, it contained a large diverse electorate of about 12,000. Although it included many of the political and social elite, the majority were tradesmen and skilled artisans who lived above their workplace.

Initially no opposition had been expected, then the Whigs put up Lord John Townshend to run in tandem with Fox. Tooke's soberer friends, who had been delighted when he concentrated on philology, were startled to find him back on the hustings supporting Hood. The ministers were believed to have bribed and intimidated on a large scale, while the Foxites raised a huge sum to back their candidates. Riots equalled those of 1784: once more butchers and chairmen confronted real or pseudo sailors. Hood's supporters considered that Tooke, if rather too much of a demagogue, spoke well. He reminded his audience that men were still relying on Pitt to introduce reform.

Tooke produced a highly popular pamphlet, 'Two Pair of Portraits'. It concerned Fox – the turf, gaming clubs, exchanging principle for party and family connections and often changing his party too – and Pitt, his virtuous youth spent studying the constitution, risking unpopularity to transform the nation's finances. To counter the impression that Pitt was a prig, Tooke declared that only his foes falsely reproached him with excessive 'sobriety and continence'. The pamphlet ended with two questions, 'Which two of them will you choose to hang up in your cabinets: The Pitts or the Foxes? Secondly, where, in your conscience, should the other two be hanged?'[27]

Poems were written on Tooke's 'matchless portraits', which were reproduced in all the pro-Government newspapers. It was a brilliant satire, a comparison of the vices and virtues of the good and naughty boys, racy, scurrilous and unfair, with exaggerations and repetitions to catch the eye. Long afterwards, when Tooke was disillusioned with Pitt, Gillray in turn mocked him for his pamphlet's former praise of Pitt.[28]

On 24 July one of Hood's supporters, John Macnamara MP, who became a lifelong friend of Tooke, had his skull fractured. Tooke published pathetic letters purporting to be from Macnamara in hospital. When Townshend charged Hood's sailors with drunken brutality, Tooke countercharged with long lists of wounded taken to St George's, Bart's and the Middlesex hospitals. Some of Pitt's adherents deplored Tooke's propaganda, thinking it did more harm than good, but it did have one desirable effect: future elections were conducted in a far more orderly manner. After a closely-fought campaign, Fox came top of the poll while Townshend defeated Hood by 6392 to 5569.[29]

Tooke was a founder-member of the Constitutional Club, formed after the election.[30] It was intended as a counterblast to the Whig Club, and to catch young men fresh from college. Members included Pitt, Lord Frederick Campbell (a Tory peer), Lord Camden and William Grenville MP, son of George Grenville. Tooke attended small select dinners for Hood and larger club dinners. On 4 November, when 1200, including cabinet ministers, peers and country gentlemen gathered at the Constitutional Club to celebrate the centenary of the Glorious Revolution, Tooke was at Hood's table with the Marquis of Graham, Sir Francis Drake and Henry Addington, the Speaker, later Prime Minister. Tooke was well-received and his opinions approved by Tory politicians, for his very long speech was much applauded. This was one of the last occasions when Tooke mixed on more or less equal and equable terms with leaders of the Government and politicians of standing.[31]

Due to attendance at this dinner, Tooke was not present at one held the same evening by the Revolution Society, to which Tooke and many of his friends and fellow members of SCI belonged. Stimulated by the centenary of 1688, societies originally founded at the beginning of the century sprang into life again. The London one held an annual religious service followed by a gathering at the London Tavern. Originally confined to inhabitants of the City, now anyone could join who paid half a guinea and subscribed to resolutions embodying the club's principles: that all civil and political authority derived from the people, that the abuse of power justified resistance, and that the right of private judgement, liberty of conscience, trial by jury, freedom of the press and election should be inviolable. The society, which included several liberal-minded MPs and many dissenting ministers, became a pressure group which joined in the current agitation for the repeal of the Test Acts. Fox supported this, Pitt opposed any modification. Tooke had little sympathy with the dissenters' grievances, so he was still able to support Pitt rather than Fox. Tooke also supported the Government against Fox over the impeachment of Warren Hastings and the question of a Regency when George III had a bout of insanity in 1788.[32]

Jebb's death in 1786 had severely affected the SCI. Without his leadership members lost interest and Cartwright, involved in reorganising his family's Lincolnshire estate, barely attended. The Duke of Richmond had been made president but was becoming steadily more rightwing. The society supported campaigns for policing the metropolis, prevention of sailors' impressment, repeal of the Test Acts and suppression of the slave trade, in which Tooke played no part. However, when Sawbridge became President in 1787, as more founder members died or withdrew, Tooke gradually assumed control. He was assisted by the hard working secretary, Daniel Adams, a clerk in the office of commissioners of public accounts, and Michael Pearson, a highly successful apothecary, who, being a placid man unlike Tooke, was much-liked, even by his political enemies. In 1805 Tooke referred to him as 'My gentle and amiable friend, forty long years my steady and uniform accomplice and comforter in all my treasons'.[33] Soon Adams, who had a private income, gave up his job and concentrated on the SCI. The society no longer met during the summer months and attendance was low, consisting mostly of middle-class dissenters, but in 1787 Tooke began to introduce a younger, livelier, more radical membership. These included the eccentric radical Count Alvise Zenobio, a tiny man from a noble Venetian family, who had inherited a fortune from an uncle, and two Mancunians, Thomas Walker, cotton merchant, and Thomas Cooper, chemist and lawyer. Thomas Paine was made an honorary member. Another young man who often acted as Tooke's secretary and was of great assistance to him in the society's work, though he did not become a member, was Felix Vaughan, a lawyer who left Cambridge in 1790. Vaughan, who was devoted to Tooke, said that 'from Tooke's constant and early care and affection for him, he had been used to consider him as a father from his infancy'. With his encouragement these newcomers proved far more energetic than the older, more distinguished original subscribers, though MPs, country gentlemen and City magnates still attended the annual audit dinners.[34]

Note on Chapter 5

1 Stephens II, p 25; Tooke's copy of *DOP* I, p 101, Br L shelf mark C60 i15 contains list of dates in his handwriting. He gives 1784? for Witton
2 Manchester MSS 12/2/8
3 Anon., 'Facts addressed to the landholders…' (Br L T 1119(5))
4 Morgan, pp 83-4;
5 Manchester MSS 12/2/35; *Parliamentary History* XXXV 1801, p 1380
6 *DOP* I, p 109
7 Horne, 'A Letter to Lord Ashburton', 1782
8 *Edinburgh Review* XXXI 1818, pp 190-1
9 *State Trials* XX, p 715
10 Stephens II, p 357

11 Stephens II, p 44
12 Burdett MSS Eng Hist B 197, f134
13 TS 11/954/3498 f1; Horne, 'Letter to Lord Ashburton', p 8
14 Cartwright I, p 134; Veitch, pp 72-3; Political Tracts 1781-2
15 Stephens II, p 438
16 Wyvill IV, p 243
17 Manchester MSS 12/2 Various letters; *The World* 2.6.17
18 Stephens II, p 26
19 Stephens II, p 451; Losh, *Diaries*, p 10; Clayden, *Early Life*, p 268
20 *DOP* I, p 62; Rogers, *Recollections*, p 130
21 Rogers, *Recollections*, p 135
22 *Ibid.*, p 142; Hobhouse II, p 177
23 Byrne I, p 91
24 Stephens II, pp 28, 29
25 Christie, pp 219-21
26 Horne, *Letter to a Friend…* April 1787; Francis II, p 451, Stephens II, p 69
27 Horne, *Two Pair of Portraits*, 1788
28 George, M.D. VII, 9270, 1.2.98
29 *London Chronicle* July 17-Aug 5 1788
30 Stephens II, p 49
31 *Public Advertiser* 7.11.88
32 George, Prince of Wales, *Correspondence*, p 375
33 *DOP* II, p 445
34 TS 11/963/3509 f498

Chapter Six

The Radical Movement During the French Revolution

The outbreak and development of the French Revolution in 1789 profoundly affected political thought and organisations. At first, liberal-minded Britons were most enthusiastic, thinking it would prove similar to the Glorious Revolution. After the disappointments of the 1780s, the political societies advocating reform were galvanized into fresh efforts, often with more emphasis on abstract rights and democracy. At first, the London Revolution Society made all the running. On 4 November 1789, at the annual service, Dr Price preached a sermon, 'A Discourse on the Love of our Country', which provoked Burke to start work on his 'Reflections on the French Revolution'. Price was a sober, moderate man, but he had been dismayed by the Goverment's refusal to repeal the Test Acts. He criticised the British constitution for its limited religious toleration and its corrupt parliamentary system. Afterwards at dinner, under the chairmanship of Lord Stanhope, in an atmosphere of buoyant optimism, he moved an Address of Congratulation to the French National Assembly. It was welcomed enthusiastically by the French and led to correspondence between the Jacobins and British clubs.[1]

Only 12 members, including Tooke, were present at the SCI's first meeting after the summer recess on 27 November, but they too sent a message of congratulation to the French National Assembly. Twenty-six members attended a dinner on 16 December to mark the passing of the Bill of Rights. There were sixteen visitors, including St André, a member of the Assemblée Nationale. The Society then toasted the French National Assembly and the destruction of the Bastille. In a renewed campaign for electoral reform the SCI adopted a far more pragmatic and moderate approach than it had under Jebb's aegis. Henry Flood MP, the Irish statesman and the new President of the Society, introduced a motion in March 1790 proposing the addition of a hundred MPs to be elected by rate-paying householders in the counties. Pitt, who still declared he would support reform when circumstances were more auspicious, pressed Flood to drop the motion, which was opposed by a large majority of MPs alarmed by events in France. Undeterred, Flood and Tooke, who had by now lost faith in Pitt's integrity, led a deputation of six members to consult with the Revolution Society on a joint campaign for the forthcoming general election.

In Westminster the election began on 16 June. To avoid the enormous cost of previous elections the two parties agreed to compromise: Hood and Fox would be elected unopposed. This was widely regarded as virtual disenfranchisement of the borough with the largest electorate in the country and a polling place within easy reach at Covent Garden. No-one expected a contest: Hood was far too busy with public affairs to spend much time on the hustings. When Tooke unexpectedly stood up and nominated himself there was consternation: the clerks did not even have pens to register the votes. Tooke gave his reasons in a notice he inserted in the newspapers on the first morning of the election. 'The junction of two contending parties… to deprive you even of that shadow of an election, to which they have… lately reduced you, calls aloud on every independent mind to frustrate such attempts, and makes me, for the first time in my life, a candidate.' The two candidates, who had never concurred in any measure for the public benefit, 'now come forward, hand in hand, with the same general and hackneyed professions of devotion to your interest, unblushingly to demand your approbation and support'.[2] It needed a man of Tooke's courage, intelligence and self-confidence to make this first attempt, undertaken entirely on his own initative, to challenge men who assumed they should be chosen by virtue of rank and tradition. It was to be hailed by radicals as the foundation of a new spirit in the constituency, an inspiration to middling men which culminated in Burdett's election 17 years later.

Due to Tooke's intervention the election dragged on until 2 July. Tooke, some of whose speeches lasted half an hour, was a great success on the hustings – cool, prompt, master of repartee – holding the attention and gaining the goodwill of his very mixed audience. He spoke to the electors who until then had no say in choosing their candidates: 'Let us convince the Lords and Lordlings of Westminster, who fancy they come into the world ready booted and spurred… and that we are born ready bridled and saddled for them to ride upon us – let us convince these Jockies, that, though they have rode us hard, and though we have carried the burthen long and patiently, it is in our power, whenever we please, to throw them off'. Some spectators thought him deficient in force and animation. He made no attempt to curry favour or rouse mob enthusiasm. He said he was too poor to be returned by bribery. His genuine patriotism increased his popularity. Burke became worried, and wrote to his son to ask if he must come to town to vote: 'I hope they (Whigs) will really exert themselves, for Horne begins not to look so ridiculous'.[3]

A small band of his fellow-reformers campaigned vigorously. Mackintosh marched the streets canvassing with Tooke's colours in his hat, but Tooke had no official backing and only a very few MPs and men of note (including, however, Rogers) supported him. The result was therefore remarkable and cheering: Fox received 3,516 votes, Hood 3,217, Tooke 1,679. Tooke claimed a moral victory, for he spent only £28 on advertising charges, yet received nearly half as many votes as the others, who were financed by the Treasury and the Whig Club. After the election he issued a manifesto thanking the electorate for their support and saying that he would present a petition to Parliament against the return of Fox and Hood on the grounds of malpractice in previous elections. He said he would present himself again on future occasions.[4]

The election left Pitt securely in power. Both Flood and Wilkes lost their seats. Wilkes, who had never been well-disposed to Fox, voted for Tooke, who thanked him for his 'judicious and handsome conduct'. By now the two men had reverted to a moderately amicable relationship. Tooke would write letters of recommendation for his younger friends who wanted to make contact with the famous old patriot.

John Thelwall, one of his assistants during the election, was taken up by Tooke who appreciated his talents. His father had been a silk mercer, but he hated the business so tried to earn his living by journalism. Clever, brave, small and undistinguished in appearance, he was a born orator with an engaging personality though, like many autodidacts, rather humourless and complacent. He became a friend of Lamb, Coleridge and Hazlitt. Thelwall had great affection for Tooke who, he said, had transformed his life. He derived enormous pleasure and benefit from his conversation, the first man of 'capacious and highly-cultivated mind' with whom he had ever been intimate.[5] He worked very closely with Tooke for the next four years and modelled his style on Tooke who, while advocating lawful peaceful methods, used violent, emotive rhetoric.

Two weeks after the election, the Revolution Society held a monster banquet to celebrate the fall of the Bastille. Among the 652 ebullient 'friends of liberty' who attended were many dissenters and members of the Whig club. The proceedings opened with an invocation to the Supreme Being. Speeches by Price and the Chairman, Stanhope, praised France, where there was now more civil and religious liberty than in Britain. Sheridan proposed a resolution that the meeting cordially rejoiced in the establishment of liberty in France and that it beheld with peculiar satisfaction the amity and goodwill which the French appeared to feel towards Britain, so essential for the freedom and happiness not only of both nations, but of all mankind. This was received with great applause, somewhat damped by Tooke who proposed an amendment. Appreciating the danger of identifying the reform cause too completely with the French Revolution, he feared that such unqualified approbation might be misrepresented as an encouragement to revolution in Britain. He pointed out that the gentlemen present had national cockades in their hats and a piece of stone from the Bastille was lying on the table in the place of honour. He thought the meeting should declare its attachment to the principles of the constitution. The former Government of France was such a decayed vessel it could not be repaired, but the main timbers of the British constitution were sound. The Whigs, who were angry with Tooke for his treatment of Fox at the election, booed and hissed him into silence. Stanhope restored order, suggesting that they should hear Tooke first and hiss him afterwards. Tooke introduced a further motion, which was accepted: 'the... English, by the virtuous exertions of their ancestors, have not so arduous a task to perform as the French... but have only to maintain and improve the constitution which their ancestors have transmitted to them.'[6]

When cross-examined some years later about this encounter, Sheridan said he had often had the misfortune to oppose Tooke at public meetings and had frequently seen him received with 'very considerable marks of disapprobation, but they never much affected him'. In private life Sheridan and Tooke remained on amicable terms and often dined together.[7]

In September French delegates from the Jacobin Society at Nantes were entertained to dinner by the Revolution Society, chaired by John Hurford Stone, a Unitarian acquaintance of Tooke's from the days of the Quintuple Alliance. An intelligent, cultivated man, friend of Fox, Sheridan and Talleyrand, he was ardently pro the French Revolution. On 4 November Dr Price once more presided over 400 guests at the anniversary dinner of the Revolution Society. This time Fox persuaded Sheridan and other Whigs to stay away. Lord William Russell and Stanhope had resigned. Burke had just published his 'Reflections on the Revolution in France' which strongly criticised the Revolution Society, Dr Price and reformers in general for their ridiculous and dangerous enthusiasm for French doctrines. He mocked the publications of the SCI, 'a poor charitable club'.[8] Price indiscreetly proposed a toast 'To the Parliament of Britain. May it become a National Assembly'. Tooke called Burke's pamphlet 'The tears of the priesthood for the loss of their pudding', and proposed a toast that 'If Burke should be prosecuted for such a libel on the constitution, may his impeachment last as long as that of Hastings'. A heated debate took place on Tooke's motion that in future, if peers wanted to join, they should be admitted under their family names, not their titles. This was emulating the French with a vengeance.[9]

Dr Theophilus Lindsey, distinguished Unitarian divine, described the scene: 'All was going very well until Tooke interrupted the festivity and harmony by a motion to exclude all Lords and titles from the society. This would have brought much censure on the society… as if a new revolution were our aim. After much altercation pour and contre it was withdrawn. I was sorry that Mr Cooper in particular and some other worthy and able [men] supported Tooke, [who] possesses great powers to win upon a popular and mixed assembly, having wit and humour at command to soothe them.' Cooper, however, wrote to Thomas Walker, '[Tooke's] superiority to his opponents singly and jointly in point, argument, language, temper and spirit was indisputable'.[10]

On 12 December Tooke petitioned Parliament on the grounds that the 17,291 electors of Westminster, who paid more tax than those who sent a hundred members to Parliament, were disenfranchised; that at the last three elections there had been armed violence and murder, for which no redress or remedy had been attempted; that the futile scrutiny on Wray's behalf in 1784 had cost many thousands of pounds, more than appeared by recent Chancery proceedings to be the agreed average price of a perpetual seat in the Commons, 'where seats… are as notoriously rented and bought as the standings for cattle at a fair'. The committee appointed after Hood's petition had equally failed to achieve anything in over a year. It would be cheaper for Tooke to be impeached and convicted of real crimes than for him to attempt to obtain justice for himself and the Westminster electors. What use was a law that a parliamentary candidate must have £300 per annum if he had to spend £50,000 to prove himself duly elected?[11] As Tooke knew his cause was almost certain to fail, he made no attempt to conceal his contempt for the Commons.

Once more Tooke took the House aback with his insouciant effrontery. The petition was received with great indignation. Pitt thought it impudent, too low to notice. After the expenditure of much parliamentary time and several rereadings of the petition, a committee was nominated to consider it. When summoned before the committee Tooke made a long able speech but – a perennial fault – emphasised the wrong aspects and introduced too personal a note. He attacked the Speaker, Addington, who had called his petition an outrage upon decency, and suggested that Addington had not grasped the latest orders for regulating contested elections because his attention had been engrossed by another act providing him with a salary of £6,000 a year.

Pulteney had complained in the Commons that Tooke's petition was merely reform propaganda. Tooke now remarked that it was curious that this objection came from someone who had just purchased four boroughs. This caused 'A general buzz in the committee'. Finally the committee pronounced the petition frivolous and vexatious and agreed to treat Tooke, his petition and his conduct, with silent contempt.[11]

By an Act of 1789 the committee's decision meant that the petitioner was liable for all costs. Tooke considered the act unjust and unconstitutional, as it made the Commons committee sole arbiters and deprived the supposed delinquent of appeal to a jury, so he refused to pay. Hood did not trouble Tooke for his share, but Fox brought an action for the taxed cost of expenses he had incurred, £198.2.2.[12]

This was heard on 30 April 1792 before Lord Kenyon, Tooke's former fellow-student. Thomas Erskine, Whig and fellow member of the SCI, appeared for Fox. As Tooke conducted his own case he was able to digress on corrupt electoral practices and to make a few cutting remarks about lawyers who had rejected him. He referred to Fox more kindly than usual, saying that he had discharged the duty of an honest man. There was nothing mean, personal or mercenary in the question, but 'a great and important national right is at stake. The last and only security… left to the people… a real trial by jury… is now attempted to be wrested from us.'

Tooke claimed that in the 1784 and 1788 elections £200,000 had been distributed among the poor as bribes, much of which had come in effect from the taxpayer, for the ministerial faction covered its expenses by levies on members of public boards. He reminded the jury that the act under which he was being sued gave a Commons committee power to inflict absolute ruin without allowing a jury to enquire into the merits of a question. Tooke used a metaphor alluding to the extremely unpopular game laws. The act was a spring gun and spoke plain language, 'Woe to the man in future, who shall be caught in our traps, our frivolous and vexatious traps'. The jury adjourned once because they could not agree, then finally at 10pm, after four hours 20 minutes, found for Fox.[12]

Though frequently interrupted by Kenyon, in argument, in clear exposition of legal points, Tooke was decidedly his superior. Most commentators praised his skilful handling of the case. 'A masterpiece of acuteness, modest assurance and legal effect.' The proceedings were published in a pamphlet which was widely reviewed. It was republished in 1812 and reissued by his friends in 1819, along with his addresses at the opening and close of the polls at elections in which he stood as candidate. Tooke's copy contains a bitter comment he added after his arrest for treason: 'What is my station in this country? He who made this man Chief Justice and peer has made me an outlaw.'[12]

Tooke also drew attention to the unwarranted 'official' charges to candidates made by the High Bailiff. His deputy, who had demanded £400 from Tooke, later gave him an itemised account which showed that a large part of this sum had been spent on dinners for the bailiff and his clerks, so when Tooke stood again, he refused to contribute as much. This marks the first salvo of an attack on excessive election costs pursued for many years by Westminster radicals.[13] The trial caused a sensation in the country and made Tooke appear even more notorious to his enemies, but heroic to the friends of reform.

The SCI and Paine

After the Government's electoral success, and with the rejection of Fox's motion to repeal the Test Acts, reforming zeal waned again. Initial enthusiasm for the French Revolution was restrained by forebodings about the future. Dr Price died in the spring of 1791, a sad loss. Brand Hollis presided at a dinner of the SCI on 7 March. There were five visitors and only 14 members. They approved one incautious resolution: 'The National Assembly [of France] and may the Parliament of Great Britain become such'.[14]

Tooke worked hard to revitalise the society by introducing fresh recruits. In the the years from 1791-94 134 men joined, of whom 46 were proposed or seconded by Tooke. Few long-standing members of any importance remained, and most newcomers were of less distinguished social and political standing, but they were educated, respectable and intelligent, and fired with enthusiasm by the revolution in France.[15]

Though Tooke himself did not do so, several of his close friends visited France: Perry, Robert Merry, a popular poet who made several brief visits, and Felix Vaughan. John Hurford Stone took a more drastic step: he sold his business in England and set up a factory and printing press in Paris, while Dr John Warner, a distinguished classical scholar and preacher with whom Tooke had discussed points in the *Diversions*, was appointed embassy chaplain at Paris and became a keen supporter of the revolution.

The SCI had always laid emphasis on distributing literature via contacts throughout the country. Tooke now went a stage further. He introduced a resolution that it should seek correspondence with 'all corresponding constitutional societies in England, Scotland and France'. Burke's damagingly derisive comment, that the SCI's proceedings had not been accounted of any serious consequence except by itself, had enough justification to infuriate its members, several of whom produced counterblasts. They included four Unitarians, one of whom was a clever young Scot Thomas Christie, friend of Dr Johnson and cofounder of the *Analytical Review*. Tooke was active in promoting his friends' tracts, in particular the reply that was to have by far the greatest impact, Paine's *Rights of Man*, the first part of which was published on 16 March 1791. Paine repudiated Burke's defence of hereditary forms of government. Man had inalienable rights to freedom which could not be challenged by historical precedents. The revolution was justified because France had no written constitution agreed by the people. *Rights of Man* was officially welcomed by the SCI but, so that this should not be misinterpreted, they passed a resolution reiterating that their own aim was limited to reform of the existing constitution. It was largely due to the promotional efforts of the society, masterminded by Tooke, that it had such an instant, huge success.[16]

Although Tooke believed that the example of the French provided an opportunity to alter the English political system, he did not agree with Paine's republicanism. Paine and Tooke had long arguments in which, according to their friends, Tooke invariably worsted Paine. Tooke, who delighted in trailing his coat, professed his belief in preserving institutions but hanging those who administered them badly. He was for having Kings but 'cutting off the head of one of them every 50 or 100 years'. One evening when he ran on in this way, Paine, 'who was a humane man', endured it with sullen forbearance, then finally burst out indignantly, 'Ah Tooke! You are a true royalist! You love blood!'

Tooke did not think much of Paine's grammar or breadth of knowledge. However, in an expansive moment, sitting next to

Paine at a dinner party of Christie's, he said that Paine had proved himself 'the greatest political writer in the world'. When giving evidence at Thelwall's trial in 1794 Tooke said he admired Paine for rising above the disadvantages of his education. Tooke considered Paine 'the defender of the small, a man who had pointed out real abuses in a very strong manner and would in his opinion be very beneficial to the poorer and oppressed portion of the community'.[17]

Many people thought that Tooke corrected Paine's work, but Paine's writings are themselves evidence that he did not. When Paine's friends suggested he should get editorial help because critics poked fun at his grammatical mistakes, Paine said he did not wish to appear under borrowed plumage. Tooke gave advice on pruning and clarity of expression, but was too sensible to tinker with Paine's rough style. He realised that Paine's simplified political theory and colloquial language would appeal to artisans and middling people. On his initiative, the SCI issued advertisements and broadsheets publicising the fact that Paine was an honourable member and recommending his 'masterly book'. £40 was raised to cover the cost, to which Tooke contributed five guineas. Tooke now often personally subsidised SCI publications.

In May 1791 Burke split with Fox who praised the revolution for bringing liberty to France. Ministers were increasingly worried by reformist propaganda, so a number of newspaper editors were accused of libel. As a result, in June 1792 Erskine, Sheridan and Mackintosh formed another society, the Friends of the Liberty of the Press, which Foxites and members of the SCI, including Tooke, joined. Some Whigs feared Tooke would give the society a bad name.[18]

The flight to Varennes on 21 June 1791 and the King's imprisonment frightened most people and made them more antagonistic to reformers who remained enthusiastic. Once more a dinner was held on 14 July to celebrate the fall of the Bastille. The Whig club were invited, but the majority declined. The Government press claimed that the principal democrats stayed away so the company was composed of 'people whom nobody knows'. In fact the thousand guests included several country gentlemen and MPs. One MP, George Rous, was chairman. So that the dinner should not be misrepresented, it was announced in advance that there would be no discussion of public affairs. There was, however, a disastrous aftermath to a celebratory dinner on the same day in Birmingham where a 'Church and King' mob, encouraged by local magistrates, burnt and looted the houses of prominent dissenters, including that of Priestley, discoverer of oxygen, whose laboratory and papers were destroyed.

Burke called for suppression of the radical societies and publications. In defiance, commemoration of the abolition of feudalism in France was planned to be held on 4 August at the Crown and Anchor. The landlord refused his permission, so Paine drew up an address which was read on 20 August to a meeting calling themselves the Friends of Peace and Universal Liberty under Tooke's chairmanship at the Thatched House tavern. The address included two cardinal democratic tenets which Tooke among others was keen to promote, that the best government secures every man's rights and promotes the greatest happiness with the least expense, and that every nation has the right to establish such government 'as best accords with its disposition, interest and happiness'. The address was published over Horne Tooke's name although Paine later acknowledged that he was in fact the author.[19]

SCI and London Corresponding Society

Tooke was a turbulent and disillusioned man. In greater isolation from other politicians than ever before, he had no forum for his ideas. Contemporaries accused him of preferring to be captain of a band of devotees who would acknowledge his pre-eminence, rather than a valued lieutenant in a more powerful and important group. Though there is truth in this criticism, it was partly due to circumstances. During the eighties, in the Quintuple Alliance, the SCI and election campaigns, he worked as organiser, journalist, canvasser and committeeman under men many of whom were less talented than himself. It was only when it became clear that Pitt had abandoned all idea of parliamentary reform that he broke away on his own. But, being temperamentally unsuited to be subordinate to others unless their opinions accorded with his own, he found this increasingly difficult as he grew older.

There was no group which could readily accommodate him. City politics were now dominated by conservatives, not radicals. The Wilkites were a shrinking, ageing band. Townsend was dead,

Sawbridge soon to be incapacitated by a stroke. Wilkes, who had taken so little part in politics that he had been rejected by the Middlesex electors and lost his parliamentary seat, greeted the French Revolution with horror. Shelburne and his entourage no longer played a significant part in Parliament. Ironically, although Tooke no longer had any contact, he was still coupled with Shelburne (now Marquis of Lansdowne). Bland Burges, Under Secretary of State for Foreign Affairs, wrote to Lord Auckland 'Talleyrand is intimate with Paine, Tooke, Lord Lansdowne and a few more of that stamp'. Tooke met Talleyrand when he came to England on diplomatic missions in 1791 and 1792, remaining after war was declared. A list of suspect persons whose mail should be opened, issued in April 1792, included Paine, Tooke and Talleyrand.[20]

The only men with any influence who were genuinely interested in electoral reform were the close-knit group of progressive Whigs. They had been antagonised by Tooke's criticism of their leader and thought him an eccentric troublemaker. Even if he had been less obstreperous, it is doubtful if the Foxites would have welcomed him. They never accepted the more moderate brewer Whitbread; while Cartwright, advocate of universal suffrage, was tolerated on sufferance as a country gentleman.

Tooke now concentrated his activities on the SCI, the only place where he could have a modicum of power. The SCI was always short of money, but it is remarkable how much impact this small club of insignificant agitators was able to make, with the *Rights of Man* as its most powerful weapon. Under Tooke's aegis correspondence increased, old and new tracts were issued and more efficiently distributed, meetings, which were advertised in the liberal press, doubled in number; Tooke seldom missed one. He continued to promote not only parliamentary reform but the society's other longstanding interests by publishing, for instance, the barrister Samuel Romilly's pamphlet on how reorganisation of the jury system could improve justice. In 1782 the society had initiated the collection of data on the representation of the boroughs in England and Wales. The work finally bore fruit in 1792 with the publication of Oldfield's 'History of the Boroughs'. This was the first comprehensive analysis of the actual state of representation and immediately became a mine of information for the reforming party. Tierney, a barrister and statesman, published an abridged version for the Friends of the People in 1793.

The most important of Tooke's activities, which perturbed the Government as a new factor with sinister possibilities, was to foster the societies which sprang up in industrial towns across the country, largely composed of artisans and tradesmen, most of whom did not have the vote. They were indignant at their lack of rights and resented their exploitation by the upper classes. They suffered from harsh conditions created by increasing industrialisation and urbanisation. Prices had risen, and there was much unemployment as skilled craftsmen were displaced by machinery. Many joined clubs as part of their struggle for social betterment. They found an excellent mentor in Tooke. Helped by John Frost (a lawyer) and Felix Vaughan, Tooke put the fledgling societies in touch with each other, suggested constitutions, amended the rules they drew up. The clubs' letters were often muddled and ungrammatical. Tooke made sensible, minimal alterations; he corrected their English and, as a Government lawyer put it, altered 'low expressions'. Unlike other clubs, the SCI never campaigned. It was the coordinating centre from which Tooke could operate, deploying his little army strategically placed round the country. As Wyvill had attempted with the Yorkshire associators, he hoped that, though each tiny group could achieve little, the combination of many might influence public opinion. It was pioneer work of great value.

In autumn 1791 tradesmen and artificers formed a society in Sheffield and made contact with Tooke. They hoped that, to promote regular communication, some of their members could be affiliated to a London organisation. Tooke wrote a long enthusiastic reply. He would propose 12 of their society as Associate members of the SCI. 'Large and respectable manufacturing towns are the great balance to the aristocratical interests of the country.' If 'discreet but zealous acivity' prevailed in other places as at Sheffield, he believed 'our cause would be as successful as meritorious.'[21]

Tooke put Sheffield in touch with a similar group, the London Corresponding Society (LCS) founded in January 1792 by Thomas Hardy, a Scottish shoemaker, a tall, handsome man who had a shop at 9 Piccadilly. Hardy was a devout Presbyterian, a hard-working idealist and an extremely skilled organiser. Honest, brave and warmhearted, though reserved, he was liked by everyone. Fired by SCI tracts written by Cartwright, the Duke of Richmond and Tooke, which Brand Hollis had loaned him, he and a few acquaintances drew up plans for a society to which he was elected secretary. With a subscription fixed at 1d a week it would cater for a different class of person to the SCI. Within a fortnight 12 had joined and by the end of the year there were about 800 active members.[22]

Hardy sought an introduction to Tooke after a typically Tookian episode. In 1790 Gow, a watchmaker in Duke Street, having heard of Tooke's reputation for tackling difficult problems, came to ask his advice. His brother, with several other passengers on an American ship, had been captured by a corsair and taken into Algiers where they had been enslaved. Tooke recommended him to apply to the Privy Council, but Gow said this had already been tried with no success. Tooke said in that case the captives would have to be ransomed. He appointed an attorney to receive donations, subscribed himself and solicited contributions. His efforts were successful, and several hundred pounds were collected, his friend General Murray giving £25. Gow's brother, redeemed from slavery, called to thank Tooke dressed in Algerian costume. So when Hardy told Gow he needed advice on drafting rules for his society, Gow recommended him to ask Tooke.[23]

Tooke was unfailingly kind and helpful to Hardy, who described him as 'a steady and intrepid champion of freedom whose friendship was a real honour'. Tooke introduced Hardy to Cartwright who, though his usual relationship with plebeian radicals was that of officer to other ranks, also became his friend. In a speech at his trial after his acquittal, Tooke gave a disingenuous impression of his connection with the LCS, claiming that it was merely in his capacity as candidate for Westminster. He formed far closer links than this would imply. Hardy said that Tooke had nothing to do with founding the LCS or drafting its regulations, but Tooke certainly acted as unofficial consultant both directly and through Felix Vaughan, who drew up the society's constitution and asked Tooke for his comments before discussing it with Hardy.[24]

Hardy hoped to attract men of standing to the LCS, but had little success. Besides Tooke's protégés, the only educated gentleman who played an important part was Maurice Margarot, aged forty-seven. In spring 1792 he was appointed LCS chairman. He was self-important and unstable, with a chip on his shoulder, a passionate fighter for his political beliefs. Over the next two years Margarot was in constant contact with Tooke, but there is no indication of any intimacy. In 1793 he represented LCS at the British Convention in Edinburgh, where he was arrested and sentenced to 14 years, transportation to Australia.[25]

Part II of the *Rights of Man* was published in February 1792. About 50,000 copies of Part I were sold. Part II was far more successful; including abridged editions it had an enormous circulation.[26] Part I had been comparatively moderate; Part II contained more controversial matter. Paine criticised the futility of petitioning Parliament and produced a comprehensive plan for free education and social benefits – old age pensions, maternity and family allowances – to be financed by cutting defence and central administration and the introduction of progressive income tax. These schemes, though far in advance of their time, were not subversive, but Paine also advocated the abolition of titles and primogeniture and virulently criticised the Government and the King. The upper classes, already frightened by events in France, thought such ideas would encourage the poor to seize their property. Several leading reformers such as Dr Lindsey and Cooper welcomed Paine's call for a liberal alliance betweem Britain, France and America. Humble reformers, who were not particularly interested in the niceties of electoral reform, were most enthusiastic about Paine's suggestions for social welfare. *The Rights of Man* became their Bible.

In March SCI issued a resolution which concentrated exclusively on reform and thanked Paine for publishing the *Rights of Man*. 'The Society does ardently recommend it to all their fellow citizens… to confer seriously and calmly with each other on the subjects alluded to.' As Judge Eyre pointed out at subsequent trials, Manchester, like the SCI, carefully confined its approbation to specific objects in Paine's work, separating good from bad. Other clubs, run by less-educated men, were not so cautious in their praise.[27]

The LCS did not publish its approval until August. They were preoccupied with a declaration of principles. Hardy consulted Tooke. Paine offered to draft it, but could not find time. Although Margarot produced the final version, he would not sign it as he was afraid it would affect his chances of employment in the City. Hardy felt he was too obscure: someone more influential was needed. Tooke settled the matter when Hardy submitted the address to SCI for approval. At a meeting on 1 April, when Captain Sampson Perry of the *Argus* was present, Tooke wrote Hardy's name and gave it to Perry who published it. It contained the usual complaints of oppressive taxes, unjust laws, restrictions on liberty, waste of public money. The goal was universal male suffrage and annual parliaments, but no details were given as to how this was to be accomplished. The only weapons were to be reason, firmness and unanimity. This was a far more moderate line than Paine's. There was, however, one sentence which could be construed to carry subversive connotations: society was a voluntary organisation and government a trust; if government did not operate for the benefit of the governed, the trust was broken. Man was not bound by oppressive actions and had an inalienable right to resist oppression.[28]

Tooke's Political Opinions

Though he touched on it in his speeches and writings, Tooke never made a comprehensive statement about his political creed. He said publicly that if a law was bad he would disobey it and work to get it repealed. In Part II of *Diversions*, published in 1805, he endorsed the LCS dictum, 'I follow the law of God (which is laid down by Him for the rule of my conduct) when I follow the laws of nature; which, without any human testimony, we know must proceed from God; and upon these are founded the rights of man, or what is ordered for man. I revere the Constitution and constitutional laws of England; because they are in conformity with the laws of God and nature; and upon these are founded the rational rights of Englishmen. If… the corrupted sham representatives of a people order… anything contrary to that which is ordered… by God, human nature, or the constitution of this government, I will still hold fast by the higher authorities.'[29]

Both Tooke and the LCS were doing no more than restating a traditional argument based on Locke's theories. Locke and the more progressive Whigs had envisaged the people delegating power to those qualified to rule, men of property and education. All individuals had the right to have their persons and property secured by law, but did not have the positive right to participate in politics. The radicals changed the emphasis. They said the constitution gave the people the right, which had existed since Saxon times, to choose their own representatives and take part in government. When the slogan 'rights of man' was first promoted, those rights were taken to be the political and religious rights of the middle classes; later they were claimed to include universal suffrage, then gradually extended to encompass the economic and social rights of the working classes. Tooke publicly opposed universal suffrage, thinking, like almost all his contemporaries, that it was unsuited to society at that time. Enlightened men should take charge of affairs on behalf of the nation.

Paine abandoned the historical argument. Each generation must be free to act as it thought best, which implied that it could remodel government. He compared the principles of British government unfavourably with the new written constitutions of America and France, and declared a democratic republic the only possible solution. Tooke's opinions were of an earlier and more conservative vintage. Paine wanted to change the constitution, Tooke to reinforce the people's legal right for it to be restored to its former purity.

It is difficult to be certain what were Tooke's real opinions. He enjoyed making mischief and misleading people. Holcroft said that he frequently heard Tooke mutter sentences at SCI meetings 'the first part of which would have subjected him to death by law but for the salvo that followed: and the more violent they were, thus contrasted and equivocatory, the greater was his delight'.[30] One could argue that by this means Tooke was able to express his seditious views without fear that they would be taken seriously. Tooke was a contrary person who, when faced with serried ranks of cautious Whigs, might be moved to advocate a touch of force. According to Mrs Thelwall, her husband recollected Tooke saying, 'I am too old to rebel – I am too gouty to rebel; but, if the people chose to rebel, I will sit in my easy chair and pray for their success'.[31]*

During the spring the SCI annual subscription was raised to enable a small library of political books to be purchased. Subscriptions in arrears were said to amount to £600, due from those to whom the society still sent material because they had not

* The second Mrs Thelwall never met Tooke. Her inaccurate life of her husband, which contains many factual errors, was written after his death. She based her book on Thelwall's notes written in old age. His memory, like Hardy's when he wrote his Memoirs, is not always reliable. See p 188.

formally resigned. Those members who disapproved of Tooke's policy resigned in protest, or merely let their subscriptions lapse. On the other hand there was a surge in attendance at meetings which now averaged 30. New members enrolled weekly. Mackintosh and the distinguished Glaswegian Professor John Miller were elected honorary members. Tooke both proposed them and put their names in SCI advertisements to increase the society's prestige. The American poet and political writer Joel Barlow was also elected an honorary member. Tooke had made a great impression on him when he arrived in London to watch the 1788 election: 'No man who heard Tooke then in the fight for parliamentary reform could fail to have his heart moved as by a trumpet.'[32]

Reform; Paine; France

On 11 April 1792 Sheridan's wing of the Whig Club, a group of 28 comparatively young MPs, launched the Friends of the People (FOP), a respectable, exclusive and powerful rival to the SCI. Its subscription was high, two-and-a-half guineas a year; Mackintosh, though blackballed by the Whig Club, was secretary; members, initially about 100, included Grey (the future Prime Minister), Erskine, Whitbread, Tierney and Tooke's friends Merry, Bosville, Robert Knight, Rogers, James Perry and J.H. Stone. Regarding themselves as natural leaders, they wanted to act as a brake on the popular societies and to formulate a reform programme which would appeal to moderate opinion. Initially they were welcomed by the humbler reformers who had hoped that more influential men would lead them. Twenty-seven past and present members of the SCI, including Dr Towers (coadjutor of Price), Richard Sharp, William Smith (a Foxite MP) and Capel Lofft now concentrated their efforts on the FOP. This left Tooke in undisputed charge of the SCI, but bereft of nearly all its remaining men of distinction. Tooke himself did not attempt to join. Cooper applied but was rejected. Cartwright and Brand Hollis, though pro universal suffrage, were accepted.[33]

On 30 April Grey introduced a bill for parliamentary reform in an attempt to sound out public opinion, but in June Fox told the Whig club that, though he wished for reform, he did not think it an appropriate moment. The move, in any case, came too late: by this time Pitt and Burke and the great majority of the country had become so alarmed by developments in France that there was little or no support in Parliament.

The SCI and provincial societies wrote to the FOP, hoping to arrange collaborative action. The FOP, however, feared they would get a bad reputation by associating with plebeian clubs. They deeply distrusted 'Horne Tooke and Major Cartwright's disciples'. Lord Lauderdale voiced their suspicions: 'their main aim was to vilify those who expressed their desire for moderate reform, whilst they took care to cover their own intentions by advancing general resolutions and avoiding everything that was specific'. Wyvill strongly supported the break with the SCI. He believed their conduct was dangerous and that it would be difficult to reverse fears Paine had aroused which would militate against reform.[34] Conversely, as Judge Eyre later noted, Tooke made no attempt to emphasise that though they might differ as to the extent of the remedies to be introduced, SCI goals were sufficiently similar for them to co-operate.

As a result the FOP, who made a genuine though muted effort to capture the reform movement, did not succeed in persuading either the general public or other reformers to listen to their advice. Tooke who, unlike the FOP, was keen to bring the rank-and-file into politics, therefore for the time being retained leadership of the radical clubs, a task for which, in spite of his organisational ability, he was ill-equipped. He had no position in the political world, he was too volatile and wayward, distrusted by many liberal men whom he made no attempt to conciliate. Other potential leaders such as Jebb had died. He had emerged as leader by chance rather than design.

Other clubs were formed calling themselves Friends of the People, including two in Aldgate and Southwark which Tooke and Thelwall helped found. Cartwright, representing the SCI, was present at a meeting when Southwark, of which Thelwall became a prominent member, declared its disapproval of the FOP for refusing to go farther. These proletarian societies, which welcomed Paine's interpretation of natural rights, increasingly adopted uncompromising egalitarianism. As time went on Tooke began to have reservations about the direction the LCS and other societies were taking. He advised caution, but by then they were too self-confident to pay much attention.

In March, Thomas Cooper and John Watt, son of the engineer, were enthusiastically received in Paris when they delivered a congratulatory address from the Manchester Constitutional Society to the Jacobins. At Tooke's suggestion after France's declaration of war on Austria and Prussia on 20 April, the SCI followed suit. At a meeting attended by FOP members Richard Sharp, Brand Hollis and Lord Daer, they agreed to send an address to their 'brothers and fellow-citizens of the world'. Signed by Cartwright as chairman, it was delivered by Watt on 27 May. The SCI rejoiced that Britain and France were uniting in amity. The only enemy of justice in all countries was 'a herd of courtiers fattening on the spoil of the public'. The hand of fellowship which France held out to the world had been rejected: she had been provoked into self-defence. In wishing the French success in establishing the general freedom of Europe they believed 'they uttered the voice of millions'. This was strong meat. When cross-examined Tooke said the address was sent because they 'rejoiced in the freedom of the French'.[35]

On 18 May Paine wrote to the SCI that, due to numerous requests, he had arranged for production of a cheap edition of *The Rights of Man*. Since then he had learnt that the Ministry intended to prosecute. On 21 May the Government issued a proclamation against seditious writings. The FOP considered this an attack on themselves, the SCI on Paine. The only effect it had on *The Rights of Man* was to increase its sales enormously. People asked for the book that had been banned. During a parliamentary debate on the proclamation Dundas, the Home Secretary, criticised reform societies for promoting Paine's principles, and emphasised the danger of manufacturing towns adopting his pernicious doctrines. Fox denounced the proclamation in Parliament, but criticised Paine's writings so severely that his objections appeared rather half-hearted.[36] Paine was summoned for trial on 8 June, but it was immediately postponed until December, by which time he had departed for France.

At the next SCI meeting resolutions were passed defending freedom of the press and the right of association and criticising the high cost of provisions. One resolution, a typical illustration of Tooke's logical mind, complained that the proclamation informed people of their happiness: if people were happy there was no need to tell them, and if not the proclamation would not make them believe they were. At Tooke's instigation, copies of Paine's letter and the resolutions were sent to all associated societies and published in newspapers willing to accept them. Orders poured in for *The Rights of Man* and public subscriptions were opened to pay for Paine's defence.[37]

Paine offered the SCI £1,000, his profit from the sale of *The Rights of Man*, but though they could have done with the money, Tooke sensibly declined.[38] In July, at Hardy's suggestion, and following the example of Manchester and Norwich, 12 of whose members had already been elected associates of the SCI, Hardy, Margarot, Richter and three others from the LCS were co-opted onto the SCI.

Tooke encouraged the provincial societies to set up newspapers. It was important for proceedings to be published to prevent misrepresentation of their objectives and opinions, to announce dates of meetings and provide information on current affairs. In order to be open and above-board, the clubs conducted their activities in a blaze of publicity and in the process greatly exaggerated their successes; the authorities, however, suspected that this was cunning cover for more dangerous schemes. Publication was dependent on the goodwill of editors. Government-subsidised newspapers would not carry the clubs' advertisements, but fortunately several leading radicals were printers and publishers.[39]

The upper classes feared that these activities of the SCI would boost Paine's popularity. The society's finances, however, were insecure, their efforts to drum up arrears from theoretical country members largely unsuccessful. As a result, though in the minutes there are references to huge orders for thousands of pamphlets and broadsheets, often only a few or none at all were printed. Due to increasing numbers Tooke moved SCI meetings from Adam's house to The Crown and Anchor, opposite St Clements Dane. A dining club was started on 1 June, which met every Friday at 4.30. This club was independent of the society whose formal business began at 7pm. Visitors were not admitted to the society's meetings but, as Tooke had hoped, some of those who were invited to dinner stayed on and joined. The FOP and SCI met in large respectable taverns, the LCS, with its much larger and different clientele, in humbler ale houses.[40]

Paine's friend Clio Rickman, the bookseller and writer of books on reform, was among new SCI recruits, some of whom had risen from lowly origin through ability and professional skill: Rev. Jeremiah Joyce, a journeyman glazier who studied for the Unitarian ministry and was now tutor to Stanhope's children; Alexander Wills, a prosperous dancing master, who, when cross-examined, gave as reason for joining that he wanted to hear clever men speak, not having it in his power to go to Parliament. Others were sons of landowning families, including several Scotsmen, Clive's cousin Lord Sempill, Dr William Maxwell of Kirkconnell, a friend of Burns, Charles Sinclair and Lord Daer, eldest son of the Earl of Selkirk, who also joined the FOP and LCS. Tooke helped develop their political talents. One, Joseph Gerrald, a young widower with two children, had inherited and squandered a West Indian fortune. After practising at the Philadelphia bar he had moved to London. He was highly intelligent, arrogant, one of the few radicals with the potential to be a leader.[41]

Daer, Gerrald and Vaughan had been pupils of Dr Parr at his school at Stanmore. Gerrald was his favourite pupil. Parr, though like Tooke now forgotten, was a considerable figure in his day. As a devoted follower of Fox, he lost all chance of preferment in the Church. A simpler, more straightforward man than Tooke, he described how at their first meeting, in spite of strong prejudice, he succumbed to Tooke's gentle manners, artful attentions and lively observations.[42]

Worried by Gerrald's political activities, Parr wrote to William Phillips, Gerrald's former guardian, asking him to warn Gerrald. Parr's estimate of the situation was shrewd: the Ministry, who intended to pursue harsh measures, might strain the new law to entrap those who should be safe. They would bring odium on the FOP if they could, but would reserve punishment for the SCI, which was not very respectable. Paine's adherents might not attract much compassion. In addition, Gerrald and Paine had quarrelled in America, so if Gerrald got into trouble, the SCI might not support him. Parr warned Phillips about Tooke, a pleasant companion and a 'man of wonderful abilities... He employs Gerrald, consults Gerrald, flatters Gerrald and Gerrald ought to know Mr. Horne Tooke. He may be betrayed, he may be deserted, he may be led to say and do those things which Mr Tooke will be content merely to prompt; and he should be aware that it is an avowed part of Mr Tooke's creed to avoid martyrdom in politics as well as in religion.'[43]

Parr was unaware at the time that Gerrald was also involved with the LCS, of which he became a leading member. His comments are particularly interesting because they were made long before anyone was arrested and before Tooke had done anything which could be construed as desertion.

Tooke was at pains to avoid giving an opening for prosecution, but he did not compromise his beliefs or actions through fear, and certainly never betrayed anyone. He could, perhaps, be justifiably accused of failing to restrain his more foolhardy followers. Tooke's imprisonment for opposition to the American war had earned him a place in the radical pantheon. An odd sidelight on Tooke's character was his reiteration, in speeches and conversation, that he was ready to die for his beliefs. Tooke appears to have been swayed by two impulses. In general he exercised sufficient caution to remain within the law, but on several occasions he gives the impression of having decided to challenge the Government.

Notes on Chapter 6

1 Veitch, pp 121-3
2 *Public Advertiser* 16-17.6.90
3 *Critical Review* Nov 1813, p 474; Burke, *Correspondence* VI p 122, 25.6.90; *The World* 8.7.90
4 Stephens II, p 90; *London Chronicle* 3.7.90; *Public Advertiser* 5.7.90
5 Thelwall, *Life*, p 76
6 Gooch 94; *Public Advertiser* 16 July 1790
7 *State Trials* XXV, p 390
8 Burke, *Reflections*, p 4
9 *Argus*, *The World*, *The Times*, *London Chronicle* 4-5 November 1790
10 *The Original* 1874 I, p 81; Lindsey, *Letters* III, to Tayleur 10.11.90
11 *Parliamentary History* XXVIII, pp 921-30, 1210-21; Add MS 27849 f163
12 Horne Proc. Action for Debt between C.J. Fox and J. Horne Tooke 1792. Tooke's own copies with notes in BL, shelf mark C60m 6
13 Paull, p 24
14 TS 11/961/3507 f221
15 TS 11/956/3501, bundle 1
16 TS11/958/3504; Burke, *Reflections* p 2-4; Aldridge p 152; *Times*, *Morning Chronicle* 31.5.91

17 Stephens II, p 323; Thelwall Trial in *Morning Chronicle* 4.12.94; Thelwall, *Life*, p 243; Rickman, p 102
18 Hunt, *The Fourth Estate* I, p 255
19 Horne, Address and Declaration 20.8.91; Paine, *Rights of Man* II, appendix; Aldridge, p 155
20 Auckland II, p 410; HO 42/208, 5.4.92
21 TS 11/951/3495 f38, 2.3.92; TS 11/962/3508 f54,56
22 Add MS 27814 f18-24
23 Stephens II, p 81
24 Hardy, p 19; TS 11/958/3504
25 Bewley, p 89
26 Thompson, p 108
27 Aldridge, p 159; TS 11/962/3508 f54; *World* and other newspapers 28.3 and 6.4.92
28 Veitch, p 205; Hardy, pp 11-2
29 *DOP* II, pp 309-11
30 Holcroft, *Memoirs* III, p 78
31 Thelwall, *Life*, p 243
32 Adams, p 30
33 Wyvill III, appendix, p 128; *Parliamentary History* XXIX, pp 1303-9
34 Grey MSS, to Grey 7.5.1809; to Burgh 16.7.1792
35 TS 11/962/3508 f71; TS 11/958/3504; *State Trials* XXV, pp 150-1
36 TS 11/962/3508 f75; *Annual Register* 1792 II, pp 192-4, 144
37 TS 11/962/3508 f76-87
38 TS 11/962/3508 f101
39 Goodwin, pp 220-1
40 *Ibid.*, p 218
41 *State Trials* XXIV, p 984; Goodwin, p 216
42 Losh I, p 10
43 Parr VIII, p 105

Chapter Seven

Social Life and Sunday Dinners; Political Polarisation

In June 1792 Tooke sold the lease on his house to a friend and moved to Wimbledon. It would be more economical than living in the centre of London and, now that he no longer spent long periods at Purley, he missed the country air which would benefit his children and himself. Although robust, with a tough stomach which enabled him to devour large quantities of food, he suffered from several ailments. Stephens was not explicit, but it appears that Tooke had some congenital deformation of his bowels which caused trouble in his youth and became increasingly painful with age. He also had frequent bouts of gout, though he used to say that of all bad things the least bad was gout, but when Adam Smith's assertion was quoted, that pain never called for sympathy unless accompanied with danger, Tooke, whose feet were wrapped in flannel, retorted, 'I wish this same Scotchman had been stuffed in my skin for the last 24 hours and then he would have discovered that it is not the fear… but the agony, which is assuredly distracting, that entitles anyone to sympathy.'[1]

On 20 September 1782, after Tooke had been rejected for the bar, he had bought a house at the corner of the west side of Wimbledon Common. William Tooke granted him a mortgage on the house which cost £700, a remarkably small sum compared with other sales in Wimbledon at about that time. It had stables, a coach house, outhouses, offices and a close of land, in all five acres, with a fine view over Rushworth pond across the common in front and to the distant woodlands behind. Tooke, who had presumably bought the house as an investment, let it until he moved in. It still exists, now much enlarged, and called Chester Lodge.[2]

Wimbledon was a favourite retreat for statesmen. Wilberforce lived on the south side of the common; Dundas, the Home Secretary, next door to Tooke.[3] Tooke was very happy at Wimbledon, his only settled home. Till then his 'things were moved and removed six times in 15 years'.

Tooke offered his son's Cambridge rooms to Thelwall, the result of a sad story of which once more it is only possible to glean a few hints. There is a poignant note in the diary Tooke kept when imprisoned in the Tower: 'My confinement in King's Bench (in 1777) ruined my boy, God send that the Tower produces no future mischief to my girls'. Tooke gave his son Sidney Montague a good classical education, then sent him to Cambridge where he was extravagant and dissipated. Tooke twice had to pay off his debts. One day in 1788 Sidney called on a fellow student, Basil Montagu. He told Basil that he and some others, who had been drinking, had robbed a man on the highway. Though he took part in the robbery he did not know his companions' intention in advance. He was determined to go to the East Indies, but had no money. Basil offered him his purse containing five guineas which he refused, saying he knew his own character too well to trust himself with five guineas, and that five shillings was all he wanted.[4]

Tooke purchased his son a commission in the East India Company for £1,000, told him that was the last thing he would do for him and that he did not wish to see him again. In June 1789 Zenobio sent Tooke a letter from a friend describing his son's safe arrival at Madras. According to Stephens, Sidney made good in India. Samuel Rogers, however, has a far more depressing version of his career. In 1797 Tooke's son returned from India, dismissed from some military situation for misconduct. He called in the evening at his father's gate. Tooke was away, and when he returned refused to see him. Sidney then enlisted as a private in the dragoons.[5] In 1812 Basil Montagu said nothing had been heard of Tooke's son for a long time and that he was probably dead.[4,5]

Tooke once told Rogers that in disputes between father and son he almost always sided with the father. 'The son's extravagance was generally the cause, and it was hard that the father should suffer for the folly of two youths – his son's and his own.'[5] Whether Tooke was correct in attributing Sidney's failings to the effects of his imprisonment, he must have felt himself partly to blame, an additional reason for his increasing antagonism to ministers and judges, the officialdom which had imprisoned him.

Tooke much enjoyed his daughters' company. Luckily they were both intelligent with a sense of humour. He was fond of young people and paid them attention. They in turn found him sympathetic, a benevolent, wise old man. He taught his daughters languages. Charlotte he said knew as much Latin as most bishops, a double-edged compliment.[6]

Tooke employed a keen SCI member, William Sharp, the internationally famous engraver, to teach 'my girls' drawing. Tooke worried about their future. He would have little money to leave them and hoped this would provide them with a livelihood. They were each set to copy the same subject and their efforts pinned up for visitors to criticise. These must have been at least competent, as some of their pictures hung in the sitting-room for many years. Sharp would stay for a week or two at a time. While he worked at his engraving Tooke wrote in the same room, mostly further material for a new edition of the *Diversions*.[7]

Tooke kept a piece of stone from the Bastille in his study. There were mementos of friends, portraits and caricatures hung in the drawingroom. A collection of cartoons of himself, by the time he died a large number, covered several walls, ranging from a young man in clerical garb defying the bishops to a hoary old Jacobin attempting to blow up Parliament. Tooke was unperturbed by cartoonists' mockery: he wanted the world to notice him and here was proof that it did. Gillray, by far the most brilliant cartoonist of the day, who drew character sketches from life, gives a vivid impression of Tooke's vigour and powerful personality. Thick-set, with a large head and wide mouth, he had a lively, sardonic expression some would call engaging, others sly. Godwin thought it one of 'superiority'.[8]

Bentham complained that 'Horne Tooke had a narrow mind. His library was narrow. A man may be judged of by his library.'[9] Tooke had a small but valuable library. He did not have Bentham's financial resources so he concentrated on subjects which most interested him, philology and politics. He cared little for fine bindings, books were there to be read. He acquired a Shakespeare first folio in order to read Shakespeare as free from tampering by later editors' or printers' errors as possible.[9,10]

Tooke's Sunday dinners became famous. A motley collection of his acquaintance from all walks of life would stream out from London, arriving between two and four and leaving between seven and eight. Politicians who might dislike his political views but enjoyed his brilliant conversation, artists, distinguished authors and scientists, journalists, bankers, classical scholars, men about town, artisans with little education and rough country manners, would mix happily together, due to Tooke's gifts as a host, genial and exuding bonhomie.[11] He was egalitarian in the best sense. Usually a few women and sometimes children were present. Bosville, a celebrated *bon viveur* and ardent Whig who contributed toward the cost of Tooke's entertaining and sometimes brought food with him, dined every Sunday in spring and autumn for many years, driving out in a coach and four. People solicited invitations. Tooke's friends could introduce their friends. On weekdays Tooke sometimes had small parties by special invitation.[9,12]

A superb though malicious deflator of pomposity, Tooke handled his outstanding gift for raillery with good humour. He would support extreme radical opinions with a nonchalant air, and settle disputes with an amusing joke, unless they were on subjects about which he held strong views, such as the constitution. He was a cruel tease, one of his less pleasant minor failings. Having a sharp sense of the ridiculous, he would pounce unerringly on his victim's particular foible. 'His intellect was like a bow of polished steel, from which he shot sharp-pointed arrows at his friends in private, and his enemies in public.'[11]

Godwin made Tooke's acquaintance at this time, while he was writing *Political Justice*, though he said it was too late for Tooke to help him as it was nearly printed before he had the pleasure of meeting 'this extraordinary and admirable man', but he was greatly indebted to his 'etymological conversation and various talents'. Tooke, 20 years his senior, poked fun at Godwin with amused contempt, self-opinionated, a slow conversationalist who revelled in abstractions. Coleridge said, 'Tooke was always making a butt of Godwin who nevertheless had that in him which Tooke could never have understood'.[5,13,14]

Tooke declared that Godwin and Holcroft, who were close friends, had their heads full of plays and novels and then thought themselves philosophers. Both touchy and querulous, they perpetually wounded each other's feelings. On one occasion, when Tooke had tormented him beyond endurance, Holcroft shouted in a paroxysm of rage, 'You are the greatest rascal in the world,' at which Tooke, who realised he had carried his raillery too far, turned round without moving a muscle in his face, and calmly said, 'Is it Friday or Saturday that I am to dine with you?'

'Saturday.'

'Then you may depend upon it that I shall be there at the appointed hour.'[14]

One notorious episode from which neither protagonist emerged with credit occurred when Tooke called for a toast, and Porson, who often turned disagreeable when he had been drinking, gave, 'The man who is in all respects the very reverse of John Horne Tooke'. When Tooke vehemently objected, Porson threatened to kick and cuff Tooke. Tooke suggested they should settle the dispute with brandy. By the time the second quart bottle was half drunk, Porson had disappeared under the table.[15]

Ministerial circles regarded Tooke's house as a hotbed of intrigue. Though much SCI business was settled at Wimbledon, political discussion at mealtimes was convivial rather than conspiratorial, and politics was not all-pervasive. Tooke's friends ranged through the political spectrum from republicans such as Cooper through Foxite MPs to General Murray who supported Pitt. Still, Wimbledon was a mecca for pro-reform intelligentsia. Godwin, who disapproved of political associations which 'spread restlessness and could obscure the truth', listed fellow guests in his diary. They included SCI members Sempill, Joyce, Merry – who had returned safely from France – and Thomas Banks, one of the most notable sculptors of the day, whose highly-successful career was affected by his political affiliations. Godwin also encountered Archibald Hamilton Rowan, a huge, vain, flamboyant Anglo-Irish landowner who had joined the United Irishmen and was making a great noise in Dublin over their campaign for electoral reform. One newcomer to the circle was William Frend, a fellow of Jesus College Cambridge, who became a Unitarian.[16]

Political Polarisation

Events on the Continent had an extremly adverse effect on the societies. On 25 July 1792 the Duke of Brunswick issued a manifesto declaring that the Austrian and Prussian armies would restore Louis's legitimate authority. His army moved slowly forward, crossing the French frontier on 12 August. A popular insurrection broke out in Paris, the Tuileries was stormed, the royal family imprisoned in the Temple, the monarchy suspended. The British Ambassador was recalled from Paris. The September massacres had a deep emotional impact on the British. The radicals, by protesting at the allied threat to their French brethren, the champions of liberty, became apologists for French excesses and so were progressively ostracised. Walpole wrote to Hannah More, 'Thank providence for the tranquillity and happiness we enjoy in this country in spite of the philosophising serpents we have in our bosom, the Paines, Tookes and Wollstonecrafts'.[17] To add fuel to this attitude, on 26 August French citizenship had been conferred on Paine, Priestley, Bentham, Washington, Wilberforce and Mackintosh. Later it was given to Cooper, Christie, Barlow, Tooke and George Rous MP.[18]

At the beginning of September Dr William Maxwell, whose Catholic father James had fought for Prince Charles in 1745, returned from Paris. Maxwell had met the French Minister of War, offered to equip a company with rifle-bored guns and suggested forming commando units equipped with pikes, daggers and shields. He went to Birmingham where he ordered 3,000 daggers and hoped to order more, dependent on a public subscription. Maxwell put an announcement in the London press that a subscription would be opened at his house in Great Portland Street on 12 September. A hostile crowd gathered, and other people turned up curious to see what would happen. Colonel Glover, a pugnacious courtier notorious for quarrelling with the bigamous Duchess of Kingston, arrived early in the morning, before the appointed time and thoroughly intimidated Maxwell, who took down his doorplate and fled. Glover waited to confront potential subscribers but Tooke, a more seasoned campaigner, arrived, saw off the Colonel, marched those who had come to contribute back to Richmond Buildings and, with characteristic energy though doubtful judgement, took over as sponsor of the subscription in the name of the SCI. In a few days £1,151 had been collected, Tooke and some of his friends subscribing £50 each, a sum which Tooke could ill afford.[19]

Margarot, backed by Hardy, wrote to Tooke suggesting that, instead of supporting the subscription, it would be more satisfactory if all the societies joined in a declaration assuring the French of their friendship and determination to do their utmost to keep the British Government to a policy of neutrality. This would not impede the subscription, but might prove more useful as ten thousand signatures would carry more weight than ten thousand pounds which might be subscribed by only ten men. It would demonstrate the reformers' strength and check ministerial oppression. Tooke agreed.[20]

Meanwhile the French defeated the Austrians and Prussians at Valmy, proclaimed a republic and summoned a National Convention, elected by universal male suffrage, in which Paine took his seat. The LCS, joined by three other societies, sent a rousing address which declared that Britain had been 'deprived of nearly all its boasted liberty', swore eternal friendship to the French, hoped they would defeat the German despots and with England and America bring freedom and peace. Eleven more societies drew up their own addresses, which were handed to the French Ambassador and presented to the National Assembly. A committee of Barlow, Sinclair and Tuffin had drawn up the SCI's address. Tooke was present at the meeting when it was approved and signed by Lord Sempill as chairman. It declared that France's continental neighbours were waiting for her to deliver them from oppression. Although the address was more restrained than that of the LCS, the republican Barlow's preliminary remarks about an English convention, introduced on his own initiative, gave it a far more subversive flavour.[21]

Reformers resented the fact that the French had obtained rights which they were denied. In spite of flamboyant phraseology, their intentions were harmless, but it was a foolish moment to express such enthusiasm for the French. By the time the addresses were presented, the French had opened navigation in the Scheldt which breached an international treaty, guaranteed by Britain, and on 19 November they issued an edict of fraternity and assistance to people struggling for liberty. When, in addition, French societies sent appreciative letters offering to help the British clubs in their struggle, containing such heady phrases as 'together we shall free the universe from the yoke of tyrants', and the SCI formed a committee for foreign correspondence headed by Tooke, the Government was understandably alarmed. British citizens were praising a foreign constituent assembly which had set up a republic. Here was confirmation of their fears that the reformers were in league with French revolutionaries who were stirring them up to rebel.

Celebratory dinners, when guests were intoxicated by excitement, wine and conviviality, replete with Jacobin songs, republican toasts and exhortations for Britons to burst the bonds of slavery, also created a bad impression. Tooke invariably played a prominent part, with his renderings of 'Ça ira' and ribald versions of 'God Save the King'. On 5 November the Revolution Society held its annual commemorative dinner 'imbued with a divine glow of patriotism and universal freeedom'. About 500 people were present and 1,000 more were unable to get into the London Tavern. Lebrun, French Minister for Foreign Affairs, had sent over copies of the Marseillaise as a tribute to the society, which was sung ecstatically. There were toasts to French victories and the revolution of the world. It was agreed that an address should be sent to the National Convention. A group of aristocratic French and Spanish merchants were in the room underneath. Tooke's sarcastic request for the company not to wound the tender feelings of the gentlemen by too much festivity was received with colossal applause.[22]

On 9 November, the SCI opened a second public subscription for the French, which raised over £820. This was to be devoted to the purchase of shoes for the French army. Altogether about 7,000 pairs of shoes were bought, of which 6,000 were delivered to the French army via Calais.[23] After war broke out between Britain and France in February 1793 the subscription was closed and no further shoes were despatched.

In spite of increasing harassment, the last quarter of 1792 marked the high point of the SCI. Large numbers attended meetings and more men enrolled, among the most active a young

Scottish lawyer Stewart Kyd. Tooke attended the meetings almost every week but usually left by 10 o'clock, before the end. Fired by French military successes, new societies emerged at Coventry, Stockport and Manchester which made contact with the SCI.

Under Burke and Windham's influence most of the Whigs became increasingly apprehensive and drew closer to the Government. Memory of the Gordon riots was still fresh, and the September massacres in Paris only confirmed fears of the consequences of granting political power to the lower classes. Portland and Fitzwilliam hoped to prevent Fox with his small group of adherents from being forced into the 'arms of the Tookes and Paines'. The Foxites were equally worried that, unless Fox took the lead, opposition to Pitt would fall into Tooke's hands. On 15 November Tierney wrote to Grey, 'Fox is represented by Horne's people, whose number you have scarcely a conception of, as one of aristocracy. Fox must come forth in his true colours and speak boldly.'[24] Fox thought the radicals misguided but like them opposed Britain's collaboration with France's reactionary enemies. He continued to rejoice in the achievements of the revolution and ignored the developing terror. He misjudged the mood of the nation and only too often his attacks on Government policies were widely resented. This increasingly divided him from the majority of the Whigs. Although he still enjoyed considerable personal popularity, he was regarded as unpatriotic, motivated by thwarted ambition.

There were riots in the autumn, but though rioters shouted political slogans, their causes were economic: a bad harvest, rising prices and falling wages. Spies were placed in the societies, most of whom were paid piece-work and so concocted grossly exaggerated stories. The Government agent in Paris sent lurid descriptions of intrigues between the SCI, LCS and their French associates. Rumours spread of French spies, artisans arming. If Pitt and Dundas did not themselves believe the country was in danger they successfully exploited popular fears. Public opinion hardened against the radicals. Their francophile attitude alienated some former supporters: dissenters, liberal gentry and merchants.

Tooke made no attempt to allay such misgivings, and showed no discretion in the example he set to other societies. In spite of his age and physical disabilities, Tooke was by far the most powerful figure left among the radicals, a veteran agitator. Instead of trying to counteract loyalist propaganda by creating a sober, law-abiding image for himself and the SCI, he issued defiant resolutions couched in fiery language which gave the impression that SCI policy was far more subversive than in fact it was. He was imitated by his disciples Gerrald and Thelwall who, though urging their audiences to be sober and prudent, interlarded their speeches with inflammatory rhetoric.

A letter to the editor of the *Patriot*, agreed upon when Tooke was present and later found among his papers with interlinings in his hand, contained what Tooke may have regarded as stock phrases included for emphasis, such as 'Freedom... makes herculean efforts; and the vipers, aristocracy and monarchy are panting and writhing under its grasp'. The next paragraph, though more acceptable in tone, was equally perturbing to the authorities: 'The SCI will... be happy to correspond... with other societies or... individuals, that make the... common cause of a... real representation of the people in parliament... their end.' With Tooke in the chair, the society wrote to thank Barlow for a copy of his new treatise 'Advice to the National Convention of France', in which he called for a democratic republic based on humane principles. It 'exhibited most important political truths' and would inspire 'zeal for the freedom and happiness of mankind'.[25] A puff for a friend, but Barlow's views were widely considered as pernicious as Paine's, and publication of such a letter to a man who had fled to France did not improve the SCI's image.

On 1 December a second proclamation against seditious meetings and publications was issued and the embodiment of the militia ordered, theoretically to put down an impending insurrection in London. All over the country corporations and county meetings of freeholders voted loyal addresses to the King, some spontaneous, some forced.[26]

Another reason for Government disquiet was a convention, held in Edinburgh from 11-13 December, of delegates from Scottish societies most of which had adopted the title FOP and modelled themselves on their English namesake, although they were more plebeian in composition. Many respectable people, including Lord Daer, attended and, though some French procedures were adopted, the convention was in general unexceptionably restrained. Its main intention was to draw up a petition to Parliament.[27]

The Government initiated a campaign of intimidation and persecution of booksellers, newspaper proprietors and leading reformers. John Reeves, friend of Nepean, Under Secretary at the Home Office, founded the Association for the Preservation of Liberty and Property against Republicans and Levellers. It orchestrated a successful jingoistic campaign, built on widespread distrust of French aims, flooded the country with loyalist literature, organised pro-Government demonstrations and fuelled a reactionary panic and witch hunt.

On 18 December Paine was tried in absentia. Although after arrival in France he had published a pamphlet which derided the FOP, called parliamentary reform futile and proposed a national convention, many moderately progressive men contributed to his defence fund, organised by the SCI. They considered Paine's a test-case in the struggle for freedom of the press and thought the Government was taking excessive steps to cope with exaggerated dangers. Thomas Erskine, the ablest defence counsel of the day, was engaged. Paine sent an abusive letter to the Attorney General jeering at Mr Guelph (George III) and reiterating his desire to overthrow the British Government. This ruined Eskine's defence. Paine was convicted of seditious libel for publishing Part II of *The Rights of Man* and outlawed. As a result, any future publisher or printer of Paine's works could be prosecuted, and the SCI was deprived of its chief propaganda weapon. Early in the new year the proprietors of the *Manchester Herald* were indicted for selling Painite literature and fled to America. During the following months Paine's effigy and books were burnt all over he country.[28]

The Foxites determined to protest. On 19 January 1793 they called a meeting of the Friends of the Liberty of the Press, at which they launched an attack on the loyal associations which had been proliferating during the past two months. Over 800 were present, including members of the FOP and SCI, and many more were turned away. Erskine made a brilliant speech defending the freedom of the press while condemning the Government's second proclamation and the use of spies and informers; this was adopted as the society's declaration. When the company adjourned to dinner, a birthday toast was drunk to Fox who remained aloof from the society.[29]

The part played by Tooke is a typical example of his stormy relationship with the progressive Whigs. According to the *Morning Chronicle*, 'the Friends of Liberty were so accustomed to dread the intemperance of Mr Tooke, that his speaking was opposed by a considerable part of the meeting, while he was supported by his friends'. Finally, to avoid dissension, he was allowed to be heard. Tooke 'applauded everthing that had been done but said they should determine to protect those whom government oppressed on account of their poverty. I speak from the bottom of the room properly because I speak for the bottom of the people.' This was a point about which he felt passionately, the initial reason why he had quarrelled with Wilkes. At that time, printers, booksellers and journalists, many of whom were imprisoned and rendered penniless, bore the brunt of the struggle against censorship. 'The society should not direct their views to the principal actors only lest they might be suspected of acting in the manner of officers who, after a successful battle, retired to compliment the General upon his gallantry, regardless of the bleeding soldier whose active valour ensured victory.'[29,30]

Sheridan expostulated that Tooke was trying to foment jealousy and discontent, and claimed that 'at the hour of danger those heroes who appeared armed for the combat ... were at once unnerved... so far had Mr Tooke... evacuated his post'. Tooke had been working hard, if not conspicuously, in the SCI, but since moving to Wimbledon he was seen about town less often. In reply Tooke disclaimed any intention of ascribing unworthy motives to any man. He disagreed with Grey who had said that, if forced to make a choice, he would prefer despotism to anarchy. 'That would be to err as our ancestors did at the Reformation. They rejected Purgatory and chose Hell.'[20,29]

Great noise and confusion ensued. With cries of 'Down, down' a bottle was thrown at Tooke, who was standing on a table. 'Contending opinions drowned all the speakers,' and so many people pressed forward to hear what Tooke was saying that the table gave way. In the scrimmage, decanters were overturned, glasses broken. According to one version, Tooke landed on the floor holding a full glass of wine which he downed and continued speaking. At one point, some of Tooke's supporters, who had applauded him loudly, were driven from the room, but George Rous was sent on a peace mission to bring them back. When chaos finally subsided, Tooke who had been at the bottom of the room appeared beside Erskine at the top.[31,32]

Another public dinner meeting attended by about 500 took place on 9 March, Sheridan in the chair. Erskine and Thelwall made long speeches. After Grey had given details of booksellers imprisoned for selling Paine's works, a fund was opened for the support of the Liberty of the Press. The committee of 44 to administer it included Daer, Brand Hollis, Mackintosh and Sawbridge but not Tooke.

At the next meeting on 20 April, Grey in the chair reported that the committee, which had loaned money to persons in distress, had taken legal advice on whether they were justified by law in relieving persons accused of offences before trial. According to expert opinion they were not. At Tooke's request the legal opinion was read. He then insisted that 'the answers were not such as to deter an honourable body of men from exercising benevolence and charity to persecuted individuals'. £400 had been collected – not a very large sum – as some members disapproved. Erskine said the society must not enter into a subscription to defend all those accused. If any man committed a libel, he must be amenable to the law. The laws were open to the poor as well as the rich. The press must be free and the way to obtain laws of the people's own consent, enacted by a free Parliament of their own choice, was to be obedient to laws while in force.

Tooke disagreed. He would search for a bad act of Parliament in order to disobey it, thus destroying its authority, or put his persecutors to shame when they endeavoured to enforce it. Those who urged obedience to oppressive laws were certainly no friends to freedom. It reminded him of the fable in which the Fox was invited to dine with the Stork. Dinner was enclosed in a vessel shaped in the form of a bottle. 'It may be an excellent dinner,' said the Fox, 'But how… am I to get at it without your d__d long bill? Thus it happened with the poor man who could not sustain the expenses of a trial which often amounted to £200.' He did not want the society to help men evade the judgement of the law, but to help them to meet it fairly. Grey then strongly advised constitutional means to obtain repeal of bad laws.[33]

Tooke astonished the *Oracle*'s reporter, too young to remember the buccaneering tactics of Wilkes's time, by stating that 'there was nothing for which he had been prosecuted which he had not done with a view to provoke the prosecution'. After dinner they debated Tooke's resolution. Daer and Vaughan backed Tooke, along with a new young acolyte, Robert Fergusson, a barrister. Although many were prepared to accept the decision that it was improper to give relief to those who had been successfully prosecuted, Tooke contested it. The company voted 121 to 80 against his resolution. The company again divided 91 to 63 for adjournment. Though Tooke's faction was in the minority, it was a substantial and troublesome one.[33]

This was the last time for several years that Tooke attempted to collaborate with the Foxites whom he considered languid, aloof, faint-hearted and self-centred. In addition he was a vain man, and must have found the Whig assumption of superiority galling. On 7 May Whitbread told the Commons that the Friends of the Liberty of the Press contained undesirable elements, and emphasised that there had been no coalition between FOP and SCI members at its meetings.[34] Only 170 attended the next meeting on 15 June. Erskine and Grey spoke; Tooke was not present. There was talk of another meeting in November, but the society never met again. Sheridan blandly declared that it had fulfilled its aims, although in fact the Government had successfully prosecuted several printers, including two whom Tooke had employed. Both were sentenced to four years plus £200 fines, part of a series of prosecutions which continued for many years against the liberal press and men who, in the excitement of the times, had uttered incautious words.

An article in the *Monthly Review* on a pamphlet called 'Leading Characters of the Day' described Tooke as 'a man of independent spirit and upright character with limited connections, narrow fortune and a desire to inspire the spirit of independence in the people at large'. Although Tooke's personal attacks were sometimes extremely acrimonious, he only abandoned men and parties when he thought they deserted their principles. 'If he were to avoid an offensive appearance of personal malignity in his political contests, and rather to think of measures than of men, he would render himself less liable to the censure that in this respect he so amply deserves... His quarrels with every character of weight and influence in Parliament are totally irreconcilable with his private interest... he must be swayed by manly and disinterested motives, he has too many enemies not to be a great and good man and therefore deserves the approbation of every honest member of the community.'[35]

Notes on Chapter 7

1 Burdett to Place Add MS 37950 f124; Stephens II, p 394
2 Surrey Records Office Acc. 620
3 Milward, pp 76-81
4 Horne, *Tower Diary*, Notes & Queries 8th series XI 9.1.1897; Add MS 27817 f204
5 Rogers, *Recollections*, pp 143-5; Thelwall, *Life*, p 77
6 Rogers, *Table Talk*, p 88
7 Stephens II, p 163
8 Stephens II, p 112; George, M.D., 9270 (1798)
9 Bentham, *Works* X, p 404;
10 Catalogue of Tooke's Library 1813, *DOP* II, p 338
11 Hazlitt, Spirit of the Age, p 106
12 Stephens II, pp 293-304
13 Coleridge, *Table Talk* I, p 122
14 *American Quarterly* V, p 402, 1829; Hazlitt, *Spirit of Age*, p 111; Holcroft, *Life* I, intro XLI; Godwin Supp to Journal 24.3.93, Dep.e. 273 f2
15 Stephens II, p 315; Rogers, *Table Talk*, p 163
16 Godwin, *Diary*, Dep.e. 273
17 Walpole, *Letters* XXXI, p 373, 21.8.92
18 *Moniteur* 25.8.92; *Le Patriote François* 24.9.92
19 Goodwin, p 242, Veitch, p 228; *Moniteur* 25.9.92; *Public Advertiser* 24.10.92
20 Goodwin, p 244
21 *State Trials* XXIV, pp 522-8
22 Goodwin, p 247; TS 11/962/3508 f127; Conway II, p 471
23 Goodwin, p 254
24 Milton MSS Box 44 f4/1-12, 31.10.92; Grey MSS Durham 15.11.92
25 *State Trials* XXV, pp 612-4, XXIV, pp 524; *World* 3.9.92
26 *Annual Register* 1792 II, pp 196-7
27 Goodwin, p 284
28 *State Trials* XXII, pp 357-472; TS 11/668/2141
29 Erskine, *Declaration*
30 *Morning Chronicle* 21, 22.1.93
31 *Morning Herald* 22.1.93

32 *Oracle* 21.1.93

33 *Oracle* 22.4.93

34 *Parliamentary History* XXX, pp 884-5

35 *Monthly Review* XII, p 424, Sept-Dec 1793

Chapter Eight

War with France

Fearful that French agents might infiltrate émigré circles, the Government had introduced a bill for surveillance of aliens in December 1792. One clause (later deleted) prohibited British subjects from returning to Britain without a permit. During the reading of the bill Burke fulminated against Maxwell, dramatically casting one of the daggers he had ordered to the floor of the House. Dundas said that 'acts of the most dreadful enormity had been perpetrated'.[1]

The SCI began 1793 with a controversial move. They made St André, Barère and Roland, 'enlightened friends of human liberty', honorary members, in recognition of their part in the French King's trial. Tooke obtained copies of the *Moniteur* carrying their speeches and, after the King's execution on 21 January 1793, a resolution was passed and published in the papers that these should be inserted in the society's books, though according to Adams this was never carried out. Tooke cannot have been surprised that this action was considered subversive, as Barère had said 'The tree of liberty could not grow unless it was watered with the blood of Kings,' and St André that the National Assembly had the right to decide the King's fate, its mission being 'to destroy kings and royalty'.[2]

Although a few members of the SCI were convinced republicans, the majority were loyal to King George, while disapproving strongly of the French Bourbons and other European despots. Twenty-three years earlier Tooke had compared George III to Nero. He disagreed profoundly with many of King George's beliefs and policies, but had by now decided that he was a useful buffer against overweening grandees. At Tooke's trial various friends testified that he had always considered a republican government unsuitable for Britain: he supported a balance of King, Lords and Commons.

Tooke's praise of the French was never effusive. He admired their achievements, but was certain Britain could effect change more peacefully and did not want his country denigrated in comparison with France. He believed French excesses were provoked by other countries' hostility and that they should be free to determine their own government which, even if violently revolutionary, was preferable to those of Britain's autocratic allies. Some of his French contacts were killed or imprisoned during the terror. He condemned Robespierre – and Tallien who had concurred in many of his cruelties – but thought highly of Barère, 'one of the most honest of the French leaders'.[3]

On 1 February 1793, France declared war on Britain and appealed for help to 'British republicans'. The radicals, who had identified the cause of liberty and humanity with the interests of the French republic, were faced with a terrible dilemma. They had no further official communication with France, but were regarded with increasing suspicion as revolutionaries infected with seditious French ideas. Many intelligent Englishmen, by no means all of them radical sympathisers, disapproved of the war as they had of that against America. This time, however, since it was against Britain's traditional enemy, an overwhelming majority backed the Government with patriotic fervour.

In a defiant gesture of support, on 15 March the SCI belatedly published formal thanks to Barlow and Frost for presenting the SCI's address to the National Convention.[4] Just before Frost left for France in November, he had been accosted by Government agents in a coffee house and enticed into argument. A proclamation was issued offering a reward of £100 for his arrest on a trumped-up charge. He was alleged to have said, 'I can see no reason why any man should not be upon a footing with another,' and when asked what he meant by equality, replied, 'Why I mean no King'. When he returned to England his post was opened, and customs at Dover reported that he had been sent 'inflammatory pamphlets'.

Erskine defended him at his trial in May, on the grounds that he was drunk at the time. His attendance at Louis XVI's trial was cited against him. He was sentenced to six months in Newgate and to stand in the pillory for an hour. However, the sheriffs, using Frost's ill-health as an excuse to avoid a public demonstration, announced at the last minute that the pillory would not be used. On discharge from prison, accompanied by Tooke, Thelwall and William Sharp, he was carried in a state of collapse to his carriage. The crowd unharnessed his horses and drew the coach, stopping at the Palace, York and Carlton Houses to give 32 cheers.[5] Frost was struck from the roll of attorneys which ruined his career. Thus Tooke lost one of his most valued assistants, though Bonney, who took over his legal work, did his best to take his place.

Tooke was present at least at the beginning of almost every SCI meeting in 1793. He wrote to Richard Sharp that, though he intended to pass the summer at Wimbledon, 'I mean always to dine at the Crown and Anchor on Friday, whether in health or not'.[6] Attendance at meetings averaged 16, sometimes only six. After the war began, Tooke became far more circumspect. He instigated or endorsed various minor skirmishes, but, as Richard Ford the Bow Street magistrate told Dundas, though the SCI was encouraging meetings in country towns and Captain Harwood was active in his native East Anglia, the society was 'much on its guard'. Although ministers were swamped with hysterical misinformation, they did have a few comparatively reliable sources. Nepean, who ran a network of spies at home and abroad, had informants in the LCS. The stipendiary magistrates, in particular Ford, employed spies and reported to the Home Office. For the rest of Tooke's life Ford kept watch on his activities.

The provincial societies' correspondence shows how serious, if naive, they were. In February, at their request, 12 members of the Birmingham Society for Constitutional Information were admitted as associates of the SCI. The Birmingham chairman was later assaulted by loyalists and gaoled.[4] Tooke organised an SCI subscription on his behalf. He sent an encouraging reply to Leeds Constitutional Society, who asked the SCI to correspond with 'poor mechanics' who numbered 2,000 and were 'very regular in their conduct'.[7]

Reformers of all shades remained over-optimistic. At the beginning of 1793 the FOP, believing without justification that propaganda and petitions would have an effect on Parliament, brought out a report on the state of the franchise, and authorised Grey to introduce a motion in the Commons. The Sheffield society wrote to the SCI and LCS calling for a discussion on how best to participate. The LCS then sent a circular letter asking other societies to consider either a petition to Parliament, an address to the King or a convention. When the LCS approached the FOP, their response was chilly and patronising. Embarrassed by the eager approaches of the LCS the FOP tried to persuade other societies to leave the field to their own more skilled and acceptable hands. When it became clear they would not be deterred, 14 liberal MPs, though they did not agree with all the proposals or approve the language, presented petitions.

Nottingham was the first society off the mark, with a petition on 21 February which was rejected by Parliament. The society was severely criticised, though defended by Fox, for presenting it at such an improper time. Nottingham then informed the SCI that it had meant no reflection on Parliament and, if other petitions were rejected, they would be happy to confer on an equally legal and peaceable but more effective method (i.e. a convention). Tooke took this up, and published a statement that the SCI agreed with all the sentiments in the rejected petition and was anxious to co-operate with them in any means for the recovery of their lost representation. He also, in a markedly conciliatory attitude, paid tribute to Fox and thanked the patriots who had 'cordially and decidedly opposed rejection'.[8]

At such an inauspicious moment even the FOP's efforts were doomed, for the end of April 1793 marked the downfall of the Girondins and the ascendancy of the Jacobins. Fox, in an attempt to preserve party unity, for the first time came out in support of the FOP, making a rather ineffectual defence of Grey in the House. When the LCS asked Fox to present their petition, composed by Gerrald, he said that as he disapproved of universal suffrage he hoped they would apply to someone else. At the last moment Francis, alhough he also disapproved, presented their petition. Altogether Grey was supported by 36 petitions, 24 from Scotland. Intimidated by loyalist activities, English counties took no part.[9]

As the FOP had feared, opponents of reform ignored their very moderate petition and severely censured those from other societies, with their more precise and vociferous demands. Sheffield's was rejected as disrespectful, that from Norwich disqualified as printed. Pitt said reform was now in the hands of men who would subvert the constitution. Mansfield commented on the obscurity of the clubs' members: the LCS were 'low people'. Burke, who particularly disliked the SCI, said it propagated the doctrine that there was no constitution: the safety of the state required that the authors of such principles be punished. By persuading Grey to accept them as allies, the radicals unwittingly brought odium on the FOP. Grey's motion on 6 May that the petitions be referred to a committee was defeated by the huge majority of 282 to 41. This marked the effective end of moderate agitation for many years.[9]

Attempts were made to keep reform alive. Francis prepared a scheme advocating household suffrage. 'Knowing Tooke to be one of the most learned men in the kingdom particularly with respect to… the history and the constitution of this country' Francis asked him if any references or authorities were incorrectly stated, a particularly piquant tribute if Francis was Junius. He called on Tooke about four times and, due to Tooke's comments, 'somewhat corrected his plan', which had much in common with Tooke's 'Letter to Lord Ashburton'.[10] When Wharton, MP for Beverley and a frequent visitor to Wimbledon, made a speech in Parliament in June calling for a committee on the restoration of the lapsed articles of the 1688 constitution, various provincial societies, following the mutually-supportive system of correspondence Tooke had encouraged, wrote to the SCI giving thanks for his efforts.

Many smaller societies gave up the struggle. Landlords would not rent them rooms, or were harassed if they continued to do so; custom was witheld from reforming businessmen. Government spies also reported nervously that the common people were drilling; Sheffield reformers were arming to protect themselves from loyalist attacks. Ministerial newspapers gave the impression that Tooke, Walker and Cooper would be charged with high treason. Cooper, whose calico business had been ruined by the war, sailed for America with Priestley's two sons.

Both Hamilton Rowan and Lord Edward Fitzgerald were stewards at the SCI anniversary dinner on 29 April where a number of rash toasts were proposed. Sempill presided, and Thomas Walker and Captain Harwood were the only long-standing members among the stewards, who included Margarot, Hardy and a brash twenty-one year old mulatto firebrand Henry Yorke. Based in Sheffield, where he was a leading member of the Constitutional Society, he had presented the Derby society's address to the French Convention.[11]

In cartoons Tooke, dressed as a revolutionary 'sans culotte', is almost always portrayed as a minor accomplice of the Foxites. In one example Fox stands, a beggar, holding out his *bonnet rouge* at the door of the Crown and Anchor. Behind him are his needy followers, Sheridan and Tooke, clutching concealed daggers and also holding out *bonnets rouges*.[12] For the past three years the radicals had persistently criticised their own Government and eulogised the French. When they now tried to gain wider backing by issuing anti-war addresses, they were deemed at best unpatriotic, at worst traitors.

Many societies were considerably larger than the SCI, in particular the LCS, though its active membership had lately fallen to about 2,000. At the beginning of March, Margarot and Hardy were made honorary SCI members. There is little direct evidence to show precisely how far Tooke and Margarot agreed, or how strongly the two powerful personalities differed over aims and tactics. There was no open clash, but Margarot never went to Wimbledon. Hardy, who did, may have acted as buffer. Sometimes Tooke clearly disapproved of other clubs' proposals; on other occasions he may have privately approved of actions he did not wish the SCI to endorse publicly for fear of prosecution.

At the end of August two leading Scottish reformers, Thomas Palmer and Thomas Muir, who had played a conspicuous part in the Scottish convention held the previous winter, were tried for seditious libel. At what were really political trials of doubtful regularity they were given, on extremely flimsy evidence, unprecedented and astonishingly harsh sentences of transportation, Muir for 14 years, Palmer for seven.[13] This put a far more dangerous complexion on the English societies' interest in a convention which, now that petitioning had failed, appeared to many of them to be the only remaining option.

In May, Margarot and Hardy had made contact with William Skirving, secretary of the Scottish FOP. Since then, the war had gone badly; the Duke of York had been defeated at Dunkirk and a French embargo put on British goods. Many educated men had been frightened away; Muir and Palmer were in gaol and Daer had tuberculosis; only Skirving remained as leader of the Scottish reformers. He was a farmer, an honest well-meaning man, but not a forceful personality. At the beginning of October, Skirving invited the English societies to send delegates to another convention to be held in Edinburgh at the end of the month. The LCS held its first open-air meeting in Hackney, at which Margarot and Gerrald were elected delegates. Gerrald had just completed a pamphlet, 'A Convention, the Only Means of Saving Us from Ruin', which advocated a convention based on indirect manhood suffrage.[14]

On 28 October an extraordinary general meeting of the SCI was called to consider the propriety of sending delegates to the convention. Tooke disapproved of the scheme and refused to attend, as did several of his friends. There were 17 members, including four delegates from the LCS: Hardy, Margarot, Richter and John Martin. Sinclair was in the chair. The original draft instructions for the SCI delegates, which were precisely worded and demanded specific actions, give indications of having been drawn up, or at least edited, by Tooke. The delegates were to assist in bringing forward a petition basing their demands on the Duke of Richmond's pamphlet, Flood's motion in the Commons and Tooke's defence against Fox's action for debt. The final instructions, similar to those issued by the LCS, were far less moderate. There was no mention of a petition. They were to demand 'general suffrage and annual representation' and payment of MPs, and to stress the people's inalienable right to reform. Evidently the LCS delegates must have carried the day. From Tooke's actions, he appears to have made it clear that he opposed sending delegates but, to avoid a dangerous split among the radicals, did not attempt to dispute the matter. It was resolved that Sinclair and Yorke, both impetuous enthusiasts, should be sent to Edinburgh. They were to be paid seven guineas travelling expenses and three guineas a week subsistence, but some members refused to subscribe. They believed it contrary to the aims of the SCI and an unprecedented departure to send delegates to a political meeting. There was only enough money for Sinclair, so on the pretext of illness Yorke dropped out. Tooke wrote discouraging letters to both young men, saying there was no money, many members disapproved, and they had better stay at home. The SCI's income at the time was a derisory £60, its outgoings £50, leaving £10 to play with.[15]

Adams informed other societies that the SCI was sending delegates. The Birmingham society replied that it had no money: war had annihilated trade, and many members had crossed the Atlantic. Norwich was unable to send a delegate so nominated Margarot to represent it. The Sheffield Constitutional Society had several thousand members, but the vast majority had been affected by the war. Brown, who went as a delegate representing Sheffield and Leeds, accused the SCI and FOP – 'great bodies... which we little folks in the country look up to for examples' – of apathy.[16]

Giving evidence a year later, Tooke said that he opposed participation. 'I saw no benefit from it... [It was] not large nor respectable enough.' Had there been any reasonable prospect of success, he would have been the first to agree to sending delegates to a convention for the purpose of more 'effectually collecting the sentiments of the people... His dislike was founded merely on this reason, and on no suspicion that it was intended by that Convention to usurp the authority of Parliament.'[17]

Schemes for associations such as Cartwright and Wyvill's delegate meetings had been tolerated in a calmer political climate. Tooke had worked in the Quintuple Alliance to bring pressure to bear on Parliament, but he never supported the proposal canvassed by Jebb and other advanced reformers to form a private assembly which would be more representative than Parliament and therefore should supersede it. Tooke opposed promotion of such ideas when they appeared more dangerous in the context of the French Revolution. Gerrald, however, had promoted Jebb's suggestion that, if a convention's demands were not met, it could force a dissolution of Parliament. Tooke might, perhaps, be faulted for not attending the extraordinary general meeting with his friends and, even if it meant a split with Margarot and Hardy, obtaining a majority vote against sending delegates.

Meanwhile on 4 November the Revolution Society, which had sunk into obscurity with the outbreak of war, held its annual dinner with Morgan the actuary in the chair. Tooke gave a toast 'May the people of this country never forget or forsake the present family on the throne unless they shall appear by their conduct to have forgone or forsaken the principles that seated them on it'.[18] This was reckless, given that Marie Antoinette had recently been guillotined.

The Scottish Convention was over by the time the English delegates arrived, but Skirving recalled it for 19 November. Its 180 delegates then sat for a fortnight. The English took control, and Margarot in particular broadened the original intention to draw up a petition to Parliament by initiating a plan for a united front which would form a powerful extra-parliamentary pressure group. Procedure for future joint conventions was defined and it was resolved that, in the event of suspension of habeas corpus, a bill to prevent popular meetings or the arrival of foreign troops to impose martial law, they would reassemble at a secret location. There were fiery speeches, Gerrald's the most impassioned and idealistic. Delegates addressed each other as 'Citizen', and French revolutionary procedures were used. After Muir and Palmer's trials such behaviour was foolhardy and misguided. The convention, far too reminiscent of the French National Assembly, shocked and frightened many people. On 5 December Margarot, Gerrald and Skirving were arrested and released on bail. The following day the other leaders were arrested.[19]

The SCI continued to evince little enthusiasm for the convention. Tooke was present when they met on 8 November and 6 December, when a report from Sinclair, written some days before his arrest, was read and a committee of correspondence appointed to reply. They adjourned until 10 January. On 17 January the SCI held a meeting, Tooke in the chair, 22 present, to express their indignation at sentences of 14 years' transportation which had been passed on Skirving and Margarot. Gerrald, a potential martyr, took part as an associate member. He had been released on bail to attend to urgent business in London. Letters from Sinclair describing the Scottish trials were read. Then a series of challenging resolutions were passed. The first three condemned the Scottish judges: 'law ceases to be an object of obedience whenever it becomes an instrument of oppression'. Judge Jeffreys's fate, 'torn to pieces by a brave and injured people', was recalled 'with deepest satisfaction'. It was agreed 'that those who imitate his example, deserve his fate'.[20]

At this point Tooke left the chair and Gerrald took over. Under his auspices further resolutions were passed which verged on sedition: they approved the convention, affirmed their solidarity with the Scots, and saw 'with regret that the period was fast approaching when the liberties of Britons must depend not upon reason… but on their… undaunted resolution to oppose tyranny by the same means with which it is exercised', a thinly veiled threat to use force if necessary.[20] Tooke has been accused of inciting his disciples to undertake dangerous work while himself avoiding responsibility. It was Gerrald, not Tooke, who was determined to introduce the resolutions, as it was Gerrald and Sinclair who, contrary to Tooke's warnings, insisted on attending the convention. If Tooke wanted the resolutions passed without accepting responsibility, it was a clumsy way to go about it. It seems far more likely that Tooke thought it unwise to adopt the other resolutions, deferred to the majority who were in favour, but once more showed his disapproval by abstention.

After the Edinburgh débâcle Tooke could have maintained that the delegates had brought their punishment on themselves by their foolish behaviour, but he had always fought for those wrongfully imprisoned, and the sentences imposed by the Scottish courts were unjustifiable. They had caused widespread astonishment and dismay. Under Tooke's leadership the SCI threw themselves wholeheartedly into a campaign of protest and support for the English delegates in an attempt to get their sentences rescinded. This involved implicit approval of the second convention.

Thelwall, who had asked Gerrald to introduce him into the LCS, had joined the Spitalfield division on 17 October and became its representative on the General Committee on 21 October, three days before delegates were chosen for the convention. He was in favour of the LCS sending delegates and was proposed as one himself, though disqualified by membership rules. He began a series of political lectures whose enormous success worried the Government. Part of the proceeds went to pay Gerrald and Margarot's legal costs. After their arrest, Thelwall and Hardy ran the LCS. Vaughan continued to attend LCS meetings occasionally as a visitor and legal adviser, warning them if their petitions and addresses could be construed as treasonable. Thelwall kept in close contact with Tooke, dining once a week at Wimbledon. He later wrote that, though he would not suffer Tooke 'to make me his tool for the execution of whatever he might dictate, or the promulgation of whatever doctrine he might wish to propagate, I never proposed a measure without consulting him, nor published a single instrument that had not openly or covertly received his sanction'.[21] Ministers were convinced that Tooke really ran the LCS. It is difficult to assess from the available evidence to what extent he now prompted their actions or left them to go their own way.

On 20 January 1794 at the LCS anniversary dinner, attended by over 1,000, 'An Address to the People of Britain' was approved. This was written partly by Tooke and partly by a lawyer, John Martin of the LCS, for, now that Margarot was no longer in command, Hardy turned once more to Tooke with his skill and experience at propaganda. The address painted a gloomy picture of Britain, where public and private rights had almost disappeared, war was ruining trade and beggaring artisans. A dangerous resolution was passed that, on the introduction of a bill inimical to the liberties of the people, the LCS general committee was to summon a convention of the people.[22]

After the break-up of the convention, the Scottish societies mostly faded away and membership of English clubs shrank considerably. Tooke asked Thomas Thompson, MP for Evesham, to join the SCI as more members of consequence were needed.[23] Thompson, who lived in the country, usually left, like Tooke, before the meeting broke up. He defended reformers when they were criticised in Parliament. Holcroft was saddened by the SCI's decline: meetings were thin, resolutions feeble, adjournments long.

At the beginning of February Tooke sent a carefully worded circular letter asking for contributions towards Sinclair's expenses. It stated that the SCI highly approved of Sinclair's moderate behaviour. In contrast to the SCI's former reluctance to contribute to his expenses, Sinclair was now sent 20 guineas, then a further seven.[24] Sinclair had played an important part at the convention. As a Scot he had been admirably qualified to undertake co-ordinating secretarial duties and had introduced some of the more advanced resolutions, but had not attracted the notoriety of Margarot and Gerrald. A few days later Gerrald and Sinclair returned north to stand trial. Gerrald had tuberculosis, so was unlikely to survive a long sentence. Friends suggested he should jump bail, but he refused and was sentenced to fourteen years. He remained in prison in London until May 1795 when he was sent to Australia, dying soon after his arrival. Of the five men transported only Margarot survived, to return penniless in 1810. He and his wife were befriended by Hardy.[25]

Sinclair's trial, fixed for 17 February, was postponed several times, then quietly dropped. The SCI were lucky. They did not have to bear the stigma of their delegate's conviction. His release was almost certainly due to pressure brought to bear by his powerful family: his uncle, Sir John Sinclair, was the first President of the Board of Agriculture. Sinclair himself said that 'the authorities dared not attack any man of connexions and estate in Scotland: that had he himself been condemned, or sent to Botany Bay, his connexions would have risen to a man'.[26]

While avoiding co-operation with the radicals, the Foxites were pursuing the same policies without any greater success. They embarked on a campaign in Parliament on behalf of Muir and Palmer who were held in the hulks at Woolwich. Their case was a better one to plead than the English delegates', for the first convention had been moderate in tone, and they could have had no inkling that their participation would incur such severe punishment. However, a motion for a royal pardon failed.

Activities Leading to Arrest of Radical Leaders

Radicalism was now widely equated with treason. Exaggerated reports from spies encouraged the Government to overestimate the influence and republican sympathies of the societies. An insurrection or French landing in Ireland was a far more genuine danger. Ministers had reason to be alarmed by another episode with which Tooke was indirectly connected. At the end of February the Rev. William Jackson, a member of the Anglo-Irish community in Paris, arrived in London masquerading as an American. Jackson, born in Ireland, had been educated at Oxford and ordained into the Church of England. He had been a preacher in London, secretary to the notorious Duchess of Kingston, editor of the *Public Ledger* and the *Morning Post* at the time of the 1784 election when he supported Pitt. He acquired a rather dissolute reputation and fled to France in 1788 to escape his debts. Jackson had come to find out what assistance French invasion forces would receive in Britain and to make contact with the United Irishmen. He carried letters from John Hurford Stone to his brother William, a prosperous London coal merchant. John Stone totally identified himself with France and the Girondins. For ideological reasons, he took part in Irish and French intrigues against Britain and was employed in an advisory capacity by the French Foreign Office. His letters to his brother were coded, in that political matters were disguised as commercial, but their true meaning is not difficult to discern. He warned William that the Committee of Public Safety were planning a raid. The French had far too optimistic a view of the numbers of British who would support them. He himself was suspect for telling them they were mistaken, and he wanted William to obtain corroboration of his views.

William introduced Jackson to his many close friends among the Foxites who, though against the war, assured him the nation was totally loyal. The MPs William Smith and Benjamin Vaughan, son of Tooke's friend Samuel, gave him written reports confirming this. William Stone drafted a letter to the Committee of Public Safety warning them that they had misjudged British public opinion; but he assured them that they had many friends in England and urged them to initiate peace talks.[27]

Jackson crossed to Ireland with a friend and former colleague, John Cockayne, who introduced him to Hamilton Rowan, imprisoned in Dublin, and to other leaders of the United Irishmen, while at the same time betraying him to Pitt. Jackson was arrested on 28 April, William Stone in England on 3 May. Those who had given Stone information were summoned before the Privy Council. Benjamin Vaughan fled to Paris, then, after a short spell in Switzerland, sailed to America. Jackson was tried for high treason in April 1795 but committed suicide by taking poison in the dock. William Stone, also charged with treason, was allowed to remain in an apartment in Whitehall to await trial.[28]

Among the papers Jackson carried with him, found when he was arrested, was a letter from Hurford Stone to Tooke. Hurford Stone wrote that he had not been in touch due to the Traitorous Correspondence Bill. He knew that Tooke's 'prudence keeps some pace with [his] patriotism', but could assure him of Jackson's integrity. Stone had fulfilled Tooke's commission to buy his daughters bonnets. This had been delayed by events, which was no loss as the fashion had now much improved, and they would be sent when an opportunity arose. 'God bless you, we shall meet under happier circumstances than our last and drink a cool bottle of good Burgundy under the shade of our trees, an early day next summer.'[29]

Many of Tooke's friends were having a difficult time. Thomas Walker was tried with nine other Manchester reformers on 2 April for conspiring to overthrow the Government and assist a French invasion. The local Association for Preserving Liberty, Order and Property had been engaged for six months in concocting a case against them. Walker was defended by Erskine. He exposed the chief prosecution witness, a drunken Irish weaver who had been bribed by the Manchester authorities to give false evidence, so the case collapsed. Tooke sadly said goodbye to Priestley, who stayed with him before emigrating to America. 'A more amiable man never lived; he was all gentleness, kindness, and humility.'[30] Tooke told Rogers that Priestley, now sixty-one, left reluctantly at the insistence of his wife who was afraid that he and their family would be persecuted. Tooke was not in favour of emigration to avoid persecution. 'Our ancestors in the last century who fled from slavery loved liberty well; but they who stayed and by their sufferings… established it, loved it better and deserve better of posterity.'[31]

Tooke, who attended all 15 SCI meetings bar one held in 1794, produced an SCI address to Margarot and his fellow reformers awaiting transportation. At the same time he proposed John Wharton, 'a friend in whose opinions he placed the greatest confidence', who was duly elected to the SCI. Originally Tooke had dissuaded Wharton, a Whig, from joining, because 'he would be liable to imputations from the conduct of others which he could not control, and he could not promote the society's objects so well in Parliament as if he appeared unconnected with them'. Now Tooke told him that 'the society was rather falling into disrepute and it was thought a credit to it that he should belong'.[32]

The LCS decided that the time had come to act. On 27 March Hardy wrote to Adams in peremptory tone: all friends of freedom must declare whether, due to the 'late illegal prosecutions', they would abandon their cause or press on. Did the SCI agree on the necessity of a convention 'to obtain in a legal method a redress of their grievances'? He also wrote to Sheridan, chairman of the FOP, asking them to co-operate in a convention to promote electoral reform, but they declined.[33]

At a meeting of 20 SCI members it was agreed 'there should be immediately a convention of the People, by delegates... from the different societies...' The LCS was invited to send a delegation to the next meeting when, at Tooke's suggestion, a joint committee of five delegates from each society was appointed to co-ordinate plans. Thelwall led the LCS contingent, the SCI one consisted of William Sharp, Joyce, Holcroft, Kyd and Thomas Wardle.[34]

Tooke had apparently abandoned his objections to a convention. His reasons can only be conjectured. Once more he may have deferred to a majority verdict. The LCS were determined to hold a convention: if the SCI held back they would lose their position of authority. Agitation had achieved nothing. Tooke and his SCI colleagues may have become convinced that a London convention was the only means left to rally the discouraged provincial societies and show the reformers' strength. Another reason for Tooke's change of heart and his increasingly cantankerous attacks on the Government could have been despair, belief that the societies he had worked so hard to promote would soon be smashed, and they might as well protest as vehemently as they could while still able to do so.

SCI members were interrogated by the Privy Council in May. Their evidence is thin, contradictory and inconclusive. Sharp said the majority were against a convention, yet resolutions in its favour were carried with a show of hands.[35] When discussing Hardy's letter, Tooke said that the LCS members were honest, well-meaning men. He said the joint committee did not achieve a great deal. At the first meeting Holcroft introduced a philosophical disquisition on the powers of the human mind which lasted for an hour and a half. SCI members were not notified about the next meeting and did not attend. At the third Thelwall produced a tentative plan for a convention; a majority, including all SCI delegates, were against such an emotive word as 'convention' and wanted to substitute meeting or assembly. It was retained at Thelwall's insistence. Tooke made a characteristic comment on this discussion: it was all nonsense, merely a dispute about the use of Latin or English words.[36]

Sheffield Constitutional Society was the first to follow up the LCS initiative. They held an open-air meeting on 7 April at which they claimed nearly 10,000 people were present. The Chairman Yorke introduced a defiant resolution that the people

1. RIGHT. Horne Tooke in 1791, engraving by Thomas Hardy. (Courtesy National Portrait Gallery)

2. BELOW. Cartoon by Roberts, November 1802. Napoleon graciously receives 5 Englishmen. First Sheridan offering medicine, then Fox, then Tooke presenting his new Botheration Dictionary, followed by Burdett and Bedford. (Courtesy of British Museum)

3. ABOVE. Chester House, Wimbledon, 1810 by William Porden. (Courtesy of Wimbledon Society)

4. LEFT. Frontispiece Diversions of Purley. (Courtesy of British Museum)

5. ABOVE. Two pair of portraits by Gillray in Anti-Jacobin Review 1.12.98. (Courtesy British Museum)

6. BELOW. Cartoon by Gillray 15.3.01. The Old Brentford shuttlecock between Old Sarum and St Steevens. In a small space between the House of Commons and a rustic house Lords Temple and Camelford play battledore and shuttlecock with Tooke's head. The opposition side of the House is visible through the doorway. (Courtesy British Museum)

7. LEFT. Burdett by William Ross, circa 1840. A bust of Tooke by John Bacon the Elder stands on the table. (Courtesy National Portrait Gallery)

8. LEFT. The Misses Hart with the bust of John Horne Tooke by Chantrey. Pastel by John Raphael Smith.

should demand universal representation as a right and would therefore petition no more.[37] On 14 April LCS held a meeting at Chalk Farm, chaired by John Lovett and attended by large numbers of reformers and curious observers, while police and soldiers hovered in the background. Lasting for several hours, it was calm and orderly, partly due to first-rate organisation by Thelwall who was also the chief speaker. A moving address to Gerrald was approved, which Tooke was said to have helped compose. The fifth resolution, that any attempt to violate remaining laws should be considered 'as dissolving entirely the social compact between the English nation and their governors... that the safety of the people is the supreme, and in case of necessity, the only law', made the Government suspect LCS were contemplating illegal action.[38] Tooke and his colleagues were involved in LCS plans, but there is no trace of any contact over the Sheffield meeting. They did not go to Chalk Farm.

Tooke at his most intransigent and indiscreet was, however, the central performer at the widely-publicised SCI fourteenth anniversary dinner on 2 May, which was to prove the society's swan-song. Nearly 300 took part, only a small proportion of whom belonged to SCI. Free tickets were issued to a number of LCS members who could not have afforded 7/6 for dinner, and a few were reputed to have behaved 'improperly'. Wharton was in the chair, Thompson a steward. Tooke was next to Wharton, flanked by Lord Daer and Frost. A number of journalists were present. The company was less distinguished than in the past, but not in general of 'inferior class'.

The dinner was a jovial affair. The band played the 'Marseillaise', 'Ça ira' and the 'Carmagnol', greeted with deafening applause. There were traditional toasts, some with a republican flavour, others ritual slogans, 'Rights of man', and 'Equal laws and liberty'. When examined by the Privy Council, Wharton admitted that some toasts were unwise: 'The armies contending for liberty'; 'May the abettors of the present war be its victims'. Knowing the members, he thought they should not be interpreted as disloyal: they were foolish, not criminal. As for one to 'Persecuted patriots', the men referred to were being persecuted.[39]

Tooke made a ferocious speech, received with great enthusiasm. One reason for his bitterness was that on this day a convict ship had set sail with Margarot, Muir, Palmer and Skirving. Neither he nor many other reformers had till now believed that they would actually be sent to Botany Bay. Tooke began by taunting Government spies. The present House of Commons was 'a scoundrel sink of corruption'. He begged the company to note that he was not inebriated, and would repeat it for the benefit of the informers. Groves, solicitor at the Old Bailey and a reasonably reliable witness, who had joined LCS as a spy and slipped in as a guest, reported that, though Tooke was patently not sober, he kept cool command of himself. In a diatribe against Pitt, Tooke declared that he and his supporters had betrayed 'that poor man the King' and the hereditary nobility, who had lost their influence to upstarts such as Dundas and Thurlow. He himself was now of little use but to read or write, and that availed nothing: more decisive means must be used. According to one spy, Tooke 'had been of the opinion that Parliament would not reform itself, but the time was not far distant when it would be reformed with a vengeance from without'.[39]

When Wharton proposed 'That steady friend to liberty John Horne Tooke', Tooke's reply, if events had taken a different turn, would have been only too prophetic: 'This was the last time his health should be drunk. His ambition was that thereafter his memory should be given.' More time was spent on songs than speeches. Tooke sang one he had composed, 'Come drink to a Free constitution... to the downfall of all Tyranny', the company singing the chorus. He introduced one of his parodies on the National Anthem, 'See George the Good and Wise roll round his stupid eyes'.

Many diners were far too engrossed in jollification to pay much attention to the significance of toasts or songs, and it was hard to hear the speeches above the din, but garbled reports encouraged the authorities to believe it a most subversive occasion. A friend told Windham that Wharton had hurriedly adjourned the meeting when Thelwall jumped onto a table demanding equalisation of property. The two open-air meetings, this dinner and the recent discovery that Sheffield reformers were collecting weapons to defend themselves against patriotic mobs determined Pitt to prevent the summoning of a convention and led to the arrest of leading reformers.[40]

Notes on Chapter 8

1 *Parliamentary History* XXX, p 189
2 *State Trials* XXIV, p 540
3 Farington I, p 279
4 *State Trials* XXIV, p 547; XXII, p 521; Thelwall, *Life*, p 201
5 *Morning Chronicle*, *Lloyds Evening Post* 20.12.93; Veitch, p 270
6 Beinecke MSS Yale, Osborn Files 38.42
7 TS11/953/3497 28.5.93
8 TS11/962/3508 f141
9 *Parliamentary History* XXX, pp 465, 775-925
10 *State Trials* XXV, p 372
11 *State Trials* XXIV, p 790
12 George, M.D., 8331 12.6.93
13 *State Trials* XXIII, pp 231, 376; Bewley, p 81
14 Add MS 27814 f56
15 TS11/962/3508 f151-4; 957/3502 bundle 1; *State Trials* XXIV, p 556, XXV 87
16 Parliament, 2nd Report Cttee Secrecy House of Commons 1794 appendix 128, 1.11.93
17 *State Trials* XXIV, pp 556-8, XXV 86-7; TS11/953/3497; *Morning Chronicle* 4.12.94
18 *Morning Chronicle* 5.11.93
19 *State Trials* XXIII 414-42; *Edinburgh Gazetteer* Dec. 93
20 TS11/962/3508 f154-8; *State Trials* XXIV, p 558
21 Thelwall, *Life*, pp 115, 122, 352
22 *State Trials* XXIV, pp 441-5; XXV, p 221
23 TS11/962/3508 f159, p 165
24 *State Trials* XXV, p 204; TS11/952/3496; 962/3508 f163
25 Bewley, pp 68-84
26 Brightwell, p 44
27 *State Trials* XXV, pp 1260-3
28 *State Trials* XXV, pp 783-890, 1155-1438; TS11/555/1793; 965/3510 A/3; Goodwin, pp 322-4
29 *State Trials* XXV, p 846
30 Goodwin 337 n166; Rogers, *Table Talk*, p 86
31 Stephens II, p 228
32 *State Trials* XXIV, p 562; TS11/962/3508 f168; 963/3509 f250
33 TS11/952/3496; 955/3500B; *State Trials* XXIV, p 562; Parliament, First rep. Cttee Secrecy 1794, pp 22-31
34 TS11/962/3508 f170-2; PC2/140-337
35 PC 2/140-201; TS11/955/3500B; TS11/963/3509

36 TS11/955/3500B; *State Trials* XXIV, 564; PC2/140 f202, 305, 337

37 Parliament, 2nd Report Cttee Secrecy, p 79

38 Add MS 27814 f70-6; *State Trials* XXIV 50-3, 735-41; House Commons Journal XLIX 608-9; Parl Hist. XXXI, pp 492-6

39 TS11/954/3498 15-17.5.94; 965/3510A/3 f36; 955/3500; *State Trials* XXIV 571; *Morning Post* 3.5.94

40 TS11/955/3500; Add MS 37876 f116, Rev. Exon labelled 21.5.96 but must be 1794; Veitch, p 304

Chapter Nine

Arrest and Imprisonment in the Tower

Leading reformers throughout Britain were arrested, starting with Hardy and Adams on 12 May 1794. Their papers were handed to a 21-man Parliamentary Committee of Secrecy, packed with Government supporters. It included Pitt as chairman, Dundas, the Attorney and Solicitor Generals (Scott and Mitford) and such passionate anti-reformists as Burke and Windham.

Joyce wrote Tooke an enigmatic note, intercepted by the Post Office and handed to Pitt by William Mainwaring, MP for Middlesex: 'This morning… citizen Hardy was taken away… They seized everything they could lay hands on… Is it possible to get ready by Thursday?' Tooke claimed at his trial that he had been collecting from the Court Calendar a list of titles, offices and pensions enjoyed by the Grenville family with the support of Pitt. The next day Joyce was arrested while teaching Stanhope's sons at Chevening. Thelwall was also taken up.[1]

The day before Hardy was arrested, Godwin and Thelwall had dined at Tooke's. On Thursday 15 May, Tooke dined with Michael Pearson at his house in Spitalfields, where he was to bring the extracts from the Court Calendar. When a troop of light horse passed by, it was suggested that they were keeping an eye on Tooke whose carriage had been followed from Wimbledon. A spy reported that Tooke and Frost also called at Thelwall's. Tooke was seized early the following morning. As he did not keep a living-in servant, he was worried about his daughters, so sent a note from Whitehall to a friend asking her to go to Wimbledon to look after them. He had made no attempt to conceal or destroy the numerous SCI papers in his study. Either he did not believe he would be arrested or did not consider there was anything incriminating. Although Tooke always sailed very close to the wind, he had a far cannier appreciation of what was permissible than less experienced men such as Hardy or Thelwall. In his words and actions at this time he appears to have been veering between hoax and rebellion, daring the Government to take him on.[2]

On 16 May, pikeheads and battleaxes were discovered in Edinburgh, intended for a genuine but hairbrained plot for an insurrection organised by a wine merchant, Robert Watt, *agent provocateur* turned radical. The same day the Committee of Secrecy issued its first report which claimed that the societies had been pursuing 'a settled design intended to subvert the constitution'. Pitt immediately introduced a bill to suspend habeas corpus for a limited period. In spite of bitter opposition from Fox and his adherents it was passed on 22 May. This meant that the arrested men could be kept in prison without trial.

Altogether about 30 men were rounded up in the first two weeks on charges of treason, and 11 more later, plus ten on less serious charges. Some were released when they agreed to become crown witnesses. By the end of May, 13 LCS members had been arrested; of the SCI, John Martin, a lawyer, was already in prison for debt, Bonney and Kyd were held, Hodgson and Wardle evaded their warrants.

Privy Council interrogations went on till late in the evening. There is an unpleasant difference between the urbane treatment of those who were gentlemen and the unscrupulous bullying of working-class men. When Richter asked for a glass of water, Dundas insinuated that it was guilt that caused his thirst.[3] Most prisoners, some very young men, were not intimidated in spite of being faced by cabinet ministers. Joyce, Thelwall and the lawyers who knew the ropes, Bonney, Kyd and John Pearson, refused to give evidence. Adams, who made a bargain with the authorities and agreed to authenticate SCI documents, was released on bail and never charged. At subsequent trials he gave fair and accurate evidence. Hardy also talked freely and identified LCS papers.

Several SCI members were summoned for interrogation but not detained. These included Banks, the sculptor, and Dr Towers, who 'had joined the SCI ten years ago but only attended once in the last six months. I only knew Tooke, Sharp, Joyce and Holcroft.' The two MPs, Wharton and Thompson, were questioned closely about toasts at the dinner. Frost, detained briefly on 30 May, said he had not taken part in politics since he was released from prison. William Sharp produced no incriminating evidence, and was ultimately dismissed though held under guard at his house.

Hull and John Williams, weak men who agreed to talk, had nothing irregular to reveal. Williams's statement that he could remember nothing about committees, because so many were formed that never acted, confirms the impression that much of the SCI's business was wind rather than deeds. His father-in-law pulled strings which obtained his speedy release. Christopher Hull, a barrister who sounded thoroughly disgruntled, said that when he joined three years earlier the SCI had been most respectable. Since then he had quarrelled with Harwood and Frost, and he did not think Tooke trusted him. Felix Vaughan said it would be highly improper for him to give evidence against Tooke since he regarded him as a father. He volunteered that there were 'bad men belonging to the societies' and warned the Privy Council not to pay too much attention to their evidence. Vaughan had been given the LCS journal for safe keeping. It was never found by the authorities.

Tooke, a man of letters and a political figure since the days of Wilkes, was by far the most important of the detainees. He arrived at the Treasury at 3pm on 16 May, where Nepean was extremely civil. At 8.30 he was examined by the Privy Council, some of whom he knew. His interrogators included the Lord Chancellor Loughborough, the Duke of Montrose, the Marquis of Buckingham, the Earls of Camden and Chatham, Viscount Sydney, Lords Grenville, Amherst and Auckland. Pitt was not present. They trod warily, treating him with correct reserve. Dundas said that he intended to examine him to remove the suspicion that he was guilty of treasonable practices, because he was a leading and active member of the SCI and LCS (Dundas slipped up here) whose object was to supersede legal government. Tooke was far too downy a bird to be taken in by this. He asked if it could be imagined that this was sufficient to justify holding him in custody, taking possession of his house and seizing his papers. If the Lord Chancellor, Dundas or any other member of the Privy Council would on their honour assure him there had been information upon oath against him for practices full of treason, he would answer any questions that might be put to him. When told no such assurance could be given, he refused to be examined. Not another word, bar complaints about his treatment, did he utter. He complained that his family were at the mercy of those who had executed the warrant against him, but conceded that they had behaved perfectly correctly, and told Dundas that, if a traitor he had been used too well, if not, too ill. Although the Privy Council continued to examine witnesses until July they secured no evidence of an insurrectionary plot.[4]

In one of those espionage sub-plots which occur in every age, Stephens and the anonymous author of an article in *Tait's* magazine give differing accounts of the part Wharton played in Tooke's arrest and prosecution. Tooke clearly embellished the version he gave Stephens. According to this, Tooke realised that Wharton gave information to the Ministry, hoping to gain advancement. Tooke therefore embarked on the dangerous course of giving him a greatly exaggerated account of the strength and revolutionary aims of the societies, culminating in the story that armed rebellion was planned, with himself at the head of the conspiracy. Wharton reported this, precipitating Tooke's arrest.

Tait's version, written in 1853 long after all the protagonists were dead, gives a more dramatic version. Once again the details cannot be entirely correct. One evening a tall man, muffled in a cloak with his hat slouched over his face, called on Tooke in prison. He revealed that he was a member of the Privy Council who had come to explain the real cause of his arrest and to warn him of the danger to which he was exposed. Wharton had introduced an abortive reform motion in Parliament which had been planned at Wimbledon; over dinner in May 1794, a more specific motion was mooted for increasing naval pay. One guest feared the scheme would create a mutiny among seamen. Wharton relayed Tooke's response: 'That's exactly what we want'. The Privy

Council had agreed that Wharton should recount this at Tooke's impending trial.

What seems most likely is that Tooke's penchant for joking and mystification misfired and led Wharton, who was genuinely pro-reform, to take Tooke's misleadng exaggerations at face value. Then Wharton, whose patron had joined the Portland Whigs who were about to support the Government, became alarmed under interrogation. In the recorded evidence before the Privy Council, Wharton spoke up for SCI members who 'from personal knowledge of some gentlemen have no wishes against the country'. In June, however, he voted for the royal address condemning the societies. 'He had been at only one meeting, and there he was sure nothing unconstitutional had appeared in the proceedings. He had now seen enough to convince him that... he now totally disliked the societies' conduct.'[5]

There is no trace of Wharton in the Treasury solicitor's dossier of evidence against Tooke, but in August an LCS member who had been arrested made his first visit to the LCS after being discharged on bail. He reported that one of the witnesses against Tooke was a man who had often dined with him, that Tooke knew who he was and warned the members to take care who they admitted to their tables.[6] According to *Tait's*, the Privy Council could not decide whether to call Wharton as a prosecution witness or allow Tooke to call him for the defence, when the damning evidence would be produced under cross-examination. They decided on the latter course when Tooke subpoenaed Wharton, but Tooke stymied the prosecution by not calling Wharton who was then unable to give evidence against him.

On 19 May Tooke was sent to the Tower, followed by Joyce, Kyd and Bonney, plus Hardy, Thelwall, Richter and Lovett of the LCS. Minor LCS fry were put in the more plebeian Newgate. On Tooke's arrival at the Tower, guns were firing a salute for the capture of Guadaloupe. He enquired whether this formed part of his reception. Wilkes pooh-poohed a false report that Tooke had burst into tears when imprisoned: 'I knew he was a knave but I never thought him a coward'.[7]

Tooke had an unpleasant time when he first arrived. Iron bars were put up at his window. He was refused writing materials or newspapers. Richard Ford, who had been authorised to remove and examine Tooke's papers from locked cases and drawers at

Wimbledon, came to collect his keys. Frost and Vaughan were present to make notes of what was taken. Tooke began to keep a diary of his life in prison, written in pencil on his copy of Chaucer. When, by order of the Privy Council, he was issued on 24 May with tea, paper, ink, sugar and lozenges for his cough, he continued in ink on his interleaved copy of *Diversions* which he was emending for the forthcoming second edition.[8] Tooke's notes reveal his anxiety for his daughters and guilt over the effect his arrest might have on them, his bitterness as he surveyed the vicissitudes of his stormy life, coupled with his indomitable determination. Incarceration in the Tower, accused of treason, was a far more serious matter than his previous imprisonment in the King's Bench.

Tooke chafed at the unnecessary petty humiliations of his restrictive custody, 'closer than was used in the Bastille'. At first he had two warders with him day and night, plus an armed sentinel at the door and one on the staircase. Every two hours a corporal and sergeant burst into his room. Later he was allowed to sleep alone with only one warder. Morning and evening he was visited by the chief warder, Kinghorn, to whom he took a great dislike: 'Gaoler, but not Gentleman Gaoler', who gave 'fawning words and most savage treatment'. When Vaughan came, Kinghorn 'sat close. He says he has the Governor's order to hear every syllable that passes'. He timed Vaughan's half-hour visit with his watch, and joined in the conversation unasked.

Friends were only allowed to see the prisoners with the Privy Council's permission which was granted to few. Tooke was understandably distressed when, after Vaughan was examined, permission for his visits was rescinded on 6 June. At first, Tooke chose not to apply for his daughters to come as he did not want to submit them to an unpleasant ordeal; visitors had to pass a barrage of soldiers' ribald jokes. A sergeant was present when visitors came; later a warder replaced the sergeant, but it was impossible to have a private conversation. Towards the end of August, when Tooke had been imprisoned for 14 weeks, having no idea how long his imprisonment might continue, he changed his mind about his daughters coming.

The Governor, Marquis Cornwallis, had under him two deputy governors, gentleman gaolers and warders. Dressed as Yeomen Warders when on duty, the warders were with a few exceptions civil and attentive. At first the military were very rude, as a report had been spread that the prisoners planned to attack them in the Tower, then march out to massacre the soldiers in barracks. When the soldiers realised this was nonsense, they were very kind and turned people out of the Tower who tried to insult them.

Thelwall was in a room above the western gate, Hardy in a small one next door. Tooke was not in the same tower, but so near that he and Thelwall could talk from their respective windows. Tooke, Kyd and Bonney could also chat by leaning out of their windows when no-one was about. Joyce was in a room with a window over Tower Wharf. Initially passengers jeered at him as a dirty Jacobin, but soon spectators began to pity the prisoners. The Government had launched a propaganda campaign of handbills, songs, slogans and, as Tooke mentioned at his trial, even abuse on earthenware. Their efforts to have the reformers branded as traitors did not entirely succeed, for many people, though opposed to radical agitation, disliked such harsh measures.[9]

The Government allowance for alleged traitors had been £1, but that had been cut in 1780 at Burke's instigation to 13/4 a week as a measure of economy. When the prisoners discovered that, if they rejected it, the Governor would pocket the money, they decided to accept it.[10] 'At last,' wrote Tooke, 'they have found out a method to make me a pensioner against my will'. But the money did not go far: Tooke reckoned his expenses at seven to eight guineas a week. All the men were poor. In particular, the LCS was extremely short of funds and found it difficult to provide money for imprisoned members' families. Many of Tooke's papers seized by the authorities are covered with financial accounts and calculations jotted down on the backs of letters or envelopes. During imprisonment he noted his expenses on the margins of the *Diversions*, these included regular payments of £10 to Mrs Hart. Friends came to his rescue: Vaughan advanced money which he gave to Tooke's daughters. In one entry Tooke records with relief, 'Mr (William) Tooke's heart smites him at last'. He sent £100 which would enable Tooke 'to pay [his] attorney and subpoena witnesses'.

Due to increasing discomfort from a defect or obstruction in his penis, Tooke had only spent one night away from home during the past seven years. In the Tower his health declined. On 9 June he wrote to the Privy Council asking for two close friends to be allowed to visit him: Henry Cline, a distinguished surgeon of Guy's Hospital, later President of the Royal College of Surgeons, and his own doctor, George Pearson, Fellow of the Royal Society. 'As my private affairs have been all laid open to the Privy Council, I feel no great repugnance to lay open to them my more private bodily infirmities...I have a dropsy, or a rupture, or both... in the testicles, besides a more painful complaint in their neighbourhood, for which, as well as for swelling in my legs, and some other unpleasant symptoms, I have long had the benefit of their assistance... My health drove me to Wimbledon, where I appeared to be recovering. My present situation has increased my complaints, and I wish for their advice.' Tooke asked that their times of attendance should be 'convenient to themselves', because they had never taken fees from him; 'and I had rather lose the benefit of their assistance than put them to extraordinary inconvenience'. Dr Pearson was totally uninterested in politics, but Cline shared Tooke's political views. After some badgering of the authorities, he and Pearson were allowed to call daily to pass bougies through Tooke's urethra. This meant that, after the unpleasant gap when Vaughan's visits were forbidden, Tooke once more had contact with the outside world, although hampered by Kinghorn who, in spite of the intimate nature of the operation, stayed close to hear their conversation. Tooke contrived to irritate Kinghorn with his jokes. One day he asked his doctors, as they prepared to treat him, to extend their care 'to another neck no less valuable and no less in jeopardy'.[11] He asked Cline and Pearson to visit his daughters, but to conceal his poor state of health. One day Cline tactfully handed Tooke a letter 'to be read later' which contained £50.

Dropsy is commonly a sign of heart failure or renal disease, but Tooke lived another 18 years so this seems unlikely. His symptoms may have been due to confinement and lack of exercise. Probably he had an enlarged prostate gland which obstructed the urethra. He may also have had stones in his bladder. Treatment by bougies caused an infection of the testicles which produced swelling in the groin. This meant that Tooke was in constant pain and discomfort. At his trial it was remarked how drawn and frail he looked. Tooke was in custody for seven months. He had a strong physique and did not give way under physical pain, but he never completely regained his former vigour and mobility. Although he maintained his insouciant bonhomie to bolster his fellow prisoners' morale, the pessimism and, for once, almost a tone of self-pity in his diary may have been partially due to ill-health.

In June a barber was allowed to call, and through him Tooke was able to read newspapers in which he was amused to find himself described as a hoary traitor, ringleader of a gang of conspirators. Tooke was uncertain what charges would be brought against him until he read the Second Report of the Committee of Secrecy of 6 June in *The Times*. He then wrote a tart letter to the Clerk of the Privy Council. Since habeas corpus had been suspended he was no longer held illegally and was by law at the mercy of suspicion. He had never seen the first Report of the Committee of Secrecy, had only this moment read the second, which he described as a 'report of Horrour and by that alone am informed what sort of a picture their Lordships have drawn of me'. His objections to examination were therefore removed. 'Such suspicions are too horrid for me to remain a moment in voluntary silence. My character is worth much more than my life.' The Privy Council, however, preferred to let matters lie.

The second report made no pretence to objectivity. Based on a partial selection from the societies' documents and evidence of witnesses intimidated by the Privy Council, it emphasised the societies' francophilia and concluded that their design was to reform the Commons, if necessary by force. It stressed the lead the SCI had given, for it was inconceivable that the clubs could have flourished without the help of men of superior talents. On 13 June the House of Lords approved an address to the Crown which claimed the existence of a conspiracy to destroy the established constitution and government. Grenville announced that a plan had been discovered to massacre all magistrates and start a rebellion. Lauderdale objected that Grenville had not produced one shred of proof. Pitt grossly exaggerated the numbers of LCS members and claimed the reformers, who aped the French, had concealed their real designs. 'So formidable a conspiracy had never before existed.'

A small minority of Foxites and independents protested against such severe measures. Fox pointed out that if a convention attempted to act illegally, it could be dispersed by the nearest JP; in addition, Lord Howe's naval victory of 1 June had destroyed any threat of a French invasion.[12] Wyvill rightly blamed 'the indiscretion (possibly it ought to be called the criminal rashness) of the popular societies'.[13] All the same, due partly to spies' reports, the Government overestimated the radicals' influence and violent intentions. It is uncertain whether Pitt really believed the loyalists' gloomy forebodings, or merely wanted to remove any potential threat to unhampered prosecution of the war. The outlook was bleak for Tooke and his fellow-prisoners.

It was an exceptionally hot summer, the sun on the leads intolerable. Hardy, Thelwall and Tooke were allowed to get a breath of fresh air on the little leads at the top of the round tower while their beds were being made and rooms swept, but no two were allowed out at the same time, so the intervals there were brief. Tooke saw Joyce walking on other distant leads, and they bowed to each other. Towards the end of July, they were permitted to walk around the ramparts, each guarded by his respective warder, and not allowed to speak to each other. Three months after commitment they were allowed to speak with their doors open, then by degrees permitted to enter each other's rooms for a few minutes at a time, always taking precautions to be back in their own rooms when guards did their rounds. The rigours of their confinement were so far relaxed that they began to wonder if the Government wanted them to escape.[14]

Thelwall, reading *Macbeth* and furious that the authorities had seized his collection of prints and engravings, fretted about his wife's ill-health until she was allowed to visit him daily. Hardy's house in Piccadilly was attacked during the celebration of Howe's victory. His wife, who was pregnant with her sixth child, stuck in a window escaping from the mob. She was pulled out but suffered injury. She visited Hardy twice a week until the day she died two months later when her child was still-born. For ten days after Hardy learnt of her death he did not appear on the ramparts, then Tooke got a message through advising him to walk out to meet his friends in the various rendezvous they had arranged as it might relieve his spirits.[15]

Tooke spent seven or eight hours a day reading and writing, the same amount as at home. He worked hard at his Chaucer from which he intended to cite examples in the *Diversions*, and made critical comments on poems with a revolutionary flavour which Bonney had composed. He reread *Tom Jones* and *Gil Blas*, loaned by a warder's wife. The loss of his friends' company was one of Tooke's greatest deprivations. To make this less noticeable he rearranged his schedule, rose at four and went to bed very early. Friends supplied him with snuff which he passed round among the warders. Perry sent turtle soup, Tuffin madeira and hock, Cline a brace of partridges. Tooke distributed strawberries, peaches and artichokes from his garden among his fellow-prisoners. One day he lowered a bottle of wine on a string from his window so that Kyd's warder, whose birthday it was, could have a glass of wine. He carefully refrained from speaking to Kyd, but there was a great to-do and the warder he most disliked, Bateman, shut Tooke's window. The heat was so intense that Tooke firmly opened it again: 'To be stapled to the floor without Bateman would be more tolerable than his company'.

From his window Tooke watched life outside: the Trinity Brethren walking in procession from the Tower; a man selling peanuts from a donkey cart, belabouring the donkey when he brayed, but restrained by the Tower soldiers from maltreatment. Occasional passers-by doffed their hats to Tooke, then one July Sunday, as he looked out of the window at boats sailing by, the crowd standing on the wharf suddenly pulled off their hats. They repeated their gesture two or three times. Tooke bowed to them, then retired from the window.

5 July was Tooke's fifty-eighth birthday. On 9 July he noted that in 1777, after he had been in the King's Bench prison about seven weeks, news came of Burgoyne's surrender at Saratoga. Now, seven weeks after incarceration in the Tower, the allies were evacuating Flanders. Tooke wrote down his credo: 'In this close custody I have had time to review my life that is passed… I shall certainly die with the principles which I have always professed and I am very willing to die for them… I will resist argument by argument, reason by reason, legal means by legal means, force by force. Every man chuses to take that situation in which he can most advantageously employ his strength. As I have never possessed any power but reason, I chuse to take the field of argument.'

Tooke gave a courageous and unwavering lead to his younger and less seasoned companions. Thelwall, who said that it was from Tooke that he had principally derived 'that energy which enabled him to preserve a calm fortitude of mind when persecuted', wrote, 'Of the philosophic firmness or the playful vivacity of Tooke's mind no one will be surprised to hear; but a delightful conversation…

stolen while our guards were asleep, I shall to the last moment of my life remember'. At midnight, while the moon shone on the river between the mass of the vessels, they talked with the freedom of men who, having nothing to conceal, had nothing to fear from what might be overheard… 'We rejoiced in the conduct we had already persued… we paid discriminating tribute of approbation to the memory of those murdered patriots who had been the preoccupants of our dungeons, and comparing the fate of Sydney and Essex, rejected the cowardly subterfuge of suicide… I will, said Tooke, either live to be useful or die usefully,' which Thelwall thought a maxim for all seasons. Before they left the Tower, Tooke said through the grating of his cell, 'I fear these bloodhounds mean our death.'[16]

Bosville and Cartwright were not allowed to see Tooke. Wilkes sent professions of respect and affection via Dr Pearson. Kyd wrote the second volume of his *Treatise on the Law of Corporations* in the Tower and dedicated it to Tooke 'to pay a public tribute of gratitude for the honour of your friendship; and… to have my name hereafter mentioned in company with yours as a scholar'.[17]

In a letter to Mr and Mrs Macnamara, who returned in June after five years abroad, Tooke threw off his aggrieved tone and wrote with the warm, light touch which endeared him to his many friends. He thanked them for visiting his girls and recalled the many happy hours the three of them had spent with the Macnamaras and their son John. Tooke had got to know Macnamara during the 1788 election. An opponent of Fox, he frequently dined with Pitt and had many aristocratic friends.

While Macnamara toured the Continent, Tooke had looked after his chests, harpsichord, table and books. Macnamara gave £100 towards Tooke's legal expenses. Tooke apologised for being such a poor correspondent. He described his life at Wimbledon during the past two years. He never rode outside the gate on his horse, and went to town in a chaise about 30 times to dine in company. On Sundays in winter and spring he 'had about 12 to 20 to eat (literally mutton)'. The rest of his time was devoted to 'hard labour in the garden (which has driven off gout)' and his books, with cards every evening with his girls 'imprisoned at Wimbledon' with him. 'Horne Tooke has always been from his cradle as great a traitor as he is at this moment, and shall continue the same to the end of his life. It has been a very happy one; it is now happy, and has never been and he trusts never will be embittered by the fear of losing it.' Macnamara's friendship for Tooke need not give him any uneasiness, 'for Horne Tooke has never done an action, nor uttered a word, nor written a single sentence, nor harboured a thought of an important political nature, which (taken with all its circumstances of time, place and occasion) he wishes either recalled or concealed'.

Preparations for the Trials

Watt, convicted of treason for conspiracy, had been condemned to death in Edinburgh. There were hints in the newspapers that the reformers were to be tried for treason. After months of uncertainty, when the prisoners had not known what charges they faced or how the crown intended to proceed, on 10 September a Commission of Oyer and Terminer was issued. Tooke noted that a friend of Joyce's brother heard Pitt say that they had not been able to get anything against Mr Horne Tooke. Ministers regarded Tooke as a useful scapegoat, lacking influential protectors but of sufficient standing to be a deterrent example.

The Attorney General, Scott, had previously taken advice as to what charges might be preferred against the SCI. Spencer Perceval, the future Prime Minister, gave his opinion on 2 March: 'the same spirit of sedition and mischief seems to shew itself in equal degree through the whole while the same caution is always at work, keeping them within the bounds of misdemeanour, and out of the reach of a heavier charge'. He did not think that the society would 'proceed to any act of treason, till they have made themselves believe that they have a very near prospect of its success'. At the end of April the crown lawyers advised Scott that the actions of the SCI 'fell short of the crime of High Treason' and that since the declaration of war the society 'appears to have been much on their guard'. However, in contradiction of some witnesses' evidence, 'No member who attended need be ignorant of the proceedings, as a book containing the business of preceding meetings was laid on the table for inspection'. In the lawyers' admirably lucid reports Tooke appears as a pervasive influence, an elusive but important figure. One lawyer doubted if Tooke could be implicated in an armed force plot but thought Thelwall could.[18]

In July 1794, when all the evidence had been collected, Scott considered the best way to bring the prisoners to trial. The crown lawyers had advised that it would only be possible to prove sedition, but the judges who were members of the Privy Council thought that, in view of evidence gleaned from interrogations, he should prosecute for High Treason. Scott was a reactionary, a strikingly handsome self-made man and a very competent lawyer, and strongly backed every repressive Government measure. He believed that it was imperative to bring home to the country the dangers of a radical convention in wartime. Also, if the prisoners were indicted for sedition and then evidence showed there was a case of high treason, they would by law have been entitled to acquittal for the lesser misdemeanour; it would then have been virtually unacceptable to indict them subsequently for treason.[19] Luckily for the accused, the prosecution therefore made the mistake of attempting to prove them guilty of constructive treason: though no single act was treasonable, their intentions were and their accumulated actions would lead to treason. Ministers had perhaps not grasped that they were required by a statute of Edward III to produce concrete evidence of 'an overt act of compassing the King's death', i.e. that a convention which attempted to seize political power would force the King to resist and put his life in danger. A charge of sedition, making each man answerable for his own acts, might well have stuck.

On 2 October Sir James Eyre, Chief Justice of Common Pleas, directed the Grand Jury of Middlesex to find a true bill against 13 of the men, most of whom had been kept under lock and key while a case against them was prepared: Tooke, Bonney, Holcroft, Joyce, Kyd and Wardle of the SCI; Hardy, Baxter, Hodgson, Moore, Richter, Lovett and Thelwall of the LCS. Hardy, Baxter and Hodgson were artisans; Tooke was the only one who had been at a university; the rest had received some education, or educated themselves, were successful in their various professions and were considered 'middling' people. Hodgson, Moore and Wardle had so far evaded their warrants.

Eyre asserted 'that a traitorous... conspiracy had been formed for subverting the existing laws and constitution, and for introducing the system of anarchy... which had so lately prevailed in France'. Even if the reform associations had no more sinister object than obtaining a reform of Parliament, any assembly they called with the aim of overawing Parliament might easily degenerate into a 'crime of high treason'. Although there might not be a clear-cut case, a judicial enquiry would determine the legality of the principle of constructive treason.

On 6 October a true bill was found against all the accused except Lovett, Hardy's brother-in-law, the 12 apostles, as they were nicknamed. Holcroft, whose play *The Road to Ruin* was a recent popular success, made a dramatic appearance in court and surrendered voluntarily. This created a very good impression, a fillip to the reformers' reputations.[20]

Holcroft summoned Godwin, who was staying with Dr Parr, to his aid. Godwin now rushed up to town, saw Holcroft held in Newgate, then in two days produced an extremely able reply to Eyre, published anonymously in the *Morning Chronicle* on 21 October. The author was rumoured to be Felix Vaughan, but was soon known to be Godwin.[20,21]

Entitled 'Cursory Strictures on the Charge delivered by Chief Justice Eyre to the Grand Jury', it was a brilliant, restrained attack on the Government's attitude, which strengthened the reformers' wavering morale and convinced many people that ministers were trying to frame the accused. Printed as a pamphlet by the LCS, it sold all over the country. Godwin indignantly pointed out that Eyre's charge had no basis in established law. The prisoners were accused of publishing pamphlets and belonging to political societies, by which they 'endeavoured to change the form of government'; but there was no proof of a conspiracy. A reform association might desert its object and become treasonable, 'but so may a card club, a bench of justices or even a cabinet council'. The charge maintained 'actions either totally innocent in themselves, or criminal in a much inferior degree, shall when united amount to treason'. The prosecution intended to convict by implication and 'probably hope that the mere names of Jacobin and Republican will answer their purposes… and that a jury of Englishmen can be found who will send everyman to the gallows… to whom these appellations have been attributed'. Godwin laid the blame for this scheme on Pitt.[22]

Tooke, walking on Tower Parade, ignored the rule of silence, waved a newspaper above his head and called to Joyce, 'By God, this lays Eyre completely on his back'.[21] The following spring, when Godwin was dining at Wimbledon, Tooke, who normally teased Godwin about his 'visionary politics', for once showed his appreciation of Godwin's intellect. After a good deal of badinage and cross-questioning, when Godwin acknowledged that he was the author of the *Strictures*, Tooke asked Godwin to give him his hand. Godwin got up and went to the head of the table, where Tooke pressed Godwin's hand to his lips saying, 'I can do no less by the hand that had given existence to that production'. This action gave Godwin immense pleasure: 'The suddenness of the action filled me with confusion; yet I must confess that... this homage thus expressed was more gratifying to me than all the applause I had received from any other quarter'.[23]

An attempt was then made to prejudice the accused's case by an absurd alarm over the 'popgun plot'. After a quarrel among LCS members, one of them took his revenge by claiming that the others had planned to blow a poisoned arrow at the King through an airgun disguised as a walking-stick. Several men were detained until the following year, then discharged. With Wimbledon as base, Vaughan organised a collection for their defence.[24]

In October Tooke's favourite nephew, John Wildman, was allowed by the Privy Council to help Tooke sort out his papers and prepare his defence. A very clever man and successful Chelsea brewer, as a youth John had been employed by Tooke to deliver letters he dashed off to the press. The solicitor to the prisoners was, however, refused access to the SCI books. Weston, whom Tooke had originally approached to act as his attorney, had refused. He 'loved and respected' Tooke, but had just married the daughter of a Commissioner of Customs so did not dare accept. Tooke would contemptuously fume over the 'ridiculous imputations of his enemies' and, when allowed, rush onto the Tower walls to relieve his feelings.

According to custom the prisoners had to be transferred to a City gaol from which they would be taken to trial. Late at night on 23 October they were told they would be moved to Newgate at eight o'clock the next morning. Due to his infirmity, Tooke got up at four to be ready. At 6.30, Kinghorn, who must have been glad to be rid of Tooke, told him he was to walk through the Tower to be delivered to the sheriff. Tooke complained that it was wet – due to his gouty feet he wore thin shoes – it would be cruel to make him catch cold and 'carry me a dumb man to my trial'.

He was therefore allowed to travel in a coach. The seven prisoners said cordial goodbyes to their keepers at the Tower; Tooke in particular had been popular with the yeomen. As they travelled in three coaches, guarded by constables and accompanied by a crowd of people, they talked gaily to each other and their attendants and bowed and smiled to those who waved from pavements and windows as they passed. They were surprised by the number of spectators as their removal from the Tower was unexpected. According to the pro-Government *Morning Post* 'the strongest animation of feeling and sympathy was visible in almost every spectator's countenance'.[25]

Conditions in Newgate were appalling. Their cells were filthy, cold, damp and dark, the furniture rickety. Tooke, on behalf of himself and the others, petitioned the judges to be returned to the Tower until their trials. Bonney was returned to the Tower, the rest were transferred to rather better cells. During their four weeks' confinement the prisoners became ill; Thelwall caught some internal ailment from which he never fully recovered. Tooke perturbed the warders by singing every night at dinner time an old anti-Jacobite song his grandmother had taught him, 'Here's a health to our old constitution... To the downfall of all tyranny I long to see the day'.[25,26]

The day after their arrival, the prisoners were formally arraigned at the Old Bailey. Tooke, who intended to act with 'the spirit of a tiger and to throw off all constraint', had planned to address the court in a speech which would be circulated to all the London papers, condemning Eyre's charge and vehemently attacking his character and conduct, but he was persuaded to abandon his scheme.[27] Instead, dressed in his customary brown in the style of a substantial City merchant, he affected an air of boredom and refused to acknowledge the gravity of the proceedings. He 'said little but created a great impression'. While they waited for defence counsel to appear, Tooke complained with an aggrieved air of a cold draught which would endanger their health as they came from six months' close confinement, and asked if they could be dismissed as soon as possible. They all pleaded not guilty.[28] It was agreed that the prisoners should be tried separately, and the Attorney General announced that he would proceed against Hardy first. Initially it had been intended that Tooke should come first. Scott later made the cryptic comment that this 'would have been unfair'.[19] The real reason was that it would be easier to prove that Hardy had been actively involved in preparations for a convention and collection of arms.

At the beginning of October Scott had told Burges that, if a true bill were found against Tooke, he would 'undertake to hang him'.[29] Although the charge of treason was widely considered too severe, many people thought it probable that the men would be convicted. Bets were laid on their lives, odds three to one against. Brooks's betting book contains the entry 'General Fiztpatrick bets Charles Grey five guineas to one that Tooke is hanged before Pitt'. Lord Townshend bet an even guinea that Tooke would hang. One evening Grey and Sheridan accompanied Erskine, who had volunteered to defend the prisoners, to Newgate. Grey wrote, 'I always disliked him (Tooke) and never met him before but in contest... Our going seemed to be a real comfort to him. He is in very good spirits, and, whether the issue be life or death, I think he will conduct himself like a man.' It was rumoured that the Government had a further 300 warrants prepared. More reformers decided to embark for America. Although until now the authorities had not touched any men of consequence, the Foxites feared that, if the prosecutions were successful, there might be widespread proscription. Grey wrote to his future wife that he would attend Hardy's trial 'to learn how to conduct myself when it comes to my turn'.[26]

Notes on Chapter 9

General: minutes of the examinations by the Privy Council are PC2/140(PRO). Tooke's diary is in his copy of *DOP*, BL shelf mark C60(1)15, and has recently been published by the Leeds Philosophical Society. Unless otherwise referenced, the account of his experiences are taken from them.

1 Stephens, II, p 119; *State Trials* XXV, pp 249-50
2 Stephens II, p 120; *State Trials* XXV, pp 248-9
3 Add MS 27816 f485
4 TS11/963/3509; PC 2/140
5 *Parliamentary History* XXXI, p 931; *Tait's Edinburgh Magazine* 1853, pp 525-32; Stephens II, pp 116-7

6 TS11/965/351OA
7 Graham, p 121
8 Stephens II, pp 121-3; Robinson III, p 187; Rogers, *Recollections*, p 140
9 Thelwall, *Tribune* I, p 306; Thelwall, *Life*, pp 188-93; Joyce, appendix; Hardy, p 4; Stephens II, p 123
10 Thelwall, *Life*, pp 199-200
11 Stephens II, pp 421-3
12 *Parliamentary History* XXXI, pp 689-931
13 Wyvill V, p 206
14 Thelwall, *Life*, p 190
15 *Ibid.*, pp 184, 188, 193; Hardy, pp 35-42
16 Thelwall, *Life*, p 193
17 HO42/32, 20.7.94 (PRO); Kyd II, dedication
18 Goodwin, p 338
19 Eldon, pp 55-8
20 *State Trials* XXIV, pp 200-14; *London Chronicle* 8.10.94
21 Brown FK, pp 92-5; Hazlitt, *Spirit of the Age*, p 51
22 Godwin W, *Cursory Strictures*, pp 23-27, appendix II
23 Brown FK, pp 96-7; Paul I, p 147
24 Veitch, p 313
25 Thelwall, *Tribune* I, pp 311-8; *Morning Post* 25.10.94
26 Trevelyan, pp 84-8
27 Stephens II, pp 133-40
28 Timbs, p 446
29 Bland Burges, p 10 f117, letter to his wife 14.10.94

Chapter Ten

Trial for Treason

Hardy's trial began on 28 October 1794 before Eyre, who conducted both his and Tooke's trials with exemplary fairness. It seems that Eyre was chosen in place of the Lord Chief Justice (Kenyon) because of the latter's 'intemperence of manner'.[1] Erskine charmed the jury, browbeat the prosecution witnesses and made out a persuasive case for Hardy. Treason trials normally lasted about a day; this one took nine, the court usually sitting from 8am until midnight. The first night the jury slept on mattresses at the Old Bailey. They complained that they could not sleep and had been 40 hours in their clothes, so eventually they were found beds in the Hummums of Covent Garden (lodgings where loose women were not allowed). The trial attracted enormous interest throughout the country. In London, the Old Bailey was besieged by crowds who, though in general well-behaved, booed and jostled the judges and Attorney General and cheered Erskine. There was an air of intense excitement and anxiety.

Every morning Hardy would leave Newgate under guard, encouraged on his way by printers convicted of seditious libel – one for printing a pamphlet written by Tooke and Thelwall – who were lodged in comparative comfort, then by ironed and fettered felons exercising in the courtyard. On his return, he would greet Kyd, Tooke and Thelwall as he passed their cells, 'Goodnight gentlemen, there is to be another day'.

Scott, who led for the Crown, produced an enormous quantity of documents, including the proceedings of the LCS and SCI and every pamphlet and address they had printed, in order to prove their treasonable intentions. He started with a nine-hour speech at which Thurlow exclaimed, 'Nine hours, then by God there is no treason'. Erskine later retaliated with one that was almost as long. As Tooke remarked, 'The law never intended the crime of High Treason should take five days in proof'.[2]

The jury were confused and exhausted by the mass of evidence. Prosecution witnesses included not only LCS members turned King's evidence, but spies who created a bad impression which damaged the prosecution case. Although they had infiltrated the LCS successfully, they produced no concrete corroboration that the societies had conspired behind an innocent facade to rebel and subvert the Government. Hardy had not answered the letter from Sheffield offering pikes. Erskine admitted that some members had used menacing language, but emphasised that demands for parliamentary reform could not be equated with intention to kill the King. He pointed out that those who had been transported under Scottish law for taking part in the Edinburgh conventions had been convicted of sedition not treason. With the backing of Erskine's skilful defence, Hardy acquired popularity as a humble, honest and independent man in the tradition of Hampden.

On Guy Fawkes Day Eyre completed his admirable summing-up while the Lord Mayor called up troops to prevent rioting. After retiring for three hours the jury returned a verdict of not guilty which was greeted with widespread relief and satisfaction all over the country. Hardy turned to the jury and spoke for the first time during his trial, 'My fellow countrymen, I return you my thanks'. Rejoicing crowds carried Hardy and Erskine home. They took Hardy's coach along a circuitous route, stopping to cheer in strategic places such as Carlton House and St James's Palace.[3] The Government had overplayed its hand.

After debating for a few days, ministers decided to go ahead with Tooke's prosecution which began on Monday 17 November. During Hardy's trial the Attorney General had given a description of the SCI which was in many ways perfectly accurate. Originally its members had been respectable gentlemen of independent principles; later, people of a different type joined who conducted themselves in such a manner that almost all the original members left. The proceedings of the society showed that about 16 people attended regularly, frequently only five were present, and business was carried on in a casual manner. One constant attendant at all important transactions was Mr Horne Tooke. The prosecution still hoped to prove that, with the SCI as cover, Tooke had masterminded sinister schemes to be carried out by the LCS. They intended to adduce as proof his propaganda for Paine's works, his encouragement of provincial societies, his contacts with the Jacobins and involvement in plans for an English convention. They attributed to Tooke, 'together with others, a conspiracy to depose the King, a deliberate plan to subvert the constitution'.[3]

Once more huge crowds collected round the Old Bailey, where the hall, corridors and the court itself were thronged with people of all ranks, including many well-dresssed ladies. An engraved portrait of Tooke by Sharp was on sale for 7/-. Opinions varied: some considered him an 'arrant traitor', but the majority did not want such a colourful and cultivated figure condemned to death.

Tooke subpoenaed an enormous number of witnesses, mostly character ones for cumulative effect. Burke hoped 'Parson Horne' would let him remain at peace, 'But, as that whole Race is irregular and eccentrick in the highest degree, I am not too confident'. Later: 'I was almost an whole week in Town. Mr Horne Tooke and his advisers had the impudence to summon me as a Witness for them, the ill nature to keep me in waiting for several days, and in the End, the prudence to discharge me.'[4] George Rose, however, Tooke's coadjutor in the Westminster election, said he 'would travel by day or night to do him service'. Stanhope, another witness, told Lord Lansdowne that his three daughters, who had got to know Tooke through Joyce, had asked him to offer himself as guardian to Tooke's daughters if he were convicted. Lady Hester Stanhope said Tooke always liked her, 'with all my aristocratical principles because he knew what I meant'. She was 'sure he was not a democrat by the court he always paid me, and by his constantly making so many civil speeches to me and of me'.[5] She was too egotistic to appreciate that Tooke would not have cared who she was; what counted was that he found her interesting.

The authorities could vet special juries in advance and weed out those likely to be sympathetic to the accused. As the jury were empanelled, Erskine exclaimed to Tooke 'By God, they are murdering you'.[6] There were additional problems, as an exceptionally large number of potential jurors claimed that they were sick or had pressing business. Tooke said he was not surprised, for they had seen what happened at Hardy's trial when jurors returned day afer day unshaven and without clean shirts. This time jurors slept at the London Tavern. The court sat from 9am to 9pm with only a quarter of an hour break for refreshment. Tooke, due to his 'very painful infirmity', had to get up at 5am to be ready.

It was the custom to place bunches of sweet herbs at the bar where the criminal was to sit. When Tooke was brought in, dressed in brown as usual with an embroidered waistcoat, his hair tied, his face pale and drawn from long confinement, he indignantly swept them away with his handkerchief. 'They put you in gaol to catch the fever, then when they bring you to Court, put herbs that the Court may not catch it.'[7] Tooke told Eyre, 'like your lordship I have not many summers or autumns to spare'. After degrading and humiliating custody, 'I come to you but half a man'. He asked permission to sit by his counsel for, if his trial were similar to Hardy's, the prosecution would produce a mass of evidence and surmise 'about passages in my life' of which his counsel would be ignorant. When Eyre replied that this would be an exceptional indulgence, he retorted 'I cannot help saying my Lord that, if I were a judge, that word should never issue from my lips... you have no indulgence to show: you are bound to be just; and to be just is to do that which is ordered'. Though Tooke did add that he was 'not so foolish as to desire to give you... offence, when it is so strongly my interest to please you all'. Eyre solved the problem by granting Tooke's request on health grounds and on this basis Tooke, 'very well content to accept it as indulgence, or any other thing', bowed appreciatively when a chair was brought for him beside Erskine and Gibbs. This was an advantageous move, as not only could Tooke communicate easily with his legal advisers, but he was in a much better position to examine witnesses, and he now faced the jury.

This was the last time Tooke appeared in court and the most memorable. He was mollified by the Chief Justice's tact, patience and forebearance. Eyre allowed him considerable latitude in his questions and paid him compliments on his legal skill; Erskine and (later Sir) Vicary Gibbs, his other defence counsel, kept him in order. As a result, Tooke showed none of the rudeness, impertinence or tendency to drag in old grudges that he had before

Mansfield and Kenyon. On the third day of the trial Tooke said 'I am sure all the conduct I have received from your lordship and the prosecutor has been such as totally to change the temper of my mind, with which I first came into this court; and I shall never be able to express the gratitude I have to acknowledge for it'. Eyre, however, displayed such dislike for Erskine and Gibbs that, when the trial was over, Erskine challenged him to a duel.

Sir John Mitford (later Lord Redesdale), the Solicitor General, led for the prosecution, and opened with a long speech lasting three hours. He was as keen to convict as Scott, but there was less likelihood of this now that Hardy had been acquitted. He suggested that the SCI and LCS were acting the part played by the Jacobin club in Paris, and quoted the support which the societies had given to the Parisian revolutionaries. Another Crown counsel was Serjeant Adair, a staunch supporter of Wilkes in the SSBR split, of whom Tooke once said, 'I would rather at any time lose a cause than be condemned to hear Adair gain it for me'.[8]

Ably backed by Gibbs, Erskine handled the defence brilliantly. He planned the overall strategy but allowed Tooke to examine witnesses and make comments. Tooke enjoyed himself enormously. He cheerfully acknowledged papers to be in his handwriting before this was proved. He offered to admit all he had 'ever said, done or written, to save time', but Eyre would not allow this as no prisoner could foresee the effect of evidence produced against him. Master of irony and light-hearted raillery, Tooke passed his snuff box about with an insouciant air of bonhomie; the skill with which he followed up Gibbs's cross examinations with pertinent comments and demolished prosecution witnesses was a reminder of what a sad waste of talent his exclusion from the bar had been. 'Cool, ready at repartee', he trod the boards of the Old Bailey like an amateur actor who had at last been given a plum role. 'From the constant merriment which rewarded his sallies, it might be guessed that a madder wag never stood at the bar; yet he rarely laughed himself, but glanced around from his keen... eyes, a satirical look of triumph.'[9] It must be the only treason trial enlivened by perpetual gales of laughter.

When worsted on a point of law by the Chief Justice, Tooke apologised with patent false modesty: 'Ignorant, as I am, of the proceedings of a court of justice... I have been but forty years a student, when I shall come to be called to the bar I hope I shall know better'. When SCI approval of Barère and St André's speeches was cited to prove its members were republicans, Tooke retorted that it was lucky the society did not say there were some good things in the Koran, or they might have been charged with Mahometanism.

He objected that the indictment charged 'divers books, pamphlets... and writings... the word "divers" so loose that all the libraries of Europe might have been brought in evidence against me'. When he amused the court with comic illustrations which, incidentally, diverted attention from more compromising evidence, Eyre admonished him for making inappropriate jokes: this was 'not a case for being ludicrous in'.

With many witnesses Tooke gave the impression of holding a personal conversation, tacking explanatory comments onto his questions and drawing the jury with gestures into friendly collaboration. He concealed the purpose of his cross-examinations, so outmanoeuvred the prosecution and elicited unbiased facts from their witnesses. Some, such as Hull, maintained they could not recollect any dates or details of meetings. Joyce's letter backfired, for Sharp confirmed that it referred to sinecures and pensions held by Pitt's cousins the Grenvilles. Tooke transformed Adams and Sharp into witnesses for his defence. Through Adams he established that the income of the society was so small that 'there was about £10 a year to overturn the government with,' and that he sometimes 'only stayed to make nine for a ballot' then went home. However, Sharp for once unwittingly turned the laughter against Tooke. Tooke, having obtained confirmation that he 'would rather be governed by St James than St Giles' and 'defended every establishment of the country', then asked, 'Did you suppose me a great bigot for the Church of England, or any other church?' Sharp replied, far from being a bigot, he did not think Tooke had any religion at all.

Tooke had considerable amusement at the Attorney General's expense. At times he and Scott appeared to reverse their roles of prosecutor and defender. Scott argued that, even if Tooke only meant to compel the King to call a parliament not consitutionally elected, he would have been guilty of treason. 'The King ought to lose his life, and I trust would be liable to lose his life, rather than govern contrary to his coronation oath.' Tooke pounced: 'What! is the Attorney talking treason?' Scott was quite put off his stride by this interruption, and feebly extricated himself with the explanation that he meant the King would resist attempts to compel him to govern unlawfully. At one point the Attorney General said in exasperation, 'I am always obliged when you correct me'. When Tooke sharply questioned the integrity of his method for instituting these prosecutions, Scott, an emotional man who often extolled his honesty, said he could endure any insinuations bar those against his good name, 'the little patrimony he had to leave his children', then burst into tears. To everyone's surprise, the Solicitor General, who was made of sterner stuff, wept in sympathy. A spectator enquired, 'What is old Mitford crying about?' Tooke replied in a stage whisper, 'The thought of the little inheritance poor Scott is likely to leave his children,' at which even the jury laughed.[10]

Tooke laid an etymological trap for Scott. He asked him if, 'notwithstanding the conviction and shameful punishment of Mr Muir', he would afterwards have associated with him. Scott replied, 'I must not sit here... to hear a question put in that way – shameful punishment.' Eyre added, 'I certainly conceived the word shameful there meant... disgracing the person'. Tooke concluded, 'Certainly no other, my Lord; not at all reflecting upon those who passed the punishment'.

On the fourth day of the trial, many reformers past and present appeared in the witness box. The evidence of some who had only known Tooke before the revolution was hardly pertinent. Macnamara, Lord Camden and Lord Frederick Campbell gave evidence about Tooke's respectable period when he supported Hood and mixed with Tory peers in the Constitutional Club. Tooke told Camden that, by being a member of a club to which Tooke belonged, 'The treasons with which I am accused may fly on your lordship'. Fox and Wyvill were called to prove that Tooke was formerly for moderate reform. Scott showed his exasperation when Erskine called a fellow member of the FOP, George Rous, another barrister: 'When one learned lawyer is examining another learned lawyer... there is no end of it'. Edward May, a more recent friend who belonged to no political societies, said Tooke held the same principles drunk or sober, and considered Britain not fit to be a republic. Confusion was deliberately caused by Tooke when he called William Maxwell of Carridan, a Foxite and frequenter of Wimbledon for the past two years, as he was at first thought to be the notorious Dr William Maxwell who had opened a subscription to arm the French (see p 121).

Tooke was touchy about the support he received. Francis, who had already appeared at Hardy's trial, only grudgingly admitted that he had discussed his reform plan with Tooke in 1793. Tooke, who had known Francis for 40 years, thought that he flinched from testifying on behalf of his fellow-reformers. Tooke complained about Lord Wycombe, Shelburne's son, who was at a dinner with Tooke shortly before his arrest, when Tooke was the only person present to defend the constitution. Reminded of this by an acquaintance, Wycombe said, 'Yes, Tooke should be protected'. 'And how did he protect me?' said Tooke. 'He set off for Italy.'[11]

Tooke did not call most of his close SCI associates, as they were under arrest themselves or appeared as Crown witnesses. Scott pointed out that Frost, who was in court, was not called. The defence may have feared that as a debarred ex-jailbird he would make an adverse impression. Captain Harwood, who had not been in London since autumn 1793, admitted that he knew many of the Norwich reformers with whom Tooke was accused of intriguing. He recalled that he and Thomas Walker had keenly supported a typical Tookian scheme which Tooke proposed to a great number of friends: they should stand for rotten boroughs and petition against members who had bought the interest in them.

Cartwright, though doing his best for Tooke, had not attended SCI since May 1792. Tooke's cross-examination tended to emphasise that Cartwright's views were more radical than his own. Cartwright quoted an analogy of Tooke's: 'If I and several men are in the Windsor stage, when I find myself at Hounslow, I get out; they who want to go farther, may go to Windsor… but … no farther will I go, by God'. When Scott asked Cartwright if he would get out with the FOP at Hounslow or stay in with SCI, Cartwright replied that there was no man so bad with whom he would not sign a petition. That, retorted Eyre, might be sincere but was not prudent. Among those who criticised Tooke's dictum, Hazlitt objected that treasonable excess did not begin where prudence taught Tooke to stop: the question was how far men had a right to go according to the law. Coleridge wondered if a man would have a moral right to go half way to his destination with a burglar and so prevent his being arrested.[12]

Stanhope and Sheridan gave evidence about the part Tooke played at the Revolution Society. Tooke elicited from Sheridan that he 'was frequently received with very considerable disapproval'. Tooke turned to the jury and said, 'My question upon that head was to show that I was likely to have very troublesome subjects, after I had deposed our Lord the King, for I was constantly received with very great disapprobation'. Sheridan said that at the Revolution Society's celebratory banquet in July 1790 Tooke considered Sheridan's praise of the French could be misinterpreted, so introduced an additional loyal resolution. Tooke was triumphant; 'I beg the Attorney General will observe that I moderated the moderator.'

The proceedings were humiliating for the two cabinet ministers subpoenaed. The Duke of Richmond, who confirmed that he had met Tooke at Thatched House meetings in 1782 and 1785, had already appeared at Hardy's trial, when it was established that the LCS had followed his ideas. Although he had lost interest in politics and was engrossed in army reform, shortly after the trials he was dismissed from his post as Master General of the Ordinance. Pitt, whose memory had conveniently failed, cut a sorry figure. He gave vague answers and attemped to evade the fact that he had attended a delegate assembly. After exact details had been provided by Sheridan, Pitt was allowed to revise his evidence and conceded, when in the witness box for the second time, that he had been at a meeting at the Duke of Richmond's composed of 'delegates from different county meetings and several cities and towns'.

Granville Leveson Gower (later Earl Granville) wrote to his mother that Tooke's examination of Richmond, Fox, Pitt and Sheridan was very entertaining. Everybody was certain he would be acquitted. 'He appears… very cool, clever and witty, at the same time I cannot say his conduct appears in any way disrespectful to the Court'. Canning, who sat in court two days running, thought it was 'not easy to see Tooke to more advantage than he appears, in point of talents, on his trial. His mode of examining witnesses, his objections in law, and his whole manner of conducting the part in his cause which he takes upon himself, is the most masterly that I can conceive and infinitely beyond any professional counsel that I remember to have seen. But then he is so insolent, and does and says things so unlike the usual conduct allowed in a court of justice.'[13] Tooke kept up his banter outside the court. One night, returning from the Old Bailey to Newgate, a lady admirer pulled up the collar of his coat and wrapped a silk handkerchief round his neck. 'Pray Madam, be careful, for I am rather ticklish, at present, about that particular place.'[14]

The court was about to adjourn that evening when Tooke caught sight of his old friend Beadon, Bishop of Gloucester, and asked permission to question him for a few minutes. Tooke mentioned the move to refuse him an MA, a degree, 'as would be given to any creature that could answer to rational questions'. Eyre interposed, 'For the honour of the university you will not pursue that Mr Tooke,' to which he replied, 'I mean no joke upon the university.' The Attorney General incautiously asked Beadon, 'Do you know anything of the proceedings of the SCI or LCS for the last three years?' On his answering, 'Nothing at all,' Tooke crowed. 'Now we are even; because it must be as great a degree of insult to ask the Bishop of Gloucester about those societies, as my speaking lightly of the qualification for a master's degree': further roars of laughter.

After 15 witnesses had been called, and without consulting his counsel, Tooke closed his defence. He would not call any more character witnesses: it was repetitive, and the Attorney General asked them about events of which they were ignorant, to make points against him. This was specious. The Attorney General had established that many witnesses Tooke called knew nothing of SCI business during the crucial last two years. Eyre said there were suspicious points in Tooke's conduct he would have been glad to clear up. 'Why the prisoner had declined calling those witnesses who by their more intimate acquaintance with his proceedings could have done this was best known to himself.' Did Tooke realise that everything was going his way, with acquittal certain, and, leaving Wharton aside, not want to risk what might come out?

The final speech for the defence was made by Gibbs. It was a brilliant effort, praised by Eyre: '... a speech that was in all respects fitter to be offered to a jury... in a case of high treason.' According to Stephens it 'laid the foundations of his future fortune'.[15]

The sober picture of Tooke painted by himself, Erskine and Gibbs – a staunch supporter of King and constitution, with an unsuspected attachment to the House of Lords, and holding views less advanced than those of the Foxites – bore little resemblance to his popular image as veteran agitator. Erskine, who may not have known how much SCI business was directed by Tooke, played down his role, and Tooke himself maintained that he had far less to do with the running of the society than was in fact the case. According to Sharp's evidence, he lived quietly at Wimbledon employed in gardening, reading old books, writing or playing whist. From Adams an impression emerged of a dilettante society dominated by Tooke, who left the secretarial work to him. There were complaints that the SCI did not answer letters; Tooke's name would often appear in the minutes as present, though he had already left when resolutions were passed. Tooke may have left early, but he hardly ever missed a meeting. As Scott noted, his memory of the transactions of the SCI and LCS were remarkably accurate. Adams confirmed that Tooke had told him for the last two years that he thought 'the society should lay upon their oars and adjourn to as distant days as they could'. Undoubtedly Tooke realised that the future of the society was precarious, but that had not prevented him from doing his best to keep it going. Tooke's skilful cross-examinations prevented the emergence of a few awkward facts. In 1803, a spy reported an evening at Wimbledon when Tooke 'amused us much describing Adams's examination about the revenue of the SCI'. He had proved by Adams's evidence that the SCI was in his (Adams's) debt. 'This was a great point gained, yet what would my questions have amounted to if the enemy had asked him if the Society ever made private subscriptions? There would have been a rub I very much feared.'

Tooke did not have to establish a case of his own, only expose the inadequacies of the case against him. Erskine said that he had planned to conduct Tooke's case in a different manner, selecting only that evidence which affected him, so separating him from the other accused. Tooke had insisted that 'although not implicated himself in the alleged conspiracy', he was charged to prove that no such guilt could be brought home to others. After Hardy's acquittal, this task was considerably easier.[16]

Erskine rightly said that many of the societies' papers were rash or absurd, often contradicting one another because written by people of diverse views, but he emphasised that this did not constitute an intention to undermine the Government. Whether knowingly or not, he took liberties with the evidence, stating, for instance, that Tooke knew nothing of a committee of correspondence, whereas Tooke himself had said that he declined participation due to ill health. The chief charges against Tooke concerned written and printed documents which he had composed or amended. Here Tooke had underplayed his part, for example claiming that he had only rewritten snippets of a key letter which he signed and sent to Sheffield.

In his excellent summing up, Eyre, convinced by Erskine and Tooke, agreed that the SCI was a 'mere club', the LCS more menacing with cells constantly dividing to form new divisions. Tooke had not initiated this himself, but he had encouraged the LCS to follow Sheffield's lead. The SCI had neither numbers, money nor even zeal to usurp the Government. Eyre then made some very pertinent comments. Tooke was a scholar; such men are generally more worthily employed than mixing in factions which tend to convulse a state; yet from about the middle of 1791 he engaged in subversive politics. The addresses to the French and various strong resolutions were a direct violation of his expressed principles. 'I wish… Mr Tooke had put his case… beyond suspicion, because I see with regret a man of his cultivated understanding, of his capacity to be useful to mankind… supported by the evidence of… the Bishop of Gloucester who… would flatter no man. In such a situation I should have rejoiced if he could have put his case beyond all suspicions, but I cannot say that he has done so. There certainly is a great deal to be explained… I am totally unable to develop the character and conduct of this gentleman.'

As the trial, which lasted five days, drew to its close, there was so much noise from the crowds outside that the Lord Mayor went out to ask them to be quiet. According to Cartwright, it had been expected to take three days, and the bad air and crush had been immensely fatiguing; 'Tooke has shown himself a wonderful man'. The jury retired for eight minutes before returning a verdict of not guilty. 'This was followed by a roar, or rather convulsive scream of joy.' Almost inaudible through the din, Tooke thanked the court, Erskine, Gibbs and the jury. The jury wept, which brought tears to Tooke's eyes. He made a brief speech in a patronising, self-congratulatory manner. All witnesses describe Tooke as agitated, speaking in a low, tremulous voice, overcome with emotion and exhaustion, totally unlike his sharp, gay manner during the trial. His words could charitably be attributed to ill-health, the strain of imprisonment, the effort of conducting his defence and reaction now it was over. He was clearly piqued by Eyre's comments.[17]

'My caution, and my virtue... are the cause of those suspicions which dwelt upon his lordship's mind... being rarely present at these meetings, when my name appears in the books, I was anxious for the safety of a very honest, but not very able man. The secretary repeatedly brought to me papers... for publication... when I saw a word which was capable of... the appearance of a libel, I struck out the exceptionable parts and inserted what would avoid the danger of a prosecution.' He corrected the works of every man, of every opinion, who came to him. 'A gentleman... wrote a book against me – I corrected the book myself.' He mentioned these facts 'for the sake of the law upon which... the character of men depend. I am glad I have been prosecuted: and I hope this will make the Attorney General more cautious in future... There is no suspicion against me but by construction and inference.'

Although there were grounds for rebuking the Attorney General, after the evidence produced both at Hardy's and his own trial, Tooke cannot seriously have expected this version of his activities to be believed by anyone who studied the cases. Tooke was justified in claiming that his restraining influence had preserved the societies from many potential libel charges but, as Government lawyers who drew up a case against him pointed out, many resolutions were drawn up and proposed by him. When not on special committees himself, he named people to compose them. He was involved in most of the societies' actions. Many drafts and documents were edited in his unmistakable hand, and he introduced men who distinguished themselves by 'violent' conduct.

On other occasions Tooke made remarks which were patently untrue. Why did he make them now, when he had been acquitted? Did he want to justify himself to Eyre? Tooke always wanted to be proved right. Brougham, who admired him, thought the flaw in his character was a 'love of victory and a carelessness about truth'.[18] The SCI was done for: did Tooke wish to brush it from his life? Tooke had made no attempt to keep SCI affairs secret; it was his manner rather than his actions which gave the appearance of conspiracy. Tooke revelled in ambiguous language, shrouding his thoughts and actions in a cloud of mystery. Now, by sleight of hand, the brooding figure controlling a web of intrigue, whom the prosecution had produced from their interpretation of the evidence, emerged as a liberal parliamentary candidate anxious to help others through his greater knowledge of law and language. As Eyre said, there remained much to explain. Tooke successfully evaded any explanation.

Some people, including Hazlitt who was only a boy at the time, have accused Tooke of exculpating himself at the expense of others. This is not fair. If he as well as Hardy were acquitted it was unlikely that any of the minor fry would be convicted. Tooke laid no blame on any other individual. It is more likely that he wanted to demonstrate the arbitrariness of accusing him of actions in which he had not been personally involved.

Tooke was surrounded by well-wishers when he finished speaking. Sheridan jumped down from the bench to congratulate him. A juryman's daughter introduced herself. 'Give me leave to call you sister,' responded Tooke, 'for your father has just given me life'.[19] The beautiful young novelist Amelia Alderson, who had felt her life would be 'changed and darkened if he were hanged', flung her arms round his neck. 'I think madam I have seen you every day during my trial,' Tooke responded. 'Yes.' 'Then grant me one favour. When I am tried for my life again, which I dare say I shall be six months hence, promise me to attend my trial again every day.'[20]

After waiting for the crowds to disperse, Tooke went quietly away with his dissenter friends Samuel Boddington and his wife to Cline's house, where he celebrated and drank the King's health with about 20 people, including Cartwright who had hoped to dine with him if he escaped the 'bloodhounds'. A lane was formed for the jury to the London Coffee House, where 500 gentleman rose, took off their hats and cried huzza.[21]

When Tooke encountered the Attorney General in Westminster Hall, he thanked him for his 'humane and considerate conduct'.[22] As Tooke's trial 'had excited general attention in the most extraordinary degree' newspapers issued résumés of his trial gratis with an engraved portrait. His acquittal was popular for, despite his controversial political reputation, he was widely esteemed for his intellectual ability, especially as author of the famous *Diversions*. Wordsworth thought him blameless, but that he appeared to court persecution 'rather from a wish to vex powerful individuals than to be an instrument of public good'.[23] By his brilliant performance Tooke greatly enhanced his reputation. It is appropriate that the most famous triumph of such a paradoxical man should be his trial for treason.

The other accused SCI members Bonney, Joyce, Kyd and Holcroft were discharged, Holcroft furious that the judge would not let him make a speech. Thelwall, however, whom the Government still hoped to catch, for he was considered a more extreme demagogue, was brought to trial on 1 December. Points in the prosecution case were that he had advocated revolutionary government in letters, had run the LCS secret committee, given subversive lectures, always advocated a convention and had vociferously supported French republicanism. The trial lasted five days. Erskine and Gibbs once more defended. The chief Government witness, a spy who produced remarkably detailed reports on Thelwall's lectures, turned out to be a bigamist.

Tooke gave evidence and was more forthcoming than at his own trial. He said that if subversion of the Government had been attempted he would not have remained in the society an hour. The members had only differed as to the extent of reform; the farthest any had gone was to support the Duke of Richmond, and latterly the aim of universal suffrage had been dropped. The first he had heard of the convention's design to usurp the authority of Parliament was when he found himself in the Tower. He never thought Thelwall 'capable of anything violent but in words', and then only in the harsh tone of his voice and vehement manner. A few people have accused Tooke of disowning Paine in his cross-examination. Once again this is unfair. When Erskine asked Tooke his opinion, he said, as he had always done, that there were parts of Paine's writings he admired and others with which he disagreed. The jury took an hour to decide that Thelwall was not guilty, and the other members of the LCS were then released.[24]

These trials had an importance beyond the fate of the individuals: they posed a threat to English liberty. Lord Holland believed that, if Tooke and his associates had been convicted, 'the first men in the country... would have followed victims to their fate'.[25] Many thought that Francis and Sheridan would have been the next to be prosecuted. The King blamed Loughborough, the Lord Chancellor, for the fiasco. 'You have got us in the wrong box.' When the Solicitor General expressed his dismay at Tooke's acquittal, Addington said he saw no cause for uneasiness: 'It is more important to maintain the credit of a mild and unprejudiced administration of justice, than even to convict a Jacobin.' Burke doubted that the innocence of the accused had been established. Many people, encouraged by hacks in Government-subsidised newspapers, continued to believe them guilty.[26]

Imprisonment and the trials placed a great financial burden on the reformers. The LCS collected several hundred pounds for their members, and a subscription was opened under the auspices of Cartwright, Gilbert Wakefield, Frend and William Maxwell which raised £1,429. The defence of Hardy, Tooke and Thelwall cost between £3,000 and £4,000. Vaughan wrote to Thomas Walker after dining at 'the citizen's' (Tooke's) on the anniversary of his arrest, 'Our subscription goes on well.' If they could raise £1,000 more they could pay all defence costs. Vaughan thought that he escaped as a lawyer, 'they being for some reason or other more formidable in the eyes of Government than other people'. Well-wishers helped Hardy, whose defence left him penniless, to open a shoe shop in Tavistock Street. Tooke was seriously out of pocket, his total expenses coming to over £1,000. Luckily he had received a legacy from his friend General James Murray, whose funeral in Westminster Abbey he had attended.[27]

Tooke enjoyed himself hugely dining out afterwards, when he proudly declared that he was the only man in Britain to be accused of both sedition and treason. At the Athenian club, whose 25 members included Sir Joseph Banks, he described the hardships of life in the Tower and said enormous fees had been paid to the law officers, Eyre £500 a day, the other judge £100, counsel £1,000 each. Stanhope held a lavish celebration at Chevening in honour of Joyce's release, 200 to dinner, 400 friends and tenants to a ball. On 30 November, Cartwright attended a 'joyous' dinner and afternoon at Tooke's. There were two women besides his daughters and a large party of men, including Hoppner, Banks the sculptor and Sharp the engraver. 'Busts, medals and other commemorative souvenirs are under contemplation.' Several medals were struck. One, with Hardy, Tooke and Thelwall on one side, Gibbs and Erskine on the other with the names of the jurors for each defendant encircling them, was sold at £1/11/6. for a silver version and 1/6 for copper. Tooke derived malicious pleasure in proposing the King's health as Pitt and his prosecutors were being entertained next door by his neighbour Dundas. Dundas and Tooke had greeted each other affably after the trial. Tooke always expressed gratitude and admiration for Erskine and Gibbs's conduct of his case. He held a feast each year at Wimbledon to celebrate his acquittal, which Erskine attended. Once, as Erskine was walking in Tooke's garden, he sprang over the haha to talk to Pitt and some other ministers in Dundas's garden.[28]

The trials temporarily brought the Foxites and radicals closer together. When the new parliamentary session opened at the end of December Sheridan introduced a motion to repeal the suspension of habeas corpus, arguing that the acquittals showed there was no need for it. The Solicitor General, however, said if the juries had been as well informed of the facts as he was, they would have acted differently. Fox said it was monstrous that law officers of the Crown should deny the justice of trial by jury and claim that the accused were only let off on technicalities. Pitt said 'these persons' were party to a crime as dangerous to the rights of Parliament and tranquillity of the country as treason or any other offence could be. Windham (Minister at War) attacked 'an active party infected to the bone with French principles. He wished them joy of the innocence of an acquitted felon'. When called to order, Windham said that, although in the opinion of the jury there was no legal evidence they were guilty, this by no means proved they were free from moral guilt.[29]

On 4 February 13,000 Friends of Freedom celebrated the acquittals at the Crown and Anchor. Stanhope, who was in the chair, flanked by Thomas Thompson, inveighed against Windham's speech. Tooke gave Sheridan's health, then made a long speech in which he announced that he would not stand for Parliament again. After this a celebration was held every 5 November, a new anniversary for the reformers on a familiar date. Cline, a rich man, also gave an annual dinner for Tooke for many years.[30]

In spite of the acquittals, the Government had dealt a severe blow to the reformers. Members of provincial societies who had been brought to London as witnesses played no more part in politics when released, others were sent to prison by local magistrates. The SCI ceased to function. Holcroft published further plays under a pseudonym which were less successful and for a time he lived abroad. Although the LCS continued, Hardy played no further part in it. He died in 1832 at the age of 80. The radical societies suffered under continued Government pressure; the suspension of habeas corpus was extended until 1801.

Tooke bitterly resented his imprisonment. James Losh, a liberal lawyer and close friend of Vaughan's, who did not admire Tooke, said that Tooke thanked him for 'standing by him nobly'; he had been deceived and betrayed by Pitt and his friends, and should consider himself a 'degraded villain' until he was revenged.[31]

Tooke withdrew to recuperate at Wimbledon. Imprisonment had been a shock to his body and a blow to his pride. He was now wary, his speech more guarded. Some people thought he became timid; circumspect would be nearer the mark. Men who spend their lives in political strife are often less bold in old age. Tooke noted in the margin of a book the days he had spent in prison: 1774, House of Commons 2 days; 1777-8, King's Bench 336; 1794, Privy Council three, Tower 148, Newgate 30, making a grand total of 519. According to Stephens, he 'banished from his table several violent men whose practices he suspected'.[32]

One unfortunate result of the trials was that Tooke broke with Thelwall. Tooke tried to persuade Thelwall to give up political campaigning. Thelwall refused, taxed Tooke with coldness towards him, and they quarrelled. The breach became known and was made much of by the Government press. Godwin, too, quarrelled with Thelwall, disapproving of his outspoken agitation. Thelwall did not attend further LCS meetings until autumn 1795, but continued his political lectures with diminishing success. In 1796 his magazine, *Tribune*, was suppressed by the Government, and he was ejected from his lecture rooms. He took refuge with Coleridge and Wordsworth at Nether Stowey where his views were too much for the locals who suspected them of being spies. Eventually he settled down to a highly successful career as a teacher of elocution and speech therapy.[33]

In November 1795 Thelwall gave a civic oration in commemoration of the acquittals. He spoke magnanimously of Tooke, whom he still loved and revered: 'Before I was born, his voice was uplifted in the cause of liberty'. In 1796 Thelwall campaigned for Tooke when he stood for Westminster. His bitterness increased with the years, culminating in a sonnet he wrote in 1820 on Tooke's ingratitude. Only Thelwall's point of view is known, recounted by his second wife who married him in 1819, seven years after Tooke had died. It is understandable that she should have been prejudiced against Tooke, but her version of events should be treated with caution.[34]

Mrs Thelwall claimed that, unlike Thelwall, Tooke had a succession of patrons and, as Tooke lost his own independence, he hated that of Thelwall. This is nonsense. William Tooke had been his patron long before he met Thelwall. Sir Francis Burdett gave Tooke financial assistance, but Tooke never lost his independence: it would have been totally out of character for him to do so. Mrs Thelwall quotes a note written many years later in which Thelwall said that if Tooke valued his posthumous reputation he had reason to wish Thelwall's memoirs should not be completed. He accused Tooke of helping to drive him from society: 'The principal demarcation between us was that I was open and sincere, he subtle and hypocritical'. Thelwall complained that during the years of distress to which he was exposed by political persecution, no-one of Tooke's connexion, excepting Bosville, helped him. Tooke could have retorted that if Thelwall had followed his advice, he would not have suffered such persecution; besides Tooke, always a generous man, was himself extremely hard-up for some years after his release. Tooke's circle collected money for men who were imprisoned. There seems no pressing reason why they should have befriended Thelwall, who was never arrested again.[34]

Thelwall believed, probably correctly, that one reason for Tooke's attitude was that he had thought Thelwall foolish to marry a young girl of seventeen instead of going to Cambridge, and that Tooke had resented Thelwall's rejection of his offer to educate him. Tooke was a masterful man who liked to dominate his entourage. On the other hand, Mrs Thelwall's claim that Tooke had pressed Thelwall to join the Church seems extraordinarily unlikely.[35]

Notes on Chapter 10

The trials of Hardy and Tooke appear in *State Trials* 24 and 25. Quotations are from these unless otherwise stated.

1 Campbell, *Lives of the Chief Justices* III, p 52
2 Hardy, p 112
3 Wharam, p 193; *Morning Chronicle* 6.11.94
4 Burke, *Correspondence* VIII, pp 66, 78
5 Stanhope and Gooch, p 135; Stephens II, p 151; Stanhope, Lady II, p 23
6 Cartwright I, pp 206-9
7 Rogers, *Table Talk*, pp 125-6; Mitford Add MS 32566 f4
8 Rogers, *Recollections*, p 139
9 Townsend II, p 24
10 Lovat-Fraser, p 57
11 Stephens II, p 391; Cartwright I, pp 208-9
12 Hazlitt, *Spirit of the Age*, p 117; Coleridge, *Table Talk*, p 121
13 Gower I, p 105; Canning, p 148 (19.11.94)
14 Stephens II, p 150
15 Stephens II, p 147
16 Stephens II, pp 145-6; Burdett MSS Eng. Hist. B200 f18-20
17 *Morning Chronicle*, *True Briton* 24.11.94; Cartwright I, pp 208-9
18 Brougham, *Historical Sketches* II, p 119
19 Rogers, *Recollections*, p 147
20 Wilson and Lloyd, p 53; Abinger MSS b210/6, 28.10.96
21 Cartwright I, pp 209-9; *Times* 24.11.94
22 Twiss I, p 282
23 Wordsworth, *Early Letters*, p 128, Dec. 1794
24 Thelwall's trial is missing from *State Trials*. Refs are: Thelwall Life App. 444; *True Briton*, *Morning Chronicle* 2-6.12.94; Cestre, *Thelwall*
25 Fox, *Further Memoirs*, p 296
26 Campbell, *Lives of the Lord Chancellors* VI, p 267; Pellew I, p 132; Burke, *Correspondence* VIII, p 423; *Parliamentary History* XXXI, p 1029
27 Farington, p 279; Stephens II, p 324; *Morning Chronicle* 23.3.95; *The Original*, pp 86-91
28 Farington I, p 276; Stanhope and Gooch, p 150; Bindman, p 192; Townsend II, p 30; Stephens II, p 305, Cartwright I, p 211
29 *Parliamentary History* XXXI, pp 994-1029, 1050
30 Stanhope, p 151; Stephens II, p 328
31 Losh I, p 10
32 Stephens II, p 154
33 Cestre, p 115; Thelwall, pp 346-7
34 Thelwall, pp 348-54
35 Thelwall, p 78

Chapter Eleven

Last Election Campaign: Burdett

One incident gave Tooke particular pleasure on his arrival home after imprisonment for nearly six months. He had a large tom cat whom he used to pet and feed after dinner. While he was in the Tower the cat did not appear, as was his custom, at four o'clock. The day Tooke returned he entered the parlour, went up to Tooke seated in his usual place at the head of the table, perched on his shoulder and purred loudly throughout the meal.[1]

Tooke plunged back into gardening. Vaughan wrote to Cooper in America, 'Sharp and Tuffin are very prudent and I believe meddle with nothing but their private pursuits. Tooke digs in his garden till out of breath, by which he has certainly increased his health.' Tooke thanked Thomas Walker for sending gooseberry bushes and potatoes. 'I will not spare manure. Justice shall be done to them – and the same I promise to any other things, or persons, which you may at any time put into my hands. Justice to Red Traitors.'[2] Although Tooke slept at home he dined out frequently. Sunday lunches were soon in full swing again. Ex-SCI colleagues who were personal friends reappeared, though William's nephew Harwood had retreated to farm in Norfolk.

After the trials, the LCS were very short of funds and many moderate members resigned. The following summer its numbers began to pick up again. The proportion of members holding extreme views now became much higher. The new leaders of the LCS with whom Tooke had dealings were John Gale Jones, John Binns and Francis Place, all young men in their twenties. Binns, whose prosperous family played a part in Dublin politics, earned his living as a plumber. He proved as powerful and popular a speaker as Thelwall. He also joined the United Irishmen. Gale Jones was an intellectual, born in Middlesex and trained as a surgeon. He too was a first-rate orator. Place was a tailor who, after a hard struggle, founded his own flourishing business. A brilliant organiser, he became famous for his work in the Westminster constituency.

1795 was a bad year: military campaigns were disastrous, a poor harvest exacerbated food shortages so prices rose, leading to widespread rioting. When the King rode to Parliament people cried, 'No war, Bread, Peace,' and a stone smashed his carriage window. This was attributed to the LCS.[3] The Government, who had only the armed forces to deal with disturbances, feared that mass meetings and rioting could, if manipulated by unscrupulous men, lead to revolution. In November, using the attack on the King as pretext, Pitt and Grenville introduced two acts which further curbed rights of free speech and public meetings. The Treasonable Practices Bill, a direct result of the treason trials, modified the law of treason to include writing or speaking against the King and constitution. The Seditious Meetings Bill forbade meetings of over 50 people unless prior notice was given in the newspapers signed by seven resident householders. If magistrates considered speeches at such meetings were seditious, they could break them up, and resistance was punishable by death. In addition lecture rooms had to be licensed.

The majority of the population was quite prepared to tolerate these 'Gagging Acts' as a wartime measure, but there were widespread protests from liberals and radicals who for a short time made common cause. Fox called for nationwide petitioning, the FOP emerged briefly from quiescence, Wyvill organised meetings in the north and the LCS held a great open-air meeting on 7 December attended by many MPs. A resolution of thanks was passed to the Foxites and about 15,000 signed a petition. Altogether about 94 petitions were presented to Parliament. Edward Malone, one of the Shakespearean editors Tooke ridiculed, complained to Windham, 'What if all the principal landowners... and merchants of London call for a certain measure to repress sedition... all these names are to have no more weight than... such wretches as Mr Thelwall or Horne Tooke [who] may assemble... in St George's Fields!' The SCI met for almost the last time on 14 December, when they passed resolutions condemning the bills and declared that 'the Whig Club, FOP and LCS had merited the thanks of their country'.[4]

At the anniversary dinner to commemorate Hardy's acquittal, Tooke said, 'He should resist oppression but it must be the resistance of the anvil to the hammer'.[5]

In January 1796, the Stone brothers were finally tried for treason. William was acquitted, John Hurford found guilty in absentia. The trial did not improve the reputations of the Foxites, several of whom were summoned to give evidence, and Tooke's friendship with a convicted traitor was publicised.

Tooke Again Candidate at Westminster

At the general election following the dissolution of Parliament on 20 May, Tooke, who had rapidly recovered his enthusiasm for politics, stood once more as independent candidate for Westminster. Although Hood had been made a Viscount, the agreement between the two parties held good and the seat was to be shared between Fox and a Ministerialist who once more was an Admiral, Sir Alan Gardner, formerly MP for Plymouth.

In his election manifesto Tooke said that he was the last person to choose, 'If the purpose of your election were to choose a master or promote a minister... but if your purpose be to appoint a servant... I may with confidence offer myself'. He made capital out of his trial: 'It is only in times like the present... that the progress of a candidate can possibly be from the hustings to Newgate, and from Newgate back to the hustings'.[6] Bosville composed for the poll breakfasts a song which became a hit.

> Unbribed by pension or share in a loan
> Your rights he'll maintain though he stand up alone
> Fast wed his great spirit to liberty's cause
> He'll scorn to betray you for courtly applause

> Come then to the hustings and loudly proclaim
> John Horne Tooke for ever! Yes, Horne Tooke's the name.
> No jobbers, contractors or placemen I say,
> But Horne Tooke and freedom for ever hooray.[7]

Tooke was nominated by Vaughan and Samuel Rogers's brother-in-law, the brewer Sutton Sharpe. He stayed with Bonney and was often drawn to his lodgings from the hustings by 'the rabble'. Tooke's committee was largely composed of ex-SCI and LCS members who helped canvas and summon electors to the polls. 'The gentlemen who were in the dock at the Old Bailey are the most active participants on the hustings,' in particular Thelwall and Gale Jones. 'I understand you have all the blackguards in London with you,' said a shady Irishman, O'Brien. 'I am glad to have it Sir on such good authority,' retorted Tooke.

The hustings were outside St Paul's Church at Covent Garden. The crowd in a picture of the scene in the piazza consists mostly of well-dressed men, Gardner in naval uniform, Tooke sporting white woollen stockings, and Fox standing with hat in hand. Many more electors than ever before came to listen to the speeches and debate political issues.[8]

This was Tooke's public swan-song. The proceedings were orderly, but there was a constant 'roar of that lion the populace' for and against Tooke who 'spoke in a very diverting manner'. All newspapers reported his speeches at length. They were incomparably better than his opponents', for Fox, though magnificent in the House, was not a hustings man. To Ministerialists, they were full of personal resentment and pique at recent persecution, artfully seasoned with illiberal abuse. Tooke's speeches were, in fact, less bitter than on previous occasions.

Tooke was in his element, imperturbable, good-humoured, quelling hecklers, dexterously employing motley snippets of information. Though his voice was not powerful, every word could be heard as he spoke with clear enunciation, in a slow composed manner. Binns thought him a remarkable and very peculiar public speaker: 'He accompanied what he said with scarcely any action. A rich vein of wit and sarcasm… told more effectually than those of any other speaker I ever heard. I have… heard him illustrate his subject with such… humour as to convulse his whole auditory, gentle and simple… all would be laughing heartily while the face of the speaker would look cold and unconscious as a metal rapper.' Stephens compared Tooke to Ulysses, 'Artful, insinuating and dauntless; at first his appearance was unpropitious, but, gaining on his audience by degrees, after some time he seized and retained possession both of their hearts and understandings.'[9]

Although they mistrusted their potential allies, Cartwright, Thelwall and other radicals were keen to retain the tenuous links forged with the Foxites during the Two Acts campaign, while Fox, with only a small band of faithful adherents, needed extra-parliamentary support. Fox wrote to Lord Holland, 'I think we ought to go further towards agreeing with the democratic or popular party than at any former period for… we as a party… can do nothing and the contest must be between the Court and the democrats'. If the Whigs did not assist the democrats, they would either be too weak to achieve anything or, if strong enough, 'unmixed with any aristocratic leaven and full of resentment against us for not joining them, will go probably to greater excesses, and bring on the only state of things which can make a man doubt whether the despotism of monarchy is the worst of all evils'.[10]

Fox and Tooke's positions had more in common than at any earlier period. Fox, who was passionately keen to uphold personal liberty which had been eroded by emergency wartime legislation, shared Tooke's belief in tolerance, the right to free speech and political association. Both played down the dangers of French expansion in Europe and the risk of French occupation of Britain. Public opinion was in favour of the war, so their opposition was regarded by the majority with deep suspicion. At other points they diverged. Fox, preoccupied with the independence of the Commons, wanted to restrict what he considered the evil influence of the Crown. Having little sympathy for the 'generality', he was equivocal about parliamentary reform. Tooke was opposed to those who oppressed the man in the street; in the days of Wilkes it had been the Crown and Court party, now it was Pitt. In the context of the Westminster constituency, Tooke was more forward-looking than Fox. He appreciated that it was the best base from which to make the first steps towards more democratic elections.

Bosville, one of Tooke's principal backers, was on very amicable terms with Fox but was unable to modify their personal antagonism. Fox, 13 years his junior, never turned his potent charm on Tooke. Rogers was present at a dinner party given by William

Smith when Fox did not take the slightest notice of Tooke, 'would not look at him, nor seem to hear any of the good things he said. It was the most painful scene.'[11] On the political front, however, there was considerable rapprochement. At the last election Tooke had attacked Fox. This time he repeatedly spoke warmly on his behalf.

Electors had two votes. They could either give a 'plumper', give both votes to one candidate only, or give one vote each to two candidates. In the previous election, when Tooke stood against the coalition, any shared votes he got were also given to Hood. This time he shared nearly 2,000 with Fox and only a handful with Gardner. Tooke said that if a man fastened two horses to a cart, one at the head the other at the tail, his journey would not be swift. This would be the electors' fate if they chose Fox and Gardner. He would recommend them to vote for Fox who had opposed the Two Acts rather than Gardner who had condoned them.[6]

Tooke coined a phrase later adopted as a radical slogan: 'A nation that has been treated as this has been has a right to demand two things, security for the future and justice for the past. Mr Fox... has given you full reason to be satisfied that he will exert his utmost to obtain them both for you.' At a dinner for Fox on 2 June, Thelwall lamented the 'little jealousies and obstacles between the parties which, if they did not coalesce, would cause their enemies to triumph'.[12] On the last day Tooke was very brief, for he was 'not disposed to contest anything with a man who had spoken as Fox had done'. Fox also was conciliatory, saying that those who had voted for Tooke were, like his supporters, against the Government's war policy.[6]

The Government-subsidised press made much of these friendly gestures. Fox was said to canvas for Tooke, Tooke to hope for respectability through Fox. Editors cleverly raked up Tooke's and Macnamara's posters and letters attacking the Foxites during the 1788 election. They reprinted Tooke's pamphlet 'Two Pair of Portraits', emphasising that Tooke's judgement could not be as sound as he made out if a few years after lauding Pitt and execrating Fox he now did the reverse. Tooke was the 'most restless man of the time and never wasted a drop of ink to praise any man, but... wastes oceans to traduce'.[13]

As the poll lasted 15 days, Tooke had scope to expound his views. His platform was war, economic distress, taxation, the Two

Acts. He wanted to show ordinary citizens that there were men who respected them and that in an open constituency the election was theirs to decide if they chose. He criticised the Government's contemptuous habit of putting up a popular hero whose candidature would flatter the electors and win votes, perverting the professional talents of brave men. 'If the Admiral were to question me about the rigging of a ship, I should certainly make a very scurvy figure; and I strongly suspect, that if I was to put two or three questions to the Admiral about the rigging of a constitution, he would not make a better.'[6] 'In our present struggle between liberty and slavery… who are the persons oppressed, beggared, dishonoured, vilified and ruined? Who are languishing and rotting in their gaols?' A voice from the crowd cried, 'Horne Tooke'. 'It is true I have been frequently in prison, but at present I had forgotten myself, I was thinking only of you. Who are… flogged… sent as felons to Botany Bay?' There were cries of 'The people'. 'You say true. It is we, the privates in the ranks. Where all this while are our political generals?… Safe in the rear, reposing on their beds of pension and privilege. You cannot entertain the smallest hope of success unless at your elections you pass by these lords and lordlings… and choose your representatives from amongst the privates in the ranks.'

At the poll Wilkes gave Tooke his 'plumper' on the first day, and so did Rogers who did not vote again for 22 years, the constable who had arrested Tooke, and Macklin, a famous old actor of 'upward one hundred and six years' who was brought to the hustings in a chair. At the end of the poll Fox had 5160, Gardner 4814 and Tooke 2819. Since the last election, Tooke had increased his vote by 1,110. In general there was little change at the election. Fox's 60 supporters were returned.[6,14]

Tooke's election expenses came to £660 and were covered by a donation of £1,000 from a well-wisher. The first time Tooke stood for Westminster, the Bailiff told him that Fox and Hood had deposited £400 for the hustings and so must he. Later he discovered they had not, and most of his deposit had paid for the Bailiff and his clerks' dinners. This time he was determined not to pay for dinners and deposited £150. When the Bailiff demanded £250 more, Tooke refused to pay.[15] Tooke's post-election advertisement was pessimistic. He looked forward to meeting his supporters at another election when taxes would be heavier. 'Be moderate and firm. If we can do no better for our country, let our carcasses at least manure the soil which has fed us.'[16]

Tooke's two campaigns in Westminster had far-reaching consequences leading to the emergence of an independent radical platform. Members of the Westminster Committee which achieved Burdett's election in 1807 and politicians such as Cam Hobhouse paid tribute to Tooke's efforts which laid the foundation for their successes. Place believed that, if the election had taken place before the state trials, Tooke would probably have been elected. It was in fact Fox's death which greatly weakened competition, combined with the formation of a local party machine, that finally enabled the seat to be captured.[17]

On 28 June a post-election dinner was held for Tooke and his supporters. Charles Lamb called it a dinner of condolence, but the 700 who crowded into the Crown and Anchor considered it a triumphant celebration. In his speech Tooke stressed the principles of liberty and justice which must stand above individuals and party. He deftly side-stepped an LCS member's request for him to explain Fox's real opinion on reform by saying he could not speak for someone who was not present though, now the election was over, he did reveal his doubts: 'I think the best and hope the best of Mr Fox, although there are some things left unexplained by him. However, it is possible the moment will arrive when you and I and all of us may compel him to explain himself.' Tooke's interlocutor assumed that if he were in Parliament he would be with the minority, but he said 'both majority and minority would be unanimous to hang me'. Certainly Windham would have done so. He wrote to Mrs Crewe that if there were a violent concussion which substituted Fox for Pitt, Fox would be succeeded by Sheridan, Horne Tooke… the long dynasty of murderous democrats and proconsuls of France. A memorandum from London to the French Foreign Office of 27 April gives some insight on the situation. 'M Pitt n'a qu'une éspèce d'honneur à craindre: ce sont ceux que la loi écarte des fonctions politiques, les prolétaires: ceux que des vexations ou des passions particulières lui ont aliéné. A la tête de ces hommes révolutionnaires est surtout Horne Tooke. Cet homme d'une complexion forte est doué d'une imagination vaste et d'un grand courage. A ces conceptions révolutionnaires il ajoute une haine profonde contre les membres du gouvernement actuel.'[16,18]

One of Tooke's popular compositions was sung at the dinner, 'The Birthday of our Liberties'. It contained several of his popular themes.

> ... They are conquer'd, they perish, no tyrant survives,
> And the day of their deaths is the first of our lives...
> Equal rights, equal laws, equal blessings shall nourish,
> Peace, justice and plenty, henceforward shall flourish:
> O guard them with jealousy, spurn from this hour,
> The bribe of corruption, the menace of power,
> And be this our decision whilst freedom survives,
> That the day of its death be the last of our lives.[19]

Burdett: Foxites Secede from Parliament

In the autumn of 1796 a young man was introduced to Tooke by Robert Fergusson, a liberal barrister, through whom he was to continue the political work which he was now too old and infirm to pursue with vigour, and who was to help make his old age in many ways the happiest period of his life. Francis Burdett had recently bought a house a few hundred yards from Tooke's on Wimbledon Common. Three years earlier, aged twenty-three, he had married Sophie, the youngest daughter of Thomas Coutts the banker who bought him the parliamentary seat of Boroughbridge in 1796. In 1797 Burdett inherited a baronetcy and several large estates from his grandfather.[20]

In spite of differences in character and background, Burdett became devoted to Tooke whom he regarded as a father. Burdett's mother had died when he was young, his father was a foolish, ineffectual man. Tooke in turn found in him a substitute son, a far more suitable filial figure than Thelwall, for Burdett had wealth and social standing to counterbalance Tooke's intellectual dominance. The conspiratorial atmosphere at Wimbledon was exciting for Burdett. At this stage he held wild views, veering towards republicanism. Although Burdett knew many Foxites and thought Fox 'the wonder of the age', he took an independent line on entering Parliament. Tooke, who had accepted Burdett's friendship with Fox, was relieved when he was blackballed for the Whig Club two years later. Tooke now described himself as 'A friend to the monarchical part of the constitution but an enemy to the aristocratic power which has grown to so great a height... as to control both King and people'.[21] Burdett, who combined a patrician temperament with humanitarian instincts, found his political creed congenial.

Many deplored Burdett's espousal of radicalism but, as Bentham remarked, 'Tooke was of great use to Burdett. He gave him some degree of intellectuality.'[22] Burdett was handsome, kind, generous and altruistic, but silent in company, and treated humble men with aristocratic aloofness. Tooke introduced him to men from all walks of life. Soon Tooke's ménage became the focus of Burdett's life. At Sunday dinners, to the cost of which he contributed, he sat at Tooke's right hand, but not invariably on more intimate occasions.

In 1797 the future looked bleak. Tooke wrote to Cartwright, 'This war is intended to put, and is likely to put, the seal to the deed of transfer of the British constitution. I think the cause of reform is dead and buried.'[23] The previous autumn, after Spain had declared war on Britain and Napoleon had inflicted a series of crushing defeats on the Austrians in Italy, Pitt, with the enthusiastic support of the Foxites, had sent a peace mission to Paris. In December the French suddenly changed their tune, rebuffed Pitt and despatched expeditions which made abortive landings in Ireland and Wales. This lead to a panic run on the Bank of England which, already affected by wartime inflation, stopped payments.

In April and May 1797 there were mutinies in the fleets at Spithead and the Nore provoked by genuine grievances over poor pay and appalling conditions. At Spithead, Lord Howe negotiated a peaceful settlement granting improved pay and conditions, but the revolt at the Nore had more revolutionary and ominous undertones. A squadron threatened to blockade the Thames, ships carrying cargoes to London were seized and officers tarred and feathered. The mutineers disagreed among themselves as to whether to accept a free pardon and finally surrendered. The ringleaders were executed or transported and 33 others were sent to Cold Bath prison in Clerkenwell. Though there is no clear evidence, the United Irishmen and possibly more extreme members of the LCS may have helped foment the mutiny. Confidence was not restored until the navy destroyed the Dutch fleet at

Camperdown in October. Austria had by then made peace with France, and Pitt once more initiated peace overtures. He was willing to recognise France's European conquests and to hand back French overseas territory which Britain had won, but in addition the French demanded the surrender of territory taken from the Dutch and Spaniards. These terms were unacceptable, once more negotiations were broken off, and Pitt was forced to soldier on alone.

Fox who, like Tooke, pooh-poohed invasion scares, blamed Pitt for continuing the war. As in the eighties, he took up electoral reform which he considered a 'sleeping question', because he wanted popular support in launching an attack on Government policies. Although he did not expect it to succeed, he backed Grey's plan for a motion calling for triennial parliaments and uniform household franchise. All remaining reformers rallied round Fox, since for the past few years he had consistently protested against Pitt's policy of repression.

On 18 May 1797 1,000 dined at the Crown and Anchor: Foxites, Tooke's entourage and members of the LCS. Burke considered that the club at the Crown and Anchor was as treasonable as the United Irishmen, and what was worse MPs openly showed themselves there.[24] Burdett 'recommended union among all those who wished for parliamentary reform, whatever differences of opinion… as to the specific form in which that measure ought to be adopted'. Some LCS members, however, insisted on universal suffrage. Tooke, in the unlikely role of 'genius of conciliation', urged them to make common cause with Fox. To insist on universal suffrage would be 'to prescribe to the people what they should choose… Those who wished to impose upon the people any positive rule by which they were to be guided in a reform of Parliament are themselves as great tyrants as those whose power they profess a wish to destroy.' Tooke's plea was successful. Always a great one for songs, Tooke received much applause when he sang one with the refrain:

> What the gallows for Pitt?
> Yes, there's nothing so fit
> For that insolent, false, hypocritical Pitt.[25]

On 31 July, the LCS, in a last effort, held a large public meeting to draw up a petition to the King. This was broken up by the magistrates and the six occupants of the platform were arrested but later released. After these further setbacks, Thelwall retired to the country while the moderate members resigned from the LCS which had increasingly become dominated by men with secret republican objectives. Fox criticised the dispersal of the meeting before the people had proceeded to any business. He announced that he would no longer attend Parliament because it would give countenance to the belief that Parliament was still able to check and control the ministers. Fox and his friends were to continue their secession for nearly three years, giving Burdett the opportunity to make his mark as one of the few MPs who criticised the Government. Tooke thereby indirectly acquired more influence and importance.

The following January, for the first time, Tooke, his friends and members of the LCS were present at Fox's birthday dinner. The Government press joked about reforming pickpockets to whom dinner tickets were issued by Bosville and Burdett, paid for out of Whig Club funds. After dinner Lord Oxford, Frend, Fergusson and Tooke entered the central room and were welcomed by Lauderdale. The Duke of Norfolk, who was rather drunk, introduced a tactless variant on a favourite Whig Club toast which had meant little before the French Revolution: 'The Sovereignty of the people'. The Duke gave, 'Our Sovereign's health – the majesty of the people,' and compared the 2,000 present with the 2,000 who had rallied round Washington in 1775. Tooke followed with a remarkably conciliatory speech. There might be differences of opinion, 'but certainly they do not exist between me and that gentleman whose nativity we are now met to celebrate. I am most perfectly satisfied with his conduct. I do not wish to advance one step in the cause of reform beyond what that Rt Hon. gentleman has pledged himself to go. I hope he will allow me to finish the debate… by repeating the health of Charles James Fox.' Fox made no reply.[26] Pitt wrote to Lord Mornington, 'The two most distinguished toasts were a speech from the Duke of Norfolk, which I think even the Crown lawyers will hardly prove to be much short of treason, and a public profession from Horne Tooke of reconciliation and coalition with Fox, with which I think you will be delighted'. Although Norfolk recanted and apologised to the King, he was dismissed from his militia command and deprived of his Lord Lieutenancy of the West Riding. Fox was indignant at his treatment. At the next Whig Club dinner he gave an identical toast, so was struck from the Privy Council. Some Whigs feared this might drive Fox into Tooke's arms. Brougham, on the other hand, who thought the Crown and Anchor meeting had 'done a world of mischief', recognised that Fox's popularity was waning and claimed that 'Tooke (who abhors Fox) triumphs in what he considers a complete victory over him. Horne Tooke's party think they have ruined one of their antagonists and wait in expectations that the other (Pitt) will ruin himself.'[27]

Irish Rebellion; Cold Bath Fields Prison

The reputations of Burdett and the Foxites were seriously damaged in the spring of 1798 by their association with Arthur O'Connor, a member of the United Irishmen who were plotting a rebellion in collaboration with the French. Burdett and Fox were unaware that the Government had documentary evidence to prove his guilt, gained through spies and the interception of letters.

O'Connor stayed for two months in Burdett's house, and then attempted to escape to France to continue negotiations, in company with Binns and the Rev. James Coigley, a Catholic priest turned revolutionary. They were arrested at Margate in February and tried for treason at Maidstone in May 1798. O'Connor called Fox, Sheridan and others as character witnesses. They gave glittering testimonials of his probity and high ideals, subsequently shown to be false. Coigley was found guilty on the basis of documents found in his pocket, and the two others were acquitted as the Government did not wish to reveal the source of their information. O'Connor was immediately re-arrested and sent to answer charges in Dublin, where the true facts relating to his activities were revealed in August during trials of leaders of the rebellion of that year.[28]

O'Connor's confession made the Foxites look at worst accomplices, at best gullible fools, who had laid themselves open to accusations of involvement in Franco-Irish intrigues. There is no evidence that Tooke was directly involved. He had several reputable

Irish friends such as Grattan and Curran. Of the United Irishmen, Lawless frequented Wimbledon, Fitzgerald had been a member of the SCI and dined with Tooke, Binns was an acquaintance. Tooke, who appeared to some people to 'tread upon the very verge of crime', had no close contact with the revolutionary fringe of the LCS which formed links with the Irish nationalist movement. Burdett never succeeded in interesting him in Irish problems. On the other hand, though Tooke must have had a shrewd idea of what O'Connor was up to, he made no attempt to dissuade Burdett from helping his friends. Like the Foxites, Tooke would probably have wished the United Irishmen well if they could bring about Pitt's downfall and force the Government to sue for peace.

In April, before the rebellion broke out, the Government moved against the dwindling remnant of the popular societies. At least 74 were arrested in 1798, including Tooke's former associates Hodgson and Lemaitre, and the Habeas Corpus Act was suspended again. Some were released within a few days, others kept in prison for nearly three years. The following spring the societies were banned. It is hard to determine how serious a threat they posed. They were riddled with informers who exaggerated the dangers, but most remaining members held extreme views and a few plotted with the French and Irish.[29]

Radicals now concentrated on the uncontroversial task of collecting funds to help prisoners and their families. William Frend and Francis Place formed a committee and persuaded Hardy to emerge from political retirement to act as treasurer. Grey, Whitbread, Lord Holland, Bosville, Burdett and Tooke, among others, gave donations. Tooke and Fergusson promised that legal aid would be provided gratis, but it was not needed as the prisoners were never charged. Place wrote to Hodgson, incarcerated in Newgate, that Tooke and his friends were the only able men who would do more than talk. Tooke also wanted the prisoners to do as much for themselves as they could.[30]

Tooke encouraged Burdett to take up not only the cases of arrested radicals, but the general and much more politically-acceptable question of the appalling conditions and corruption in prisons, of which he had first-hand experience. Many of the political prisoners were moved to provincial prisons, but some remained at Cold Bath Fields Prison, Clerkenwell, nicknamed

The Bastille, together with forty sailors imprisoned for their part in the Nore mutiny, plus ordinary felons, debtors, vagrants, paupers and people awaiting trial. Prisoners were not classified or differentiated. Felons often received better treatment than men held without charge. The cells were tiny, overcrowded and unheated, the food inadequate, and water dripped down the walls. Better rooms were given to those who could afford to bribe Governor Aris with weekly payments.

In December, Burdett gave notice of his intention to raise the question of Cold Bath Fields in Parliament. Portland ordered an enquiry which was undertaken by a committee of the Middlesex Quarter Sessions, presided over by William Mainwaring, MP for Middlesex. This was most improper, since these magistrates were themselves accused of disgracefully negligent supervision. Both they and a subsequent parliamentary select committee produced whitewashing reports which dismissed Burdett's allegations.

The agitation was politically biased, but undoubtedly prisoners were inhumanely treated, and Aris, a friend of Mainwaring, was a rogue who fiddled the books. Fox took the matter up, as did, more significantly, John Reeves, who had for so long worked to suppress the reforming societies. Once more Wimbledon became radical headquarters. Publicity was gained with the cases of Mary Rich, mistakenly detained in prison where she was raped, and the dramatic weighing of a sailor, James Johnson, one of the mutineers, outside Jordan's bookshop. He had lost five stone in prison and was released dying of starvation. In July 1800, Burdett, backed by Sheridan, once more moved for an enquiry. One was appointed which criticised the prison regime, corroborated charges of bribery and cruelty and vindicated Burdett. Burdett and Tooke were to keep this issue before the public for the next two years. It was a justifiable cause which laid the foundation of Burdett's popularity as a radical leader.[31]

Tooke also interested himself in Gilbert Wakefield, a Unitarian minister and distinguished scholar, who had dashed off a reply to a patriotic defence of Pitt's administration written by the Bishop of Llandaff. Wakefield asserted that the common people were in such poverty they would welcome any change, and that the militia and volunteers were incompetent and reluctant to fight. He was charged with seditious libel and sentenced to two years' imprisonment. Through Wakefield's imprisonment, Henry

Crabb Robinson – barrister and diarist, then aged twenty-three, and devoted to Wakefield – came into contact with Tooke. He admitted that, 'Tooke was never a favourite of mine, but I never thought so well of his heart as from his behaviour to Wakefield, kind and respectful; and when we consider how unlike their characters are, his attentions do him the greatest honour. The day sentence was passed, he sent to Wakefield and, in his jocular way, comforted him by observing that probably a year hence he and Mrs Wakefield would be congratulating each other on his situation, "For, my dear, it has saved you," Mrs Wakefield will say, "You see Tooke and the rest of them are half way on their voyage to Botany Bay".'[32]

The Government took the opportunity to charge two booksellers for selling Wakefield's pamphlet, Joseph Johnson and Jordan, who had published so much for Tooke and other reformers. They cowed Johnson.[33] In future, he refused to publish even Wyvill, and concentrated on belles lettres. Before he was sentenced to six months, however, he produced a handsome two-volume new edition of the *Diversions*, which had by this time gained a high reputation among scholars not only at home but abroad, and had also excited considerable interest and enthusiasm among the educated public. As it was 12 years since the book had appeared there was a demand for more copies. For some time, including his sojourn in the Tower, Tooke had been refining and enlarging the book for a second edition. Meanwhile a well-known bookseller pirated the original version which he sold at a guinea a copy. Though this deprived Tooke of royalties, the extra publicity had the beneficial effect of increasing demand. Many of Tooke's friends bought copies, and he pressed them to become retail dealers in the book if they could find customers (see chapter 13).

Windham's jibe 'acquitted felons' continued to rankle. In June 1799, Tooke brought a libel suit against Wright, a bookseller who had printed the record of the secret committee of the House of Commons. Tooke himself did not appear: his case was conducted by Erskine. Wright pleaded that he had merely printed a literal copy and did not publish it to calumniate. Tooke objected to the statement that although Hardy, Tooke and Thelwall had been acquitted of treason, the evidence given at their trials established the grounds on which the committee of the two Houses of Parliament had founded their reports, and 'shows beyond the possibility of doubt that the views of these persons were… completely hostile to the existing government and consitution of the Kingdom and… subversive… of legitimate authority'. Erskine contended that the House of Commons had no right to sanction publication of this libel beyond an entry on its own journals for the use of the House. This did not give the printer a legal defence for printing and circulating copies. It was a foul libel to say Tooke was guilty of the crime of which he had been acquitted. Kenyon, who gave judgement, pushed parliamentary privilege to great lengths. He said that a report of the House of Commons could not be a libel. This was an important judgement on a constitutional question which was later opposed by other lawyers, notably Lord Denman.[34]

Tooke's Private Life

Until he was past sixty Tooke existed on slender, precarious means. Besides legacies from family and friends, he earned a little from journalism, and the *Diversions* had brought in quite a large sum, but he had no regular employment. When he first moved to Wimbledon his house was cheap to run. Prices had risen with the war, his income had not. He could no longer afford to entertain his friends, yet was loath to turn them away. He was subject to the constant caprice of William Tooke who, as Stephens said, 'affected to be his patron', but in fact gave him little of the financial assistance he had earlier promised. Tooke decided to let his house and rent a small cottage 200 yards away where he would live with his daughters and one maidservant, and where he could no longer hold Sunday lunches. No sooner had he announced this than his friends – Bosville, Richard Sharp, Boddington, Robert Knight and Rogers – rallied round, raised a subscription and bought an annuity of £600 a year from Burdett. In addition, over the next few years Tooke was bequeathed considerable sums in legacies. Felix Vaughan, in particular, who, to Tooke's great sorrow, died in 1799, cancelled Tooke's debt to him from an earlier loan. Tooke was freed from financial worries and at last considered himself independent.[35]

At the time a few people, including Thelwall, disapproved of Tooke's annuity; one or two historians have dubbed him sponger.

Stephens considered it unnecessary to vindicate Tooke's acceptance of financial assistance: he had sacrificed his prospects to serve his country. The money was raised by those who considered him a political martyr. There were many precedents for the subscription. Friends, including Tooke, had organised one for Porson, who was very hard up when he lost his Cambridge fellowship for refusing to take orders. Crabb Robinson said that Tooke's annuity, following those given to Parr and Fox, 'Seems to show all regard for public characters is not at an end'. Tooke had contributed to many collections for reformers in distress. He had spent much of his income working voluntarily for political causes. The friends who gave him money, most of whom were rich bachelors, considered it well spent.[36]

As Tooke suffered increasingly from gout, especially in his hands, he dictated most of his letters to his daughter Charlotte who acted as his secretary and would add playful postscripts to her father's letters, while Mary managed the household. Tooke's daughters appear to have been popular in the Wimbledon circle. When Tooke died, they received warm and affectionate letters from his friends. Tooke jokingly referred to his monopoly of his daughters' time but, even if he was a possessive father, they were devoted to him, eager to entertain and make him comfortable. Young people came to the house, and the sisters made friends with the children of Tooke's acquaintance, among others Sir Joseph Banks's daughter and Thomas Walker's son and daughter. Neither had married by the time Tooke died, when the elder must have been nearing thirty. It would not have been easy for them to find suitable husbands, as they were used to brilliant company but were illegitimate and had little money.

Tooke's close friends would drop in without invitation. He expected them to visit him frequently. Rogers, who often talked to Tooke while he dug in his garden, offended him once by not attending his Sunday dinners for several weeks. One Sunday, as dinner was about to be served, a Mr Baxter was announced. Tooke had no recollection of him but ordered him to be shown in, saying there must be some mistake. Baxter turned out to be a LCS member who had come to pay his respects. Tooke welcomed him enthusiastically and introduced him as a fellow-sufferer whom he had only met once before in the dock when they were both about to be arraigned. Godwin recorded in his diary that he frequently attended Sunday dinners from 1792 to 1805. He noted dinners for a few guests and 'huge gatherings' of over 18. At Christmas time in 1799 there were French visitors. Among those he encountered were Thomas Manning, fellow of Caius, a brilliant linguist; John Wolcot (Peter Pindar), critic and satirist; Anna Barbauld, a handsome radical writer; and Major Charles James, who had travelled round France on the outbreak of the revolution and was now engaged in compiling a highly successful *Dictionary of Military Terms*.[37]

Holcroft introduced Coleridge to Wimbledon, but he did not fall under Tooke's spell. Coleridge wrote to Wedgwood, 'He is a clear-headed old man, as every man must needs be who attends to the real import of words; but there is a sort of charletannery in his manner that did not please me. He makes such a mystery... out of plain and palpable things and never tells you anything without first exciting and detaining your curiosity. But it were a bad heart that could not pardon worse faults than these in the author of *The Diversions of Purley*.' Coleridge, who soon lost his enthusiasm for radicalism, 'saw a good deal of Tooke at one time: he left upon me the impression of his being a keen, iron man'. Coleridge claimed to have worsted Tooke in a discussion on one of Tooke's favourite topics, etymology: 'Tooke found he could not make a fool of me as he did of Godwin and some other of his butts'. Hazlitt, however, said that Tooke 'put a full stop to one of Coleridge's longwinded prefatory apologies for his youth and inexperience, by saying abruptly, Speak up, young man'.[38]

Hazlitt had great but not unqualified admiration for Tooke. 'He was the best intellectual fencer of his day... He said the most provoking things with a laughing gaiety, and a polite attention, that there was no withstanding. He threw others off their guard by thwarting their favourite theories' then himself remained unmoved while chafing them into madness 'with the extravagance of his assertions, and the teasing sophistry by which he rendered them plausible... He took up any topic... and played with it at will, like a juggler with his cups and balls.' No one knew better how to foil his guests or bring them out. 'It was delightful to see him sometimes turn from these waspish or ludicrous altercations with overweening antagonists to some old friend and veteran politician... to hear him recall the time of Wilkes... the conversation mellowing like wine... assenting to all the old man said, bringing out his pleasant traits, pampering him into childish self-importance, and sending him away 30 years younger than he came.' Lamb thought Hazlitt's sketch 'a matchless portrait'.[39]

Both Coleridge and Hazlitt were young men judging an old one. Tooke's contemporaries agreed that in his company everyone else's conversation appeared flat by comparison. Only occasionally did he fail to shine. Creevey records that Lady Oxford invited Tooke to dinner to meet Thurlow. The other guests were hoping for an exciting contest. 'I considered his powers of conversation as surpassing those of any person I had ever seen... I took for granted old grumbling Thurlow would be obliged to lower his topsail to him. But it seemed as if the very look and voice of Thurlow scared him out of his senses... so Tooke tried to recruit himself by wine ... and was very drunk... but all would not do.'[41]

Tooke's circle contained an increasing number of people younger than himself. He enjoyed the company of the young and had already outlived many of his contemporaries. Wilkes, who had died in 1797, had asked that his tomb should be inscribed 'John Wilkes, a friend to Liberty'. 'I am glad,' said Tooke, 'that he was not ashamed to show a little gratitude to her in his old age: for she was a great friend to him'. A few friends had changed political allegiance. Mackintosh, whom Tooke apreciated as 'a very formidable adversary across a table', was converted by Burke and offended his liberal acquaintance by lecturing against Godwin's works and the French Revolution. Still, until his death, Tooke was surrounded by devoted friends of all ages.[41]

Notes on Chapter 11

1 Stephens II, p 155
2 *The Original*, pp 46, 87
3 Place, pp 145-8
4 *Morning Chronicle* 7-9.12.95; Wyvill, pp 303-28; Windham I, p 319
5 Thelwall, *Tribune* III, p 265
6 Tooke's election speeches appear in Stephens II, pp 165-227 and in ref. 20
7 Add MSS 27837 f70
8 Hone, p 25; *True Briton* 9.6.96; Rogers, *Recollections*, p 146; George, M.D., 8815

9 Binns, p 43; Stephens II, pp 451-2
10 Fox, C.J. III, pp 135-6
11 Rogers, *Table Talk*, p 81
12 Gazetteer 3.6.96; Stephens II, p 213
13 Oracle 30.5.90; *Sun*, *True Briton* 10-13.6.96
14 Russell, p 262
15 Paull, pp 24-5
16 Jordan's complete collection of addresses and speeches of Fox, Gardner and Tooke 1796, 2
17 Add MS 27849 f163
18 Lamb I, p 33; Windham II, p 24; Archives Min. Aff. étrangères Corr. Pol. Anglaise 589/372, 27.4.96
19 Add MS 27817 f47; Stephens, appendix
20 Patterson I, pp 1-118
21 Stevens, p 399; Farington II, p 479
22 Bentham, *Works* X, p 404
23 Cartwright I, p 240
24 Burke, *Correspondence* IX, p 357
25 *Morning Chronicle*, *Times* 19.5.97; Add MS 27817 f49
26 Clayden, *Early Life*, p 378; *Express* and *Evening Chronicle* 23-25.1.98
27 George III, *Later Correspondence* III 18n; Brougham and his early friends I, pp 11, 35
28 Goodwin, pp 432-49
29 Add MS 27816 f542-61, 578; PCl/3514 f36-44
30 Add MS 27817 f84, 212; 31543 f66-7; Hone, pp 119-21
31 Hone, pp 122-8, Patterson, pp 67-79; *Parliamentary History* XXXV, pp 963-70; House of Commons papers 1799-1800 vol. 132, pp 441-562
32 *Monthly Magazine* Oct 1, 1801, pp 225-30; Robinson I, pp 55-61, 66n
33 Robinson I, p 57
34 *Times*, 4.6.99
35 Stephens II, pp 158-62
36 Robinson I, p 61
37 Stephens II, p 301; Clayden, *Early Life*, p 292; Abinger Papers, Bodleian dep e pp 201-8
38 Coleridge, *Table Talk* I, pp 117, 122-3; II, p 237; Coleridge, *Letters* I, p 560; Hazlitt, *Plain Speaker* I, p 91
39 Hazlitt, *Plain Speaker*, p 91; *Spirit of the Age*, pp 108, 111; Lamb II, p 460
40 Hazlitt, *Spirit of the Age*, p 109; Creevey, *Papers* I, p 60
41 Rogers, *Recollections*, p 143; Stephens II, p 333

Chapter Twelve

Election to Parliament

At the beginning of 1801, Tooke met Lord Camelford, a cousin of Pitt's and Grenville's brother-in-law. An endearing young man with a tinge of the madness which affected other members of his family, his ferocious temper had put paid to a promising naval career. Encouraged to befriend him by his cousin Lady Hester Stanhope, Camelford was captivated by Tooke. He pressed him to accept his pocket borough of Old Sarum. Tooke was reluctant; the offer, which might have transformed his life 20 or 30 years earlier, had come too late. Though appreciating the irony, he found it hard to reconcile himself to representing the rottenest borough of all. He was sixty-five; his poor health would prevent him from constant attendance. After three days and nights spent in discussion to get acquainted with the character and views of his potential patron, he finally consented, for although their political beliefs differed Camelford was content to give him a free rein. Tooke introduced Camelford to his circle, which he found most congenial and its members not 'proud'. Camelford preferred, however, to be alone with Tooke, saying that he derived more pleasure and instruction from his conversation than from that of anyone else he had ever met. Camelford and Tooke remained friends until Camelford was killed in a duel in 1804.[1]

The current view in society was voiced by Lady Malmesbury: 'I understand Lord Camelford asked Tooke what he could do that would annoy the Government most and he said bring me into Parliament'. Her husband thought 'Camelford should be confined for this act of madness and wickedness'.[2]

When young, Tooke had been reviled as a renegade radical cleric; now he was suspected of the far more heinous crime of treachery in wartime. He put on a brave front, being more impervious than most men, but finally gave up frequenting the coffee houses where he received slights and insults. Rogers described an occasion when he and Tooke attended a play privately performed for the Margravine of Ansbach at Brandenburgh House. During the performance, a person behind said audibly, 'There's that rascal Horne Tooke'. Tooke was so offended that he left immediately.[3]

Tooke took his seat on 16 February 1801. He had been provided with rooms in Palace Yard so that he would not have far to walk. All eyes were turned on him as he entered the chamber and sat down under the gallery, where he was greeted by friends. He was introduced by Burdett and Richard Wilson. The ceremony of shaking hands with the Speaker, Mitford, attracted much attention, for it was not long since as Solicitor General he had prosecuted Tooke for treason. Mitford shook hands with great cordiality, and they chatted for several minutes. Tooke's 'health and personal vigour appeared to have greatly declined. His countenance was pale and sickly but strikingly marked with its wonted expression of sagacity and energetic resolution. The upper part of his head is bald; but his hair… retains its former chestnut colour unmixed with grey.' Sylvester Douglas described Tooke walking about the House from bench to bench, followed by Burdett: 'Tooke looks very old and is lame'.[4]

No sooner had Tooke taken the oath than, as in his private life, enmity turned his parliamentary career into one more prosecution which, this time, he had done nothing specific to provoke. Tooke's right to sit was challenged by Lord Temple, on the grounds that he held holy orders. In the debate on 10 March he claimed that he raised the question on principle and from no disrespect to Tooke. The House was amused when Tooke remarked that 'men quite commonly act from one motive while they think they have acted from another'. Temple had many reasons for disliking Tooke, in particular for his much publicised note to Joyce before his arrest which referred to the perks Lord Temple and his Grenville relations received. When Temple mentioned his stake in the country, Tooke retorted that he too had a stake in the country, 'not stolen... from the public hedge, for I planted it myself'.

Fox came out of retirement for 'Tooke's business which I could not desert without shabbiness'. He proposed that it should first be decided whether a clergyman was eligible to hold a seat in the Commons, after which Tooke's position might be investigated. In his rambling response Tooke in vain attempted to prove that he was no longer a clergyman since he had divested himself of his orders. After a heated debate a select committee was appointed to consider precedents.[5]

On 4 May the committee reported against him. In his speech on the report of the committee, Temple pointed out that Mr Rushworth, who had been elected in 1784 and was accepted by the House, had been ordained only as a deacon, not a priest. Priests were members of convocation and were represented by their bishops in the Lords. Further, he said that under canon law priests could not relinquish their orders. Addington – who was now Prime Minister, Pitt having resigned over the question of Catholic emanicpation – on the other hand thought 'there was no distinction in reality' between the states of a deacon and a priest. He was worried that if Tooke were excluded by simple resolution of the House, the electors might return him again (perhaps he was thinking of Wilkes). He therefore suggested that a bill should be prepared specifically to exclude priests and deacons in future.

It is difficult to know whether Tooke was losing his grip or joking when he said that if he were a Jew, pagan, Mahometan, Jesuit, Presbyterian or Quaker he would be eligible. More to the point was his remark that clergy were allowed to marry. 'Shall it be said that he who can govern a wife is unfit to assist in the government of a kingdom?... Because, like a good subject, I chose to withdraw without giving my reasons and thus exciting scandal, I am forever ineligible.' It was ironic that Tooke, though not interested in religion, should twice suffer severe penalties for having been ordained. Tooke made one hit with the House when he compared his situation with that of 'A poor girl... quite destitute, who applied for admission to the Magdalen Hospital'. When questioned as to her previous history, and her life discovered to be irreproachable, the Director said, 'If you wish admittance here you must qualify yourself by prostitution'. Holy orders were apparently indelible, but 'on the night of Queen Mary's death the clergy went to bed Papists and the next morning, on the succession of Elizabeth, they rose Protestants'. Tooke raised a laugh when he claimed that 'an unanimous resolution' of 'a respectable body of constituents' was being overruled.

Addington introduced a declaratory bill making it illegal for anyone in holy orders to hold a seat in the House. Tooke proposed an amendment which would make it unlawful for clergymen elected to the House to hold any benefice or office under the Crown. This was refused. Fox, Sheridan and Erskine opposed the bill, as did Thurlow in the Lords. Thurlow, who as Attorney General had clashed bitterly with Tooke when prosecuting him for libel in 1774, opposed the statute as unprincipled and a needless restriction of the franchise. The bill was, inevitably, passed on 19 May. In the *Diversions* Tooke sarcastically expressed astonishment that Parliament had not yet passed an act to make him conform to the liturgy and to prohibit his 'meddling with any words out of it'.[6] So, to keep one individual out, Parliament disqualified all those who had ever held holy orders, and the disqualification continues to this day.

While the process of evicting Tooke from Parliament ground on, he took part in debates and voted with the opposition. He made his maiden speech in support of Charles Sturt's motion of 18 February 1801 demanding an enquiry into the failure of the expedition to capture Ferrol, a naval base in North West Spain. 'If the House refuse to go into a committee of enquiry, with what propriety can they enter into the merits of Old Sarum and its member?' *The Oracle* considered his speech a good example of the mixture of 'satire, sarcasm, irony and subtlety' for which he was distinguished. Government supporters, however, quickly reported that Tooke had failed to make his mark. Malmesbury said no notice at all was taken of him, Lord Granville Leveson Gower that 'Horne Tooke spoke very ill last night, and showed no appearance of being a formidable antagonist in the House of Commons'. Pitt reassured the King that Tooke's speech 'seemed to aim only at quaintness and singularity… and deserves very little remark'.[7]

Often, successful Commons speakers have made no impression with their maiden speech. There were various reasons why Tooke did not make the impact which many had expected. In those days many MPs were suspicious of lawyers and journalists; Tooke was a lawyer *manqué* and a successful journalist. He had always employed a cold manner, concentrating on teasing antagonists rather than warming hearts and wooing supporters. He was diffuse and boastful; he did not gesticulate, and his articulation was monotonous; his dry, pointed sayings fell flat. Used to dominating mixed crowds at the hustings, he was too old and infirm to tackle the totally different style of oratory needed for a more sophisticated audience accustomed to debate important matters of policy, almost all of whom, moreover, held him in contempt. In the law courts Tooke had tended to introduce too many personal grievances; he did the same now. He caused offence by enquiring what kind of malady could be produced if he sat among those who were pleased to call themselves the Commons of England? Was not a quarantine of more than 30 years sufficient to guard against the infection of his original character?

Tooke might never have been successful in the Commons. Erskine failed, as did Wilkes. Lord Holland, who thought his speeches 'neat, facetious, ingenious and subtle', believed he would have been more successful if he had been elected earlier. 'His love of victory rather than of truth, of quaint logick rather than of sound sense, were not very unnatural consequences of accidents which had debarred a powerful mind and ambitious spirit from all the usual and honourable avenues to distinction.' Tooke told Lord Holland that he 'had a very different view of the House now he had been in it… I thought… and I think so still, that those who govern this country are rogues; but I had no notion that the business was done so ably, or that the members of the Commons… were so superior in talent as I have found them.'[8]

Even if Tooke's speeches were not masterpieces, despite forebodings that they would be wild and controversial they were sensible, to the point, respectful of the Ministry, on occasion positively conservative. He criticised the Government for its inept handling of the war and its failure to alleviate economic hardship. In the debate on the continued suspension of habeas corpus, which he opposed until ruled out of order, he made a typical swipe at lawyers, complaining that within the last 40 years no less than 20 peerages and £10,000,000 had been showered upon the gentlemen of the bar, but he emphasised his love and respect for Addington. The House must have been surprised to find Tooke recommending compromise in a bad-tempered debate on the Irish Martial Law Bill.

To many MPs' astonishment, Tooke declared that he hated innovation in all things, in Church, State and agriculture. 'I look to what is established and approve of it – not because it is the best, but because it is established.' Charles Abbot (Lord Colchester) found his speech 'strange and paradoxical'.[9] Tooke had not learnt how to expound his views succinctly in a manner which would hold the attention of a hostile House.

Tooke did not always appreciate the merits of new methods. He erroneously despised new agricultural practices, ridiculing landowners who 'were more intent on raising turnips, fattening swine and over-feeding sheep, than in attending to objects of national concern'. He subscribed to current liberal economic theory expressed in pamphlets by his friends Morgan and Frend. Their main theme was the evil effects of war which retarded economic activity and increased disparities of wealth and power. Cobbett thought Tooke in his speeches 'uttered more good sense on political economy than I ever heard of being uttered in that House for the last 30 years'.[10]

Tooke was allowed to keep his seat until Parliament was dissolved in June 1802, though he would have been content for the House to 'throw Old Sarum on the floor along with the other boroughs of the same description… thus they would be rid of him at once'. He continued to attend when well enough. At his final appearance on 12 April 1802 he supported Burdett's notice of a motion for an enquiry into Pitt's conduct of the war.[11]

After the dissolution Tooke issued a last bitter address to the electors of Westminster: 'It has… been discovered that something mysterious, miraculous, and supernatural, was operated upon me nearly half a century ago… which has divested me… of the common rights of a man and a citizen. I am thus prevented… from keeping my word, and offering you again my services… this, however, I regret the less, because… I am… satisfied that (constituted as that assembly at present is) nothing short of another miracle could possibly enable me to render you any service here.' Nevertheless it was an act of mercy of his old electioneering comrade (Addington), for if instead he had 'proposed to hang me immediately in the lobby, he… would have been followed by the same majority'.[12]

As a minor consolation, Tooke was now rated an expert on the new act. Isaac Corry wrote to Charles Abbot concerning the case of another man who had taken holy orders but wanted to enter Parliament: 'Both the Speaker, the Attorney General and Horne Tooke, for I communicated with that great authority also, considered him disqualified'.[13]

In May 1801, Lady Holland dined at Mrs Sharp's to meet Tooke. 'He was ill and in all probability would not have kept his engagement had he not been aware that the dinner was expressly made to give me an opportunity of seeing him, and wise as he is, he is not free from the frailty of the weak... vanity, for he was gratified at knowing he was sought as a sight. He is an infirm, exhausted old man, with a mild, placid countenance, a small penetrating eye, and a flat, broad forehead. His manners are those of a remarkably high-bred, old-fashioned man of quality; his sentences are precise, clear and short. His language obsolete and affectedly so, but often productive of a happy and singular effect, witty and brief. He so evidently laboured under the pressure of bodily pain that he only flashed, but from those scintillations I could easily perceive what he must have been in his days of vigour.' Perhaps influenced by a desire to please, Tooke told the Hollands, 'Mr Fox has taken a severe revenge. I have passed my life in attacking him, and he has now, for the second time, defended me nobly against the arm of power.' Lord Holland recorded Tooke's statement made 'with some truth and the love of point which distinguished his conversation'. 'The candour of Ministers consisted in this, that deacons and priests had sat in Parliament for more than a century; but at last one got in who opposed the Minister of the day, and then Parliament determined that there never should be any... priests admitted... hereafter.' Lady Holland entered in her journal that in Parliament Tooke was too fond of talking of himself, and his jokes were trite. On the other hand, he made a very good satirical joke in a toast, so well disguised that what was Jacobinical appeared extremely loyal: 'The brave followers of the Duke of York', meaning the French who pursued him when his army was put to flight in Holland.[14]

Burdett as MP for Middlesex; Cold Bath Fields Prison

During the 1802 election, Tooke appeared on the Westminster hustings. At first he supported John Graham (not the John Graham of page 48), the independent candidate who had replaced him, and Fox. When Fox showed his lack of reforming zeal by combining with Gardner, the Tory candidate, Tooke spoke for Graham alone. Graham, though not of Tooke's calibre and like him without organised backing, polled 1693 votes to Gardner's 2341.

Due to his advanced views Burdett was no longer acceptable as member for Boroughbridge. He talked of living abroad. In an attempt to keep him at home, Coutts used his influence to procure other seats but Burdett turned them down. He was dissuaded by Tooke who maintained that there were better things for a reformer to do than waste his time battling futilely in the corrupt Commons. However, when Richard Payne Knight, William Tooke and Michael Pearson officially invited Burdett on behalf of the Middlesex freeholders, Tooke withdrew his opposition and Burdett accepted. Byng, the sitting Whig member, was certain to be elected. The Government candidate was Mainwaring, the magistrate who had reported so favourably on the Cold Baths prison.[15]

Burdett followed Tooke in calling for the people to support the Monarchy which suffered, as they did, from domination by a corrupt oligarchy. Announcing that he would run his campaign on the issue of Cold Bath Fields prison, he accused Mainwaring of abetting ill-treament there. Mainwaring's supporters accused Burdett of consorting with traitors such as O'Connor. Much was made of Burdett's connection with Tooke, his 'Magnus Apollo', not like Wilkes a burnt-out volcano, but 'As combustible as ever, though too cautious to let anything be seen issuing from his own crater', 'The most dangerous man in this country, who has wrought incalculable injury to society'.[16]

Rowdy crowds surging through the streets rivalled the days of Wilkes. Treating, bribery and perjury were rife. Tooke had vowed to stay away from the hustings, but he dreaded his ewe lamb falling into the Whigs' hands. When Fox and Lord William Russell organised a huge meeting at the Crown and Anchor in support of Burdett, and the Duke of Bedford subscribed £1,000 towards his expenses, Tooke changed his mind and went down to

Brentford wearing Burdett's blue favours. At the close of the poll Byng was elected, followed by Burdett with 271 more votes than Mainwaring.[17]

On 9 July 1804, in response to a petition from Mainwaring, a Commons committee reported that the sheriffs had corruptly admitted 300 ineligible voters, but Mainwaring's agents had treated voters so he too was incapacitated. A new election was ordered.[18]

This time Mainwaring's son George stood against Burdett, who was backed by the radicals and the Whigs plus Lord Lansdowne. Burdett had co-operated with the Foxites during their infrequent appearances in Parliament, but they disapproved of his association with Tooke and the lower-class reformers. Creevey, who had declined Burdett's request to nominate him, thought Burdett, 'with all his political intemperance an amiable, innocent, excellent creature', who, alas, listened to the infamous counsels of 'the archfiend Tooke'. Cartoonists, who ignored these subtleties, showed Tooke driving Burdett's processional coach with the Foxites harnessed to the reins.[19]

On 6 August, the last day of the poll, there had not been time to examine all the disputed votes. The sheriffs decided that the poll must be declared as matters then stood, so Mainwaring was returned by a majority of five votes. The Middlesex freeholders, led by Bosville and Cartwright who had reappeared on the political scene, petitioned on the ground that the disputed votes should have been taken into account. A Commons select committee reported that Burdett should have been elected. Mainwaring then counter-petitioned, accusing Burdett of bribery and corruption. In February 1806, almost at the end of the Parliament, the select committee upheld Mainwaring's objection and declared him elected.

Burdett had spent nearly £100,000 on the two elections, seriously embarrassing his finances. A large proportion went on costs generated by the two petitions. Burdett had no personal objection to widespread treating. Tooke, who had strongly condemned Government bribery at Westminster, may not have realised how much money was dispensed as he spent little time at Brentford. When both sides' total costs were known, Tooke expressed dismay at the huge expenditure which was of 'no public or private benefit'.[20]

At this time Tooke played down his distrust of the Foxites. He was grateful to Fox for his opposition to the act which debarred him from Parliament, but never abandoned his conviction that they were the more dangerous of the two parties, 'for out of office they would seek the support of the people, who would trust them', only to be discarded if they got in. It seems likely that, if Tooke had not been there to keep an eye on him, Burdett would have modified his attitude and joined the Foxites.

After the 1802 election and during the Peace of Amiens Burdett crossed to Paris. There, in the company of Lord and Lady Oxford, he was reunited with Arthur O'Connor, called on Tooke's republican friend John Hurford Stone, gave Paine money and attended Napoleon's levées. Tooke was too infirm to go abroad, but entertained the Abbé Grégoire, Bishop of Blois, like Sieyès a powerful revolutionary cleric who campaigned for equal rights for Jews. Tooke owned a bust of Napoleon, who 'possessed all the qualities of a great genius and was truly a hero'. He thought the French should be content with their revolution for the benefit preponderated beyond comparison over the bad.[21]

On Burdett's return he and Tooke became involved in helping Despard. He had been imprisoned in Cold Bath Fields for suspected treason and was released when suspension of habeas corpus ended in March 1801. He immediately joined in a conspiracy with the United Irishmen and other disaffected groups. They planned to suborn guardsmen and Irish dockers, form a revolutionary army and stage a coup d'état in London. They believed that there were organisations in the provinces which would join them, and hoped all would combine with a simultaneous revolution in Ireland. A Grenadier guardsman who had taken their illegal oath turned informer. He and other spies reported every move to the authorities. Ford rightly thought it a 'mad enterprise'. Although it is possible that it was part of a much wider conspiracy supported by the French, nothing bar an abortive rising in Ireland ever came to fruition.

On 16 November, Despard and 40 of his motley collection of accomplices were arrested at the Oakley Arms, Lambeth, where they were said to be discussing plans to assassinate the King on his way to open Parliament. Despard was the only educated gentleman among them. Few of those arrested had grasped what was going on or realised that they were engaged in anything illegal, and 20 were released almost immediately.[22]

Considerable efforts were made to help Despard, a man who inspired affection and respect. He had been befriended by such respectable reformers as Bosville and Frend. Lord Moira, one of the few statesmen who won Tooke's unqualified approval through his attempts to modify laws penalising debtors, sent him £50 just before he was arrested.

Tooke and Burdett went into action to co-ordinate strategy and form a defence fund for the arrested men. Moody reported to Ford, 'Hardy, Lemaitre and myself form a kind of secret committee... to issue out the money entrusted to us... Most of the supplies come from the circle of Wimbledon, and very trifling from any other quarter.' At a meeting at 'Headquarters', 'the High Priest' gave a toast: 'The innocence of the virtuous Despard'. Among those present who gave donations were Rogers, Morgan and Payne Knight who had just been appointed High Sheriff of Herefordshire. Burdett was worried that his name would come up in the course of the trials, which 'would be damned awkward'. Tooke recommended blackening the characters of the five material witnesses, 'otherwise the prisoners would all be hanged'. The rest of the company agreed that unless the witnesses could be discredited, Despard would be convicted. Men were found willing to bear false witness, but John Foulkes, a defence lawyer at previous treason trials who was employed by the committee for Despard's defence, decided it would be unwise to use such 'infamous means' to combat 'infamous enemies'. Tooke, who had no such scruples, then condemned Foulkes as a rascal.[22,23]

Eventually only 13 men were tried on 7 February 1803. Three of those arrested turned King's evidence. Nelson appeared as a character witness for Despard and did his best to save his life. Three men were acquitted and three found guilty but pardoned. Despard and six others were found guilty and executed, though the jury strongly recommended mercy for Despard. Ford and Moody knew that several of the most extreme ex-members of the LCS who were perpetually concocting revolutionary intrigues were involved, but none of them was tried. The Government did not want to reveal its intelligence sources. Persecution had moderated under Addington's premiership. Ministers believed correctly that sedition was on the wane. The exposure of the conspiracy was a blow to the radicals. Though Tooke must have known that Despard was implicated in the plot, he may well have maintained his innocence to retrieve what he could of the campaign to present him as a victim of the horrors of Cold Bath Fields.[22]

Notes on Chapter 12

Many quotations are from Cobbett's *Parliamentary History* XXXV, pp 956-1523 (*PH* below)

1 Stanhope, Lady Hester, *Memoirs* I, p 321; Stephens II, p 237; Elliott III, pp 313-4
2 Elliott III, p 201; Harris, James (Earl Malmesbury) IV, p 9
3 Rogers, *Table Talk*, p 127
4 *PH*, p 956; Douglas I, p 171; *Oracle* 17.2.01
5 Fox, C.J. III, pp 189-90; *PH*, pp 1323-49; *Oracle* 7.3.01
6 *PH*, pp 1386-1418, 1541; *DOP* II, p 667
7 Harris, J., IV, p 13; Gower I, p 300; George III, *Later Correspendence* III, p 506; *Oracle* 20.2.01, *PH*, p 1000
8 Fox (Lord Holland), *Memoirs of Whig Party* I, p 181
9 Abbot (Lord Colchester) I, p 250; *PH*, p 1000, 1006, 1290, 1523
10 Stephens II, pp 353-4; *Political Register* XIX (1811), p 193
11 *PH*, p 1418
12 *Morning Chronicle* 29.6.02
13 Royal Commision Historical MSS 346, Lord Colchester papers 30.10.1801 (PRO 30/9, NRA 8652)
14 Lady Holland II, pp 134, 146; Fox, H, *Memoirs Whig Party* I, pp 179-80
15 Patterson I, pp 132-4
16 Bowles, p 12; *True Briton*, *Oracle* 15.7.02
17 Stephens II, pp 306-7; Patterson I, pp 136-8
18 *Parliamentary Debates 1804* II, p 959; Patterson I, pp 147-8
19 Creevey, *Life and Times*, p 20; George, M.D., 10264
20 Patterson I, pp 150-1; *Parl. Debates 1806* VI, pp 183-5
21 Stephens II, pp 414-6; *DOP* II, p 664; Alger, p 37, Patterson, pp 104-7
22 Hone, p 105-17
23 Add MS 27816 f579; Burdett MSS Eng Hist B 200 f18-20

Chapter Thirteen

The Diversions of Purley

In 1786 Tooke published Part I of *The Diversions of Purley*, briefly mentioned earlier, so called in honour of William Tooke. Most of 'A Letter to Mr Dunning on the English Particle' of 1778 was included in it. The second edition, published in 1798, had an attractive frontispiece engraved by William Sharp, of Mercury binding on his winged sandals, an appropriate illustration of its subtitle, 'Epea Pteroenta' ('Winged Words'), from the *Iliad*. Neither was a title for the uneducated. Some people mistook the book for a game or a novel. Blackwood's reviewer complained that his family were bitterly disappointed, having bought it as suitable Christmas entertainment.[1] Part II was published in 1805. Towards the end of his life, Tooke wrote much additional material which he intended to publish as Part III. However, shortly before he died he decided to burn it all (see pp 269, 270).

The *Diversions* was written as a conversation between Tooke and his two close friends, William Tooke and Dr Beadon, in which they fed him questions and Tooke always won the argument. The dialogue form was not used in grammars, but was used sometimes in philosophical studies. In Tooke's hands it was lively and piquant, helped make his arguments readable, and enabled him to avoid prosaic explanations or exposition of difficult points. Tooke's statements were not all intended to be taken literally, but to startle people into considering alternatives. Besides the radical political ideas which underlay Tooke's theory of language, the book was enlivened (for some) by jokes, puns and Tooke's mystifying games. It was illustrated with jibes at his pet bugbears: ministers, Papists and literary critics with whom he differed.

Tooke died leaving many additions, mostly to Part II, for a new edition. Richard Taylor incorporated them in his 1829 octavo edition. There was another edition in 1840, and one in 1857 with additional notes by Taylor, pointing out some of Tooke's errors and criticising some of his conclusions.

While in the Tower, Tooke made calculations about future earnings from the *Diversions*. He listed distinguished clientele who had agreed to subscribe to Parts II and III and reckoned he would receive £1,188. He made a note that 'An ample justification of the author will be given in one of the volumes for exercising by this mode of publication the only profession which the prevalence of corrupt injustice in this country have left to him'.[2] Tooke made a considerable profit, both from royalties and subscriptions, altogether between £4,000 and £5,000 for a book on which he only spent about £10 for one advertisement. This was a large sum in those days for two quarto volumes. He received subscription payments of two guineas for the unpublished third volume, which were not returned. Copies were to be sold to subscribers only. The *Diversions* was also printed in Philadelphia in 1806.

Eighteenth-Century Ideas on Language

In the eighteenth century, language was seen as one of the keys to philosophy, as a means of studying the mechanism of thought, and as a political weapon. This led to important questions – all of which Tooke intended to consider – such as the relation of language to the laws of reason and society. Did the mind have a material basis? Did mankind have a single origin? Was language given by revelation or had man invented it? If language manifested the nature of the mind, should it be possible to discover a universal grammar?

Ideas on language in the eighteenth century were greatly influenced by Locke's *Essay Concerning Human Understanding*, first published in 1689. Locke argues that human knowledge consists of ideas which are derived from experiences gained during life. Ideas not based on direct sensation are acquired by reflection on the operation of our minds. Simple ideas can then be combined to form complex ideas such as truth or honesty.

Language is the means of transmitting thought and of doing so 'with dispatch'. Locke says that we should 'note how great a dependence our words have on common sensible ideas; and how those which are made use of to stand for actions and notions quite removed from the sense, have their rise from thence, and from obvious sensible ideas are transferred to more abstruse significations... viz to imagine, apprehend... tranquillity etc.'[3] In addition to words signifying ideas of things, Locke included others, indicating 'connections that the mind gives to ideas, or propositions, one with another'.[4] These words he calls particles, each of which may have several meanings: 'most of these particles have diverse and sometimes almost opposite significations.' 'It is in the right use of these, that more particularly consists the clearness and beauty of a good stile.' Particles, prepositions and conjunctions were of particular importance to Tooke.

However, Locke noted many and important imperfections in language and in the way it is used. 'But that they [words] signify only men's peculiar ideas, and that by a perfectly arbitrary imposition, is evident, in that they often fail to excite in others... the same ideas, we take them to be the signs of.'[5] 'Besides the imperfection that is naturally in language, and the obscurity and confusion that is so hard to be avoided in the use of words, there are several wilful faults and neglects which men are guilty of... whereby they render these signs less clear and distinct in their significations, than naturally they need to be.'[6] To remedy these problems, Locke suggests that a complex idea should be defined in terms of the simple ideas of which it is composed, as the meaning of simple ideas is more readily agreed by different individuals. Later thinkers, such as Condillac and Tooke, extended this idea into a belief that a proper understanding of the etymology of the words representing complex ideas would clarify their meaning.

There was much discussion of the origin of language in the eighteenth century. Condillac extended Locke's ideas by suggesting that language had slowly developed from natural cries and onomatopeia. This 'modern', sceptical notion was opposed by traditionalists who maintained that language was such a complex edifice that it must have required a complex system of thought, but that the latter itself depended on language, the only possible solution being divine revelation to Adam. In the original perfect language, words expressed the essences of things and were far from arbitrary (until the dispersion at Babel).[7] Many, who did not take such an extreme point of view, believed that Man was innately endowed with a large number of ideas, and that the divinely-inspired characteristics of human thought implied a universal grammar. They retained enough of the old ideas to suggest that modern languages were corruptions and so inferior to the languages from which they were derived. They thought that a 'pure' language, without borrowings from other languages, would be the clearest for expressing complex ideas, since a collection of words from many sources must lead to confusion. In practice this meant a return to Latin and Greek, an expression of the eighteenth-century desire to emulate the best features of classical civilisation.

One of the most celebrated eighteenth-century grammars is *Hermes*, by Harris, 'a philosophical enquiry concerning language and universal grammar'. It is based on the grammars of Greek and Latin and most of the examples cited are in one of those languages. He considers Greek to be the most perfect language: 'And thus is the Greek tongue, from its propriety and universality, made for all that is great, and all that is beautiful, in every subject, and under every form of writing'. Another celebrated grammar is that of Lowth, later Bishop of London, written in 1762. He says in the introduction that he does not assume knowledge of any foreign tongue, but the book is set out in a formal manner like a grammar of one of the classical languages and would not have been very useful to those who had received no classical education.[8]

Emphasis on the classical languages was a characteristic of late eighteenth-century and early nineteenth-century culture. For example, 'grammar school' is defined in Johnson's dictionary as a 'school in which the learned languages are grammatically taught'. In 1805, the Governors of Leeds Grammar School applied for leave to teach arithmetic and modern languages. Lord Eldon rejected the application on the grounds that the purpose of grammar schools was correctly defined by Johnson, and that therefore no such subjects could be taught in them.[9] The classical languages were usually considered to be the best medium for expressing educated and refined thoughts. Consequently the educated class tried to mould the English language into a classical framework which was contrasted with the brutish, vulgar tongue of the mass of the people. Popular petitions to Parliament, organised by bodies such as the SCI and LCS, were often rejected on the grounds that they were couched in 'highly indecent and disrespectful language'.

Tooke disagreed with this emphasis on the classical languages. He considered grammar 'absolutely necessary in the search after philosophical truth' but did not find *Hermes* a useful guide. 'Nor can I boast of any acquisition from its perusal, except indeed of hard words and frivolous or unintelligible distinctions.' He considered *Hermes* 'a compilation of almost all the errors... which grammarians had been accumulating from the time of Aristotle'.[10]

When Tooke was writing the *Diversions*, a movement, supported among others by Richard Sharp, had sprung up which laid greater emphasis on Anglo-Saxon. Johnson, in the preface to his dictionary, writes, 'Our language, for almost a century, has by the concurrence of many causes, been gradually departing from its original Teutonick character, and deviating towards a Gallick structure and phraseology, from which it ought to be our endeavour to recall it, by making our ancient volumes the ground-work of style'. For many, this movement contained an element of patriotic pride. The constitution was founded on custom, so was the English language. Both had Anglo-Saxon origins. The lack of rigid rules in English was a symbol of liberty. Codification would give the elite more arbitrary power. Thomas Sheridan and Priestley wanted more standardisation, but in a flexible form which would enable men to communicate on more equal terms and help diminish social distinctions.

Tooke's Aims: Philosophy, Linguistics, Politics

Tooke was never an egalitarian, nor did he seek to be a popular writer. The *Diversions* was too expensive for the general public. With its classical allusions and philosphical arguments, it was directed at a cultivated audience. He presumed his readers would be 'acquainted with French, Latin, Italian and Greek'.[11] He emphasised, however, that knowledge of many languages was no criterion of intellectual potential. One of his principal aims in writing his book was to extend literacy, to make the principles of language more widely accessible and to alter the attitude of the educated to those with fewer advantages than themselves.

Tooke, following Locke whom he 'reverenced on this side of idolatry', argued that a clear conception of the nature and function of language would lead to a better understanding of philosophical and political problems. But he thought that Locke's ideas on the mind and mental processes should really be applied to language. 'The business of the mind, as far as it concerns language... extends no further than to receive impressions, that is, to have sensations or feelings. What are called its operations are merely the operations of language.' (Tooke never explained what he thought was the business of the mind which did not concern language.)[12] If 'you read the Essay over again with attention, [you will] see whether all that its immortal author has justly concluded will not hold equally true and clear, if you substitute the composition etc. of terms whenever he has supposed a composition etc. of ideas'. Tooke's materialist conception of the mind suggests that what are called mental processes are determined by the structure of language, rather than languages being determined by the innate structure of the mind.[13]

Most treatises were pedantic and technical. Tooke's was vivid, racy and readable. His style 'had a terse and poignant simplicity, as clear as Swift without being either so slovenly or so dry'. He employed English idiom rather than complicated words based on classical tongues, an example for the self-taught to emulate. He wanted intelligent men without much education to appreciate that they could acquire 'wisdom and true knowledge' as readily as classical scholars. 'A man of plain common sense may obtain it, if he will dig for it; but I cannot think that what is commonly called Learning is the mine in which it will be found. Truth... has been improperly imagined at the bottom of a well; it lies much nearer to the surface; though buried... under mountains of learned rubbish.'[14]

Tooke emphasised the distinction between customary usage and the intrinsic meaning of words, because he believed that if men understood the words they used, they would naturally learn to use the best language. 'As far as we know not our own meaning... we gabble like things most brutish.' He was irritated when words were employed out of their correct context. Throughout his work runs the theme that, though there are inevitably differences between spoken and written English, the supposed dichotomy between civilised and 'low barbaric' language was an arbitrary and erroneous imposture of the establishment. Tooke pointed out that, although language was a glorious art, 'whose influence extends over all the others', it had sprung from necessity and was 'invented by artless men'. 'People who have the poorest and scantiest language, have yet always many more words than ideas.' Deficiencies in languages were linguistic not intellectual. He wanted to encourage use of the vernacular but with usage that was skilful and grammatically correct.[15]

Locke had said, 'and it is agreed on all sides', that clearness and beauty of good style depended on the right use of particles (prepositions and conjunctions). Monboddo and Harris considered that it was essential to learn languages rich in particles, such as Latin and Greek, which were highly-developed instruments for expressing rational and abstract thought. English, deficient in particles, was only fit for crude uncomplicated ideas. Tooke disagreed, for if the nature of particles were understood, their proper use would be evident to everyone and not dependent on extensive education. Those who promoted classics were trying to shroud learning in mystification and keep it inaccessible to the uneducated. It was easier to understand grammar by studying one's native language, and most people could not spare ten years working on dead languages to learn how to understand their own.[16] He objected to the emphasis on logical purism and futile refinements suggested by 'Certain precise gentlemen' who 'will no longer permit us to call our kindred our relations: no, but our relatives'. 'But these petty fopperies will pass away… and we shall all find our relations again as safe and sound as ever.'[17] Although Tooke found Paine's style somewhat crude and ungrammatical, he appreciated its widespread appeal. Its use of everyday words showed that vernacular phraseology could be used to express important ideas in an intelligible, lively manner. Though he does not say so explicitly, Tooke clearly believed that the English character and spirit is embodied in its language. This was another reason to study it and emphasise its importance.

Tooke believed that attention to the origin of individual words would avoid the ambiguities so often present (Locke's imperfection of langauge) and throw light on the origins of languages and peoples. He gave numerous examples from old English and

Anglo-Saxon to substantiate his etymology. Most were drawn from Chaucer, Gower, Shakespeare, Ben Johnson and Spenser. Most grammarians and critics at the time were contemptuous and ignorant of Germanic languages. Tooke derided etymologists who believed English and all other languages came from Greek or Hebrew, and he sometimes rejected the derivation of words from Greek in favour of 'Gothic'. Latin was 'a mere modern language' whereas the origin of Anglo-Saxon was lost in deep antiquity.[18] Because he had determined that Latin was partly derived from 'our Northern ancestors', no historian's testimony was needed 'to conclude that the founders of the Roman state and of the Latin tongue came not from Asia but from the North of Europe. For the language cannot lye, and from the language of every nation we may with certainty collect its origin.'[19] Many of his derivations now appear to us fanciful or absurd, but we must remember that he was breaking fresh ground and was ignorant of the common origins of the Indo-European languages.

Sir William Jones, who had been appointed a Judge in India in 1783, made a detailed study of Sanskrit. In 1786, when Tooke had already published the first part of the *Diversions*, Jones read a celebrated paper to the Royal Asiatic Society in Calcutta pointing out the affinities between Sanskrit, Greek and Latin, showing that they and probably Celtic and Gothic had sprung from a common source. It took some time for Jones's work to make an impact, and Tooke does not appear to have appreciated its crucial importance. Sanskrit grammars in English were published in 1806, too late for him to consider when writing the second part of the *Diversions*.

One of Tooke's most famous and controversial entries was 'TRUTH'. 'When Pilate asked what is TRUTH, he would not stay for the answer… and from that time to this mankind have been wrangling and tearing each other to pieces for the TRUTH without once considering the meaning of the word.' Tooke says it is a past participle of the Anglo-Saxon verb to think, to trow, originally written 'TREW', that which is trowed. In Latin 'Res, a thing, gives us Reor, i.e. I am Thing-ed, Ve-reor, I am strongly Thinged and Verum is the contracted participle of Vereor'. Here Tooke allowed Burdett to exclaim, 'Who ever used such language before'. This derivation caused much mockery – to say truth was merely what is trowed was no better than saying that danger was what is feared. Tooke wanted to show that the nature of truth is not fixed but relative, dependent on the observer: the word truth was formed for and by and was applicable to mankind alone. 'If no man no TRUTH, there is therefore no... eternal, immutable... TRUTH; unless mankind... be also... everlasting. Two persons may contradict each other, and yet both speak TRUTH; for the TRUTH of one person may be opposite to the TRUTH of another.' His solution to a perennial problem was in character: 'To speak TRUTH may be a vice as well as a virtue; for there are many occasions where it ought not to be spoken'.[20]

Tooke criticised the obscurity and imprecision of metaphysical terms which perpetuated ignorance and subordination. He wanted to demonstrate that these words did not represent universal abstract ideas (whose existence he denied), but an individual's experience of law, justice etc. He considered that 'all general reasoning, all Politics, Law, Morality and Divinity' were 'merely Metaphysic'.[21]

Tooke was keen to improve the quality of education in general. However, he was afraid of the consequences if this were controlled by Government, and in 'A Letter to Mr Dunning' had attacked what he considered Monboddo's idea of the most perfect form of society 'where Government leaves nothing to the freewill of individuals, but interferes with... the private lives of citizens and the education of their children'. This would 'be the last stage of civil society, in the sense of the lady in the comedy whose lover having offered to give her the last proof of love, and marry her, she aptly replied "the last indeed: for there's an end of loving"'.[22]

Tooke's political philosophy underlies much of the *Diversions*. In addition, he uses examples and footnotes to fire overtly political squibs. For example, in the entry under 'BREAD', Tooke inveighed against substitutes for representatives, juries, money and militia. The Archbishop of Canterbury was disparaged under the word 'DOLE', which Tooke declared 'has not in itself the smallest reference to Alms or to the Nobleman's gate, or to Lambeth Palace; if indeed those places have any distinguished connection with Alms'.[23] Many others will be quoted below.

Part I of *Diversions*

Part I, dedicated to the University of Cambridge (and in particular to Rev. Dr Beadon, Master of Jesus) from 'one of her grateful Sons, who always considers acts of voluntary justice towards himself as Favours', carried a typically challenging footnote in which Tooke disagreed with both Plato and Machiavelli, 'for the experience of much injustice will cause the forbearance of injury to appear like kindness'. In the introduction and first chapter Tooke states his aims in writing the *Diversions*. 'Should you be altogether so severe upon my politics; when you reflect that, merely for attempting to prevent the effusion of brother's blood and the final dismemberment of the empire, I stand the single legal victim during the contest, and the single instance of proscription after it?' This is followed by remarks on Locke's essay and three chapters on the parts of speech, the noun and the article. The subsequent chapters relate to 'A Letter to Mr Dunning', in particular an analysis of the word 'that' and a discussion of conjunctions, prepositions and adverbs.

Tooke often presents his ideas in opposition to those of the classical grammarians such as Harris and Monboddo. He emphasises the importance of Anglo-Saxon derivations and includes a 'Moeso-Gothic alphabet' which was missing from the grammars in current use. Tooke's theory of language is based on the premise 'In English, and in all languages, there are only two sorts of words which are necessary for the communication of our thoughts – Noun and Verb'. 'I… include all the others (which are not necessary to speech, but merely substitutes of the first sort) under the title of abbreviations.' They are 'employed for despatch, and are the signs of other words'. 'Abbreviations are the wheels of language, the wings of Mercury.' 'The first aim of language was to communicate our thoughts, the second to do it with despatch. The difficulties and disputes concerning language have arisen almost entirely from neglecting… the latter.'[24]

Much of Part I is taken up with particles. Monboddo and Harris maintained that these words have no signification of themselves, but were formed to connect either sentences or words. They enable more refined and complex ideas to be expressed. Tooke disagreed. He considered a word with no signification of itself to be a logical absurdity, and said that conjunctions and prepositions were abbreviations of verbs and nouns. Thus 'IF' was derived from 'GIVE', i.e. weather tomorrow – 'IF fair, it will send me abroad; IF foul it will keep me at home' is really 'GIVE fair weather, it will send me abroad; GIVE foul weather it will keep me at home'. Similarly 'unless' is derived from 'dimiss', though from allow etc. Thus, far from having been invented, as proposed by Monboddo, they are corruptions or abbreviations. 'In this respect the savage languages are upon an equal footing with the languages (as they are called) of art except that the former are less corrupted. Savages have not only as separate and distinct ideas of those relations as we have, but... they have this advantage over us (an advantage in point of intelligibility, though it is a disadvantage in point of brevity), that they also express them separately and distinctly.' This brings out clearly Tooke's political aims, by denying that those educated in the classical tongues (drawn from the hereditary wealthy class) should alone be able to partake in public life, politics and affairs of state. Many of the examples in the *Diversions* make the same point, e.g. 'The word "Nether" is at present... rarely used but in ridicule and with scorn; and this may possibly have arisen from its former application to the House of Commons, anciently called (by Henry VIII) the NETHER house of parliament... in truth this Nether end of our parliament has for a long time past been a mere sham and mockery of representation, but is now become an impudent and barefaced usurpation of the rights of the people'.[25]

'A Letter to Mr Dunning'

Chapters 6 to 8 are a modified version of 'A Letter to Mr Dunning' which is itself included complete at the end of Part II in Taylor's edition. The letter was first published in 1778 following Tooke's conviction for libel in 1777 (see p 67). The immediate purpose of the letter was to explain Tooke's view that he had been wrongly convicted, but the substance of it had 'been amongst the loose paper in my closet for upward of 30 years'.[26] The three chapters are concerned with the word 'that', conjunctions and English conjunctions.

Tooke maintained that he had 'been made the victim of two prepositions and a conjunction'. Dunning, at his instigation, maintained on appeal that in criminal prosecutions the indictment must contain in itself a certain and explicit charge of the offence. Tooke had said in his trial 'it is simply averred, that I did write and print and publish, and cause to be written and printed and published, to the tenor and effect following'. The Attorney General, however, said that the averment continued 'he had written and published a certain false, wicked, malicious, scandalous and seditious libel of and concerning His Majesty's Government...' Tooke said that 'of and concerning' could relate to good as well as evil actions, and that the indictment had failed to aver that there was a rebellion in Massachusetts etc.[27]

Lord Mansfield (the presiding judge) quoted as a precedent 'She, knowing that Cooke had been indicted for forgery, did so and so.' Tooke maintained that the word 'THAT' had not been correctly understood. The precedent was really 'Cooke had been indicted for forgery (there is the averment literally made) – she, knowing THAT, did so and so'. Tooke was using the legal quibble to illustrate his disagreement with Harris's *Hermes* where it was maintained that conjunctions have no signification in themselves, and that 'some words, according to the different manner of using them, are sometimes articles and sometimes pronouns'. Tooke did 'not allow that any words change their nature in this manner, so as to belong sometimes to one part of speech, and sometimes to another... the words appear to me to continue faithfully and steadily attached, each to the standard under which it was originally enlisted.'[26]

Tooke devotes much space to the etymologies of words, and particularly to the particles. For 'THAT', however, he is not clear: 'for abbreviation and corruption are always busiest with the words which are most frequently in use. Letters, like soldiers, being very apt to desert and drop off in a long march.'[29]

Conjunctions, he maintains, are the imperatives of verbs. For example, '"IF" is merely the imperative of the Gothic and Anglo-Saxon verb... Gif' (see the previous section). 'I mean to discard all supposed mystery... about all those words also which Mr Harris and others distinguish from prepositions and call conjunctions of sentences. I deny them to be a separate sort of words or part of speech by themselves... By such means alone can we clear away the obscurity of errors in which grammarians... have been involved... and get rid of that farrago of useless distinctions into

Conjunctive, Adjunctive, Disjunctive, Subdisjunctive... (38 variations are listed) which explain nothing; and... serve only to throw a veil over the ignorance of those who employ them.'[30]

The last chapter of 'A Letter to Mr Dunning' is concerned with the etymology of the English conjunctions. Tooke supports his derivations with numerous examples drawn from Old English and Anglo-Saxon, and quotes equivalent words in other Teutonic languages: German, Dutch, Danish and Swedish. In the case of 'but', Tooke disagrees with Locke. 'BUT,' he says, has two meanings with different derivations. One is really 'BOT', from Anglo-Saxon to boot, i.e. to superadd, with a footnote, 'Perhaps it may be thought improper for me to address you on this subject. BUT a moment my Lords, and it will evidently appear that you are equally blameable for an omission of duty here also.' In its other meaning, as in the phrase 'I saw BUT two plants', it is derived from Anglo-Saxon Bute or Butan, Be-out.[31]

The rest of Part I of the *Diversions* is concerned with prepositions and adverbs. Like conjunctions, prepositions had been wrongly derived by the older grammarians. 'They are not little words invented to put before nouns, and to which all languages have had recourse: but are in fact either Nouns or Verbs.' For example, 'WITH' is derived from the Anglo-Saxon 'TO JOIN' and 'THROUGH' from the Anglo-Saxon for 'DOOR'. Adverbs are derived from various sources. With 'spick and span', he takes the opportunity to have a tilt at Johnson. In his dictionary Johnson says, 'This word I should not have expected to have found authorised by a polite writer – originally used of cloth now extended or dressed at the clothiers, and spick and span is newly extended on the spikes or tenters – it is however a low word'. Tooke remarks, 'there is nothing stretched upon spikes and tenters but the etymologist's ignorance. In Dutch they say Spikspelder – nieuw'.[32]

Second Edition of Part I, 1798

The second edition contained many amendments and additional political comments. For the attentive reader there were now subversive propositions on most pages, with some reference in the text or footnote to current events. Since his rejection for the bar,

Tooke's trial for treason had exacerbated his embitterment. He inserted more sarcastic jibes at lawyers, animadversions on Government food policies and sallies and strictures on ministers, 'small men in every sense of the word'. His example for the usage of the word 'ALONG' ran, 'Thanks to Pitt: it is ALONG of him that we not only keep our boroughs, but get peerages into the bargain. Curses on Pitt; it is ALONG of him that the free constitution of this country is destroyed.' He dexterously seized the opportunity to add a letter Pitt had written to him in 1782, when he called on Pitt as leader of a deputation from the Westminster Committee, which he had not been allowed to read aloud at his trial. 'When fidelity to the sentiments it contains was seriously and unblushingly imputed to me as High Treason. The original of this letter Mr Pitt, upon his oath, to my astonishment acknowledged to be in his own handwriting; although every trace of Delegation was totally effaced from his memory.' In the letter Pitt declared that he considered reform 'necessary to the independence of Parliament, and to the liberty of the people'.[33]

Income tax was the subject of a footnote to a quotation from the Aeneid 'Disce puer… fortunam ex aliis' ('fortune you will derive from others'). 'Aliis should in a modern version be translated Lord Grenville, Mr Rose, Mr Dundas, Mr Windham, Mr Pitt, Lord Liverpool etc.' who take 'a triple or quadruple (they may take half or two thirds of our income next year) additional assessment upon our innocent property; whilst their guilty emoluments of office… remain untouched'.[34]

Tooke might believe that 'Personal enmity is a motive fit only for the devil', but Windham, who had 'Fleec't the people, and splic't a rope for your own neck', he attacked with particular venom. In a typical example of his mixture of criticism and recrimination, he wrote on the subject of conjunctions: 'I say what are they? for that is the rational etymological question; and not: whence do they come – it is with words as with men: Call this Squire, my Lord; then he will be comparative: call him by the new-fangled title of Marquis, or call him Duke; then he will be superlative: And yet whosoever shall trust him… will find to their cost that it is the same individual Squire Windham still. So neither is the substance or meaning or real import or value of any word altered by its grammatical class and denomination.'[35]

In 1790 the Rev. John Bruckner, Minister of the Dutch Church at Norwich, had published under the pseudonym Cassander, *Criticisms of the Diversions* in which he praised the book as important and innovative, but deplored Tooke's slapdash methods, charged him with inconsistency and hinted that he had appropriated the work of Professor Schultens, an accusation which Tooke was able to refute. Tooke directed some 'hostile flashes' at 'My Norwich critics', largely because he suspected Windham, a member for Norwich, of having put Bruckner up to it, for a friend of Tooke's had reported that 'the present precious Secretary at War' had gossiped Cassander's criticisms in a book-shop, saying that Tooke 'had found a mare's nest'.[36]

Tooke was not yet inured to sufferings which his enemies considered self-inflicted. At this point his personal feelings overwhelmed him and 'the etymologist was lost in the persecuted politician'. He launched into a diatribe, a catalogue of woes so unrestrained and inappropriate it roused irritation rather than sympathy among many readers, though others found the passage pathetic. 'The enemies of the established civil liberties of my country have hunted me through life... because I early descried their conspiracy... and have to the utmost of my power legally resisted their corrupt, tyrannical... innovations and usurpations. They have destroyed my fortunes... illegally barred and interdicted my usefulness to myself, my family, my friends, and my country. They have tortured my body (here Tooke inserted a footnote about his seven months close custody). They have aimed at my life and honour: can you wonder that, whilst one of these critics takes a cowardly advantage (where I could make no defence) to brand me as an acquitted Felon, I am unwilling (where I can make a defence) that he should... exhibit me as a convicted plagiary and impostor? But no more of these cowardly assassins. I consign them to the lasting contempt they have well earned, and which no future Title will ever be able to obliterate from the name of Windham.'[36]

When 'A Letter to Mr Dunning' appeared, although Tooke was imprisoned for libel, it was a comparatively liberal era. The first part of the *Diversions* was published when reform was quite acceptable. By the time it was reprinted in 1798 the nation was engaged in a desperate struggle with France which included a serious insurrection in Ireland. The political climate had changed;

etymology and philosophy were still of interest, but Tooke's political posture could no longer gain sympathy. All the same, the second edition was a great success. Fox wrote to Lord Holland, 'I have just finished Horne Tooke's *Diversions of Purley* and like it very much indeed. My opinion of his abilities is much raised, for I did not used to hold him high in any other respect except wit and some humour.' The *Morning Chronicle* predicted that 'every scholar in England would hasten to procure it'. The Government was not worried by the book as, like Godwin's *Political Justice*, it was too erudite for the uneducated.[37]

Part II

Part II of the *Diversions*, also published by Johnson in quarto in 1806, was dedicated to Tooke's jury and counsel at his treason trial. It is longer than Part I and contains the etymology of about 2,000 words, illustrated by innumerable examples and quotations from English and Scottish poets such as Douglas, Spenser, Gower, Milton, Pope and Gray, and also foreign authors, including Seneca, Metastasio, Lucretius, Juvenal, Boethius, Goldoni and Tasso. The dialogue is between Tooke and Burdett.

As the text was complicated, instead of proofs being posted to and fro, Tooke went to town every day to supervise the printing. At one point the printer, Mr Bye, ran out of Greek fount. Tooke had problems with Bye who feared he would be prosecuted for seditious libel. Eventually, after many strenuous arguments, the book appeared with blanks replacing names and the most contentious remarks. At the head of the printer's errata Tooke inserted an explanation for the absence of words 'as fair, as true, as honest, as legal as any other part of the book'. The result gave some paragraphs a comic appearance and led to speculation about the missing words. They were inserted in brackets in the edition published long after Tooke's death.

In one typical instance, after mentioning that Wakefield's death, caused by his imprisonment, had precluded their joint work on the origins of Latin, Tooke launched into a fiery paragraph on the state of the country where nothing was encouraged '[but… new penalties for spies and informers] which swarm amongst us as numerously as our volunteers [in this our present state of siege] with this advantage, that... [neither taxes nor penalties, nor spies] are ever rejected on account of their principles. Good God!... What cannot an [obstinate system of despotism and corruption] achieve! America, [Ireland,] Corsica, Hanover, with all our antient dependents, friends and allies, [all lost, all gone] and in how short a time! And the inhabitants of this little [persecuted and plundered] island... besieged collectively by France from without; [and each individual at home, more disgracefully and daily besieged] in his house by swarms of [tax collectors, assessors and supervisors, armed with degrading lists to be signed]' and so on.[38]

Part II opens with a defence of the notion that men have rights, in disagreement with the views of the governing class for which Tooke gives a quotation from Canning: 'Sir, whenever I hear the word 'RIGHTS', I have learned to consider it as preparatory to some desolating doctrine. It seems to me, to be productive of some wide spreading ruin, of some wasting desolation.' Tooke's says '"RIGHT" is no other than "RECT"-um (Regitum), the past participle of the Latin verb Regere'. All uses of the word are then explained by substituting the word ordered. 'When a man demands his right, he asks only that which it is ordered he shall have.' When F. (Burdett) demands 'Now what becomes of your vaunted RIGHTS of man?' Tooke answers, 'The RIGHT I revere is not the RIGHT adored by sycophants;... the capricious command of princes or ministers. I follow the LAW of God... and upon these are founded the RIGHTS of man, or what is ordered for man.'[39]

Most of Part II consists of chapters entitled 'Of Abstraction', followed by three short chapters on adjectives and participles. Tooke maintains that abstractions, or abstract ideas, 'are generally participles or adjectives used without any substantive to which they can be joined; and are therefore, in construction, considered as substantives... Such words compose the bulk of every language. In English those borrowed from the Latin, French and Italian are easily recognised... those from the Greek are more striking; because more unusual: but those which are original in our own language have been almost wholly overlooked, and are quite unsuspected. These words, these participles and adjectives, not understood as such, have caused a metaphysical jargon and a false morality, which can only be dissipated by etymology'.

Towards the end of the book there are signs that Tooke may have changed his opinion of the value of the classical languages. He regrets the lack of four participles (which he calls verb-adjectives) in English which exist as useful abbreviations in the classical tongues, viz. the potential active, potential passive, official passive and future active. These in English are provided by the respective suffixes ive or ic, able or ible, end or and, but for the last there is no English form due to the 'penury of our language'. 'Can anything be more lame and awkward, than our… About to be, about to come… is to be, is to come etc.?' The book closes with the hope '(if the time will bear it) to apply this system of language to all the different systems of metaphysical (i.e. verbal) imposture'.[40]

Tooke's Criticism of Others

Mackintosh assessed Tooke's attitude to his contemporaries in this way: 'As to praise, he confines it to a few of his own sycophants; he praises nobody that deserves it, except Rogers. His invectives against his age, his country and his literary contemporaries are not worthy of a wise or good man; his temper is soured, and his character corrupted by philosophy and disappointed ambition.'[41] The reader of the present biography will understand the latter from his struggles to be accepted as a lawyer and a member of Parliament, to say nothing of his imprisonment in King's Bench prison and the Tower.

Harris and Monboddo were especially singled out. 'As judges shelter their knavery by precedents, so do scholars their ignorance by authority; and when they cannot reason, it is safer and less disgraceful to repeat that nonsense at second hand which they would be ashamed to give originally as their own.' If Tooke's reader thought he had treated 'Harris, Monboddo and the common-sense Drs Oswald, Reid and Beattie with too much asperity… let him recollect how they had treated the vulgar, unlearned and atheistical Mr Locke'. Tooke claimed that Monboddo could not write a sentence of common English and 'if you reason directly contrary to Monboddo… you will generally be right'. Dr Lowth got short shrift. He wrote 'an elegant little treatise ... highly useful to ladies and gentlemen for their conversation and correspondence' while being 'much better acquainted with Greek and Latin than English'.[42]

The *Diversions* abounds in harsh criticism of Johnson, 'the first in fatuity'. However poor much of his etymology, Tooke gives him little credit for the comprehensive nature of his dictionary or the wealth of interesting quotations. In his pro-Government pamphlets, in common with many Augustan writers, Johnson distinguished between the educated gentleman and the vulgar. He considered universal truths alone were of interest, and that none but the cultured could appreciate them. Tooke castigated Johnson's contempt for the ignorant, entries in his dictionary for words such as stark, 'little used but in low language', and objected to his use of long, sonorous, Latin-based words. Johnson termed the vocabulary of labouring and mercantile people 'fugitive cant', wanted to ascertain the best usage and fix it beyond the reach of corruption by innovators and those who spoke incorrectly.[43]

Tooke condescendingly admitted that Johnson's merit ought not to be denied, but considered 'nearly one third of his dictionary is as much the language of the Hottentots as of the English... an idle performance... compiled by an author who possessed not one single requisite for the undertaking'. Tooke did not appreciate that Johnson's many examples of word usage enriched people's vocabulary. Burdett suggests consulting Johnson on 'right': 'He did not indeed acknowledge any "RIGHTS" of the people; but he was very clear concerning... the inherent, hereditary "RIGHTS" of Monarchy'. Tooke dissuades him (though for once Tooke and Johnson were in agreement on derivation): 'Seek no further for intelligence in that quarter; where nothing but fraud, and cant, and folly is to be found... because it has a sham appearance of labour, learning and piety'. However, although Tooke considered Johnson's dictionary the least valuable of his productions, he rejoiced that it was the most profitable, 'for I could never read his preface without shedding a tear'. Tooke could sometimes be fair. Though his criticism in the *Analytical Review* of a book by a rival philologist Rev. S. Henshall, who dubbed Tooke 'a venomous viper of democracy', exposed Henshall's conceit, it was plain, brief and moderate.[44]

Those he admired – Locke, the French grammarians and philosophers, the Bishop of St David's, his friend Dr Warner the classical scholar – he quoted with respect. He paid his friends compliments and acknowledged his gratitude for their generosity. He defended Dr Anthony Addington who had been misquoted by the authorities as saying that bran was more nutritious than meal.

Contemporary Criticism

Contemporary criticism almost unanimously praised the clarity and scholarship of the work but deplored Tooke's political posturing. The *Critical Review* objected to 'his remarks on the celebrated author of *Hermes*... influenced by some illiberal resentment of a political nature'. Bentham thought that a universal grammar would now be possible due to Tooke's 'discovery that... the relation which has place between certain till then incomprehensible parts of speech... and certain of the better understood has been brought to view'. Part II received even wider coverage than Part I. Leigh Hunt 'at first sight of it bade adieu to the leaden *Hermes* of Harris to admire the more vivacious, engaging and informative spirit of *The Diversions of Purley*'. Brougham thought that Tooke had made an amusing book from one of the driest subjects in literature or science. He had made important discoveries, but saw roots and derivations in everything and was inclined to think he had solved a metaphysical problem when he had only found the original meaning of a word. Satirists described old Tooke as having worn out his brain studying Gaelic, 'hoping to find the difference twixt why and wherefore' in a year's time. In one of Roberts's cartoons, Tooke presents his new *Botheration Dictionary* to Napoleon.[45]

The intelligentsia were dazzled by the novelty of Tooke's ideas. Erasmus Darwin was effusive. Tooke had 'unfolded by a single flash of light the whole theory of language, which has so long lain buried beneath the learned lumber of the schools'. The *Annual Review of Literature* thought it 'the most valuable contribution to the philosophy of language which our literature has produced'. On the other hand, the *Critical Review* of 1806 slated the work. 'The art which... is constructed is fallacious, the etymology is a deception, and the inferences... are absolute sophisms.' But it conceded that 'as an auxiliary to English grammar, and to the future compilers of English dictionaries, the epea pteroenta will afford valuable materials'.[46]

An article in the *Monthly Review*, said to be by Tooke's friend Richard Sharp, was laudatory but not uncritical. 'It is somewhat diverting to see the fierce patriot is tamed into the etymologist, though now and then the old spirit breaks through. If his manner of fighting is condemned, yet no one can dispute his claim to victory.' The author asked what had happened to the 'sage of Wimbledon's sagacity' when he claimed the reign of Saxon Athelstan was preferable to the present day. Tooke, who censured and laughed so freely had 'no right to complain' if others produced 'a little ridicule at his expense'. A later piece praised the 'unspeakable value' of the *Diversions*, but deplored 'the obtrusion of politics into this work... one of its most objectionable characteristics. An abstruse etymological enquiry cannot be the field in which [the ministers'] vices or their virtues should be blazoned.'[47]

One criticism was that Tooke would have saved himself unnecessary labour if he had made more general observations instead of producing a superabundance of proofs and footnotes. Tooke, however, thought that 'the generality of minds receive conviction more easily from a number of particular instances than from the surer but more abstracted arguments of general proof'. The *Quarterly Review* thought Tooke had attempted to raise a superstructure on inadequate foundations. Many reviewers praised the vigour of thought and depth of research, but wished Tooke had been less supercilious, abusive and overconfident. There were complaints of unnecessary appeals 'to the woods of Germany' and the book's excessive length. Another complaint was that Tooke deliberately adopted no clear-cut method and seemed in some respects to wish to conceal his aims. He did not give full explanations, and evaded awkward problems with personal sarcasm or witty epigrams.[48]

The *Anti-Jacobin*, which referred to Tooke as an unfrocked priest, carried a review suggesting that Tooke was more indebted to the work of previous scholars than he was willing to admit and poison had been 'infused by the quack politician'. 'Tooke has produced such contrary ideas on the verb and the noun that we are convinced his ideas are not made up.'[49]

Tooke had compared etymology to a microscope. His philology was acclaimed in fashionable scientific terminology; he had discovered that words were 'the machines used by the mind'. more powerful and useful 'than the lever, wheel or screw'. His philosophy received more adverse criticism, in particular the importance he assigned to etymology. Hazlitt greatly admired Tooke's philology but considered his philosophical theories 'downright, unqualified, unredeemed nonsense'. Mackintosh objected to his metaphyiscal reasoning. He thought Tooke's brand of nominalism confounded a science with its practical methods. The *Diversions* was a wonderful work of great originality, but Tooke's triumphant revelation of discoveries the rest of the human race had been too blind to make, and his petty tricks to entangle the reader, were worthy of a hierophant rather than a philosopher.[50]

Initially, Coleridge was as greatly impressed as other critics. In 1796, after Tooke's defeat in the election at Westminster, he wrote a poem praising Tooke and the *Diversions*:

> Patriot and Sage! whose breeze-like spirit first
> The lazy mists of Pedantry dispersed...
> Thy struggles soon shall wak'ning Britain bless
> And Truth and Freedom hail thy wish'd success.

The breeze-like spirit referred to Tooke's 'winged words'. He suggested to Godwin that he should 'write a book on the power of words and the processes by which human feelings form affinities with them - in short I wish you to philosophise Horne Tooke's system,' but showing 'that words are things and living things too'.[51]

Later, Coleridge became more conservative, both philosphically and politically. In 1830 he called 'Epea Pteroenta' hasty words and thought that all that was worth anything '(and that is but little)' in the *Diversions* was contained in 'A Letter to Mr Dunning'. Though enlarged to an octavo and a quarto volume, the only additions were lampoons. Coleridge explained that it showed a 'base and unpoetical mind to convert so beautiful, so divine, a subject as language into the vehicle... of political squibs'.[52]

Only radicals openly accepted the political aspects of the *Diversions*. Reviewers either did not immediately grasp the political implications of Tooke's arguments, or dismissed them as irrelevant to a study of language. People found the mixture difficult to appreciate. Tooke's teasing method of presentation did not help. Holofernes complained in the *Morning Chronicle* that he 'contrives to force an Oxford Tory or a Cambridge time server to swallow a great dose of Wimbledon politics when he opens his mouth to ask what's the meaning of that'.[53]

There was widespread condemnation of the disgraceful 'offensive, factious rubbish' in the enlarged 1798 edition of Part I. Even Tooke's friends and followers objected. 'One grieves to find the same memorials of personal and political altercation which disgraced the former edition. They exhibit strong and disgusting indications of a perverse, acrimonious and vindictive spirit; yet in private life Tooke... is a most entertaining and agreeable companion.'[54] When Part II appeared there were regrets that Tooke could not be reclaimed from his old habits, though, as the climate was slightly more tolerant, some welcomed the game of guessing what the blanks represented as light relief from long lists of derivations.

Dugald Stewart was the major critic of the *Diversions*. He protested that, by throwing an air of mystery over the subtle thread of his arguments and 'amusing the imagination with the prospect of a wonderful secret' to be revealed later, Tooke gave 'to his truly learned and original disquisitions a degree of celebrity among the smatterers of science which they would never have acquired if stated concisely and systematically in a didactic form'.[55]

Stewart disagreed with Tooke's thesis that each individual word in a sentence had its own, invariable meaning, and that the meaning of the whole sentence could only be understood from an understanding, through etymology, of each word. Instead, Stewart asserted that the meaning of each word depended on the context and that many had none apart from it. 'Our words, when examined separately, are often as completely insignificant as the letters of which they are composed.' Words such as of, by and from are listed in Johnson's dictionary with 40 or more meanings, yet small children can understand perfectly well the sentences in which they occur, without any knowledge of etymology. Stewart maintained therefore that language cannot be the precise image of thought. Words merely supply hints to the reader, or suggest a train of ideas, 'leaving by far the principal part of the process of interpretation to be performed by the mind itself'.[56]

Stewart considered that Tooke had made two errors, extremely common even among the best philosphers. He had confounded 'the historical progress of an art with its theoretical principles when advanced to maturity', and he considered language to be 'a much more exact picture of thought than it is in any state of society'. Tooke's speculations did not 'relate... to the analysis of a language after it has assumed a... systematical form, but to the gradual steps by which it proceeds to that state from the... jargon of savages'.[57] Thus Stewart disagreed with Tooke's basic materialist hypothesis that the business of the mind is merely the operation of language.

Stewart complained that Tooke had availed himself of a philological hypothesis based on inconclusive evidence to decide in a few sentences... one of the most important questions connected with the theory of morals. The allocation of the same word to denote a straight line and moral rectitude of conduct was in every language he knew and could be satisfactorily explained without founding the theory of morality on a... nostrum concerning past participles.[58] Stewart did not comment overtly on the political aspect of the *Diversions*, but his essay is clearly based on a political attitude diametrically opposite to that of Tooke.

Contemporary Influence

Tooke's speculations awakened a keen interest in philology. He had many disciples, and many grammars were produced founded on new principles. Hazlitt published the first in 1810, which incorporates Tooke's ideas. The distinguished grammarian Noah Webster hailed his discoveries. Tooke, however, had left his investigation incomplete: 'I shall pursue it'. Charles Richardson was an enthusiastic exponent of the *Diversions*, which form the lexicographical basis of his extremely successful *New Dictionary of the English Language*, published in 1837. His *Illustrations of English Philology*, a critical examination of Johnson's *Dictionary* and Dugald Stewart's contrary ideas, also included many of Tooke's arguments.[59]

Godwin rewrote his essay on literature in the second edition of the *Enquirer* to explain his appreciation of earlier works such as the *Diversions*. *Political Justice* especially shows Tooke's influence. Godwin, who decried the use of rhetoric, wished to emphasise that he was a searcher after plain truth, concerned with accuracy of language and the primary meaning of words. In addition, he elaborated Tooke's ideas on aristocractic imposture and Tooke's perception that institutions had the power to infiltrate the very nature of thought.[60]

The *Advertisement to the Lyrical Ballads* (1798) was written during Coleridge's first flush of enthusiam for Tooke and the *Diversions*. 'The majority [of the ballads] were written chiefly to ascertain how far the language of conversation in the middle and lower classes of society was adapted to the purpose of poetic pleasure.' These poems mark a new direction in English literature.

The *Diversions*, with its thesis that all words were really names of sensations, gave a great boost to materialist philosphy. Tooke's matter-of-fact method appealed to Bentham and his Utilitarian followers. They believed that the vested interests which controlled society for their own ends contaminated not only politics but language itself. Bentham intended to write an essay on relations between thought and language and to include 'The discoveries half concealed or left imperfected by Tooke'.[61]

James Mill, who had analysed and discussed the *Diversions* in the *Literary Journal* in 1806, had enormous enthusiasm for the light Tooke had shed on the subject of language. In his *Analysis of the Phenomena of the Human Mind*, a psychological rather than a philosphical work published in 1829, he incorporated a large proportion of Tooke's theories of the origins of parts of speech and abstractions. He followed Tooke in believing that the presence of different words for the same object was a barrier to philosophic accuracy. Another of Tooke's admirers, Thomas Belsham, quoted him in his manual on Hartleyan logic, psychology and morals. Tooke's influence on Mill and Belsham promoted the Utilitarians' resuscitation of Hartley's associationist psychology.[62]

Peacock thought highly of the *Diversions* which he had read when a young man. He quoted from the *Diversions* – e.g. *Headlong Hall*, chapter 7 – and in his early novels introduced dramatic dialogue based on people assembling for dinner parties as at Wimbledon. Lady Bessborough's letter to Earl Granville is an example of a general reader's reaction: 'I am reading a strange book. It is impudent, ingenious, indecent and entertaining – that is, its extreme ingenuity and sometimes its impudence amuses, when its coarseness and indelicacy does not disgust or too long a list of words tire... Told in dialogue between Tooke and Sir Francis Burdett as you may imagine nothing is wanting... that may set his republican doctrine in the strongest light.'[63]

Diversions Outmoded

John Fearn, an undistinguished philosopher, published *Anti-Tooke* in 1824 which criticised Tooke's etymological logic. John Barclay followed this, in *The Sequel to the Diversions of Purley* (1826), with an extension of his work but with some adverse criticism. By 1840, the tide began to turn. *Blackwood's*, which was anyhow opposed to radical thought, in reviewing the new edition said that the *Diversions*, a fallacious and frivolous book, was full of blunders. 'It is with a mixture of mirth and amazement that we look back to the position it used to occupy; when even those who felt it to be wrong and ridiculous, could only qualify themselves to appear as its opponents by first paying homage to its ingenuity and learning.'[64]

That Tooke's work fell out of repute was due largely to the discovery of the importance of Sanskrit by Sir William Jones. His work was taken up more rapidly in Germany than in Britain; indeed, Aarsleff considers that Tooke's reputation kept England immune from the new philology until the new results and methods were imported from the continent in the 1830s.[65] Knowledge of a wider range of foreign languages led to development of a new science of comparative philology by the German school, particularly by Bopp and Grimm. Many of Tooke's derivations had been based on inadequate knowledge, particularly of old Teutonic languages, and were often made to fit his preconceived ideas. Tooke was not sufficiently scholarly, being too interested in the hurly-burly of daily life and political agitation to take a detached view. Perhaps he burned Part III because he was losing confidence in his work.

In his lectures on the science of language, Max Mueller said 'The true nature of grammatical terminations was first pointed out [by Tooke] who, however wild some of his speculations, caught many a glimpse of the real life and growth of language'. The *Diversions* showed 'how a man of clear, sharp and powerful mind… may yet, owing to his defective knowledge of facts, arrive at conclusions directly opposed to the truth'.[66] Although Tooke was inevitably circumscribed by his place and date of birth, he had the perception to work on the lines where advances were being made. Tooke's important contribution to the development of linguistic ideas was to emphasise the objectivity of language as distinct from its subjective existence as a means of personal expression. His work was one of the factors that led to renewed interest in the Anglo-Saxon origins of English, and to acceptance of the vernacular as a proper mode of expression. He struck a powerful blow against the restriction of verbal ability to a narrow class, and helped to give the common man a more important place in the intellectual and political life of the country.

Notes on Chapter 13

General note: unless otherwise stated, all references are from *Diversions* I, II, London 1840 and 'A Letter to Mr Dunning' (bound in the same volume) (ed. R. Taylor). This later edition has the advantage of including Tooke's extreme political comments in Part II which were excised from the original edition.

1 *Blackwood's Edinburgh Magazine* XLVII, 1840, p 484
2 TS11/956/3501
3 Locke III, ch. 1
4 Locke III, ch. 7
5 Locke III, ch. 2
6 Locke III, ch. 10
7 Beattie, p 101; Condillac, E.
8 Harris, *Hermes*, p 423; Lowth, introduction
9 Adamson, p 43
10 I, pp 3-4; 'A Letter to Mr Dunning', p 693
11 I, p 50
12 I, p 107; I, p 25
13 I, p 19; Aarsleff, p 53
14 Mackintosh II, p 232; *DOP* I, p 6
15 II, p 389; I, p 170; I, p 84
16 Burnet, James (Lord Monboddo) II, p 313
17 II, pp 674-5
18 II, p 505
19 II, p 403
20 II, pp 604-8
21 II, p 389
22 'A Letter to Mr Dunning', p 721
23 II, p 335; II, p 495
24 I, pp 51, 24, 13-4

25 I, pp 52-3, 70-217, 221
26 I, p 37
27 I, p 38; *State Trials* 1777, p 789, *ibid.*, p 766
28 I, p 44; 'A Letter to Mr Dunning', pp 685, 686; I, pp 41-2
29 I, p 48
30 I, pp 52, 56
31 I, pp 100-15
32 I, pp 171-82; I, p 293
33 I, p 234; I, p 109
34 I, p 288
35 I, pp 141-2
36 I, Additional Notes, pp xii, 82, 122-33
37 Fox, C.J. III, p 143; Add MS 47573f13 February 1798
38 II, pp 403-4
39 II, pp 301-13
40 II, pp 650-84
41 Mackintosh, see ref. 14
42 I, p 62; 'A Letter to Mr Dunning', pp 709-23; II, pp 366, 655
43 II, p 507; I, p 286; Preface to Johnson's *Dictionary*
44 I, p 119; II, p 303; *Analytical Review* pp 28, 360, 1798
45 *Critical Review* 1786, pp 57-60, 62; Bentham, *Works* VIII, p 185; Leigh Hunt, *The Examiner* 5 April 1812; Brougham, *Historical Sketches* III, p 144; Anon., *Sir Frantic*, p 1809; George, M.D., 9893 (1802)
46 Darwin I, p 531; *Annual Review of Literature* 1805, V, pp 675-9; *Critical Review* 1806, VII, pp 67-375; *Eclectic Review* 1806 II, pp 245-361
47 *Monthly Review* 1787, LXXVI, pp 1-13; *ibid.* 1798, XXVII, pp 423-31
48 I, p 69; *Quarterly Review* 1812, VII, p 313
49 *Anti-Jacobin* II, p 38; III p 383, 1799
50 *Monthly Review* Dec. 1798, p 423; Hazlitt, *Works* XI, p 119; Mackintosh II, p 230
51 Coleridge, *Poetical Works*, p 65; *Letters* CLI, p 625
52 Coleridge, *Omniana*, p 340, *Table Talk* 7.5.1830
53 *Morning Chronicle* May 13, p 1807
54 Green, T., p 66 9.3.1798
55 Stewart V, p 159
56 Stewart IV, pp 154-5; pp 25-7; Aarsleff, pp 103-5
57 Stewart IV, pp 38-9; V, p 160
58 Stewart V, p 161; pp 159-60n
59 Webster, N., *Letter to Dr Ramsay*; Richardson, Charles, *On the Study of Language*
60 Godwin, *The Enquirer: Enquiry Concerning Political Justice*
61 Bentham, *Chrestomathia*, pp 258-395

62 Mill, James; Belsham, p xxiv
63 Gower, *Letters* II, p 137, 28.11.1805
64 Blackwood's *Edinburgh Magazine* XLVII, 1840, p 496; Fearn, J.
65 Aarsleff, p 73
66 Mueller I, p 291

Chapter Fourteen

Social Life; More Westminster Politics

In October 1802 William Tooke died on his Norfolk estate aged 83. This resulted in the most squalid episode in Tooke's life, a typical saga of capricious testator and disappointed legatee. William Tooke had grown doddery, forgetful and ever-more parsimonious. Like so many old people, he changed his mind. He made several wills. By his last one he left the bulk of his estate to his nephew Harwood and his great-nephew Beaseley, and only £500 to Horne Tooke, though he cancelled a mortgage of £700 plus 14 years' interest on his house. In view of Tooke's expectations, the three of them agreed verbally to share the estate equally. When the time came to settle the will, Harwood changed his mind and denied having made the agreement. Meanwhile Horne Tooke had obtained an advance from Burdett to cover annuities for his daughters. When Harwood refused to pay, Burdett sued and Harwood counterclaimed in Chancery. Ultimately, in 1812, after the law's customary delays, Lord Eldon found in favour of Burdett. As so often with disputed wills, the story does not make pleasant reading.[1]

In spite of William Tooke's disappointing legacy, Tooke was now comfortably off. Rogers compared his life to a calm October sunset. In contrast to some successful men who founder in old age, Tooke, who had failed to achieve a satisfactory career, had become a famous – or notorious – public figure. He was regarded as an oracle and venerated for his sufferings by the shrunken phalanx of reformers. His courteous, slightly old-fashioned manners gave him distinction. He was still asked for legal advice. He had Burdett's companionship, and through him vicariously continued to dabble in politics. Bar three attacks of gallstones his health improved, and he had occasional bursts of great activity, though he would jocularly warn his friends, if they congratulated him on this, that 'the enemy was upon him', and sure enough he would soon suffer an acute attack of gout. Tooke believed that jolting was good for the human frame as it tended to remove obstructions. He did not keep his own carriage, but when he thought he was in need of shaking up he would hire a postchaise, cross Putney Bridge and order the postillion to drive up and down the roughest streets for a couple of hours.[2]

Samuel Miller, whose father was a shoemaker, a member of the LCS and a friend of Tooke's, gave Brougham a vivid description of life at Wimbledon where he often stayed for a week or more from the age of twelve. Tooke spent hours in his garden working or propped against his spade talking to visitors. He had water laid on in pipes divided by cocks six yards apart. When troubled with gout he would lean on Samuel as he went from one cock to another to water the flowers. He ate breakfast separately at a reading desk. Afterwards his favourite cat would climb on his shoulder to drink milk. Tooke remained in his study for the rest of the morning working on the *Diversions*. After dinner, Samuel used to help him to a recess in the garden and read *The Arabian Nights* tales in French, at which Tooke would laugh heartily. One night at supper Samuel gave an involuntary laugh. Tooke's elder daughter Mary objected, 'It is very rude to laugh'. 'Oh,' said Tooke, 'He is laughing at the story of the hunchback,' which was true. 'He was always cheerful and quite playful with us boys, that is Mr Courtenay the barrister, William Scott and myself.'[3]

As his life became more circumscribed, Tooke, benevolent despot of his household, held unchallenged sway at Wimbledon. He could quell discussion of a topic he wished dropped by his manner alone, but he was delighted if people appreciated his company. As all the best conversation should be, Tooke's was hardly ever completely serious. Long acute observation of the world, encounters with many outstanding personalities, had provided him with a fund of information and anecdote which he could relate with skill, brevity and fluency, but was not forced on an unwilling audience. He never bored and only embellished the truth for heightened effect. Tooke may have laughed at the world to compensate for his lack of power in it, but his judgements on politicians, though carping, were shrewd and entertaining. If his portraits were caricatures they 'bore a striking and amusing resemblance to the originals'.[4]

Several close friends were already Whig MPs. Grattan entered the Commons in 1805 and a year later Richard Sharp did the same. Old acquaintances reappeared. In 1802 Barlow travelled to Britain for a brief business visit. At first he lay low: 'I knew if I broke loose among my democratic friends I could not avoid running the gauntlet of all their dinners, getting my name in the papers, and becoming an object of jealousy with the government'. Later the same year he spent longer in London, and renewed his friendship with Tooke.[5]

Tooke's version of past events was sometimes rather fanciful, and, whether done with tongue in cheek or not, there were changes in the emphasis he laid on his opinions. His enemies dubbed it whitewashing. In Part II of the *Diversions*, Tooke declared, 'I tremble at the very name of reform. Bosville and I have entered into a strict engagement to belong for ever to the established government, to the established church, and to the established language of our country: because they are established. Establish what you please... and, whilst that establishment shall last we shall be perfectly convinced of its propriety.'[6]

Tooke believed princes had been wise to promote the crusades which rid them of their tiresome nobility. Nations were most servile 'when the secular and ecclesiastical powers were united in the same person, as no degree of absurdity then appeared too gross'. Would anyone have believed Herodotus if he had written of 'a boy-god surrounded by priests, who sold pastils composed of his excrements to his infatuated worshippers who... devoured them?' Yet this was true of the Dalai Lama, to whom Hastings had sent an embassy.[7]

Godwin, hypersensitive and distressed by his waning intellectual reputation, created scenes with his faithful friends over imagined slights. In December 1803, he left Tooke's house in a fury because he was not shown upstairs immediately. His letter of complaint has not been preserved, but Godwin kept Tooke's reply which shows what a forbearing and helpfully critical friend he could be. For once, Tooke answered promptly: 'I return an immediate answer, that you may not have an uneasy… moment by my fault. What happened… to you… happens to every one of my friends… every day.' Tooke explained that Bosville and three of his friends had been chatting to Tooke in his study. When they left, Tooke discussed important business with William Scott. At this point Godwin arrived. Tooke sent word that he would soon dress and come down. Bosville returned, mentioned that Godwin was in the garden and 'I immediately begged them to call to you out of the window… I had quite forgot that you were there. You… ought to be ashamed of such womanish jealousy.'[8]

Hoppner thought Tooke had no feeling for poetry or painting. There is no record of which painters Tooke admired. He had little money to acquire paintings and despised those who went abroad merely to acquire artistic souvenirs of dubious merit. Tooke frequently quoted from Horace and Virgil. His favourite poets were Spenser, Chaucer and Milton, all unfashionable at the time. He relished the plays of Ben Johnson, with whom he had an affinity. Tooke believed that Shakespeare, whom he started to read at the age of seven, understood the innermost recesses of the heart, the springs of human action. His works were the best from which to learn the duties of private life. 'There is a tune in all good prose, and Shakespeare's was a sweet one.' Hoppner also complained that Tooke introduced 'stories of a gross nature, told in a vulgar manner… when the subject of conversation does not lead to it', but he cannot have found them too distasteful, as he frequently dined at Wimbledon.[9]

Tooke thought one of the great evils of the times the lack of a rational occupation for 'our opulent youth' who, when they left school and college, had nothing to do, so spent their time with pugilists, their money on wagers, and were only learned in the pedigree of a horse. Formerly, when they travelled to Paris and Rome, if they acquired nothing more than the languages, these were 'inlets of human reason. The mere sight of foreign countries, too, enlarges the ideas of the inhabitants of a little island… apt to undervalue strangers.'[10]

Tooke was eager to encourage talented young men. Before Humphry Davy's reputation was established, Tooke formed a high opinion of his abilities and once more enlisted Dr Pearson to bring him to Wimbledon. Tooke was so impressed by Davy that he promptly commissioned Chantrey to model his head. Tooke and Chantrey had a warm regard for each other. The first successful work Chantrey undertook was a brilliant head of Tooke which served as a good advertisement for his work.[11]

Westminster Election of 1806

When Pitt died in January 1806, Grenville and Fox combined to form the Ministry of All the Talents. The Grenvilles were notorious sinecurists, opposed to both economic and parliamentary reform, but the Foxites outnumbered them two to one so many liberals had high hopes of the new administration. Fox had denounced Grenville's politics for many years, and Tooke considered this alliance a piece of opportunism on a par with the North coalition. Almost all reformers became disenchanted when Fox introduced a bill enabling Lord Grenville, First Lord of the Treasury, to retain a sinecure office as Auditor. Though they did not publicise the fact, the Foxites intended to shelve reform, an unrealistic and hopelessly unpopular objective in wartime, and concentrate on efforts to end the war.

Burdett wrote to his chaplain that he believed, 'and so does Tooke, that peace will be made, because it must, and a base and dishonourable one it will be'. He had a political scheme to support and avenge the oppressed and expose the mean and selfish: 'but I must not commit my thought to paper until matured by conversation with the Wizard of Wimbledon'.[12] After Austerlitz, Napoleon was triumphant; Fox's negotiations failed and he too died in September 1806.

An election was called that autumn after the death of Fox, and Burdett agreed to stand for Middlesex again. His election address at the beginning of November caused a furore. He attacked the memory of Fox by saying 'Whenever the Leaders of contending parties... unite... it is... always at the expense of the people... Neither of the parties will descend to particulars, and inform you what [they] have... done, or will... do, for you. What they have done for themselves we know and feel.' Burdett announced that he would stand as popular independent, and would spend no money on his election. This was greeted with derision: Burdett now setting himself up as Coriolanus because he had been convicted of bribery at the last election, and could not afford such largesse again.[13]

The Middlesex freeholders passed resolutions supporting both Burdett and Byng, the other sitting member, who this time refused to combine with Burdett. The Foxites were in a quandary when asked to support the third candidate Mellish, a crony of 'Cold Baths' Mainwaring, instead of Burdett. Lord Holland wrote to Grey that this would be 'playing Horne Tooke's game and turning over all our real interest in the community to him or to opposition'. Burdett found himself opposed on the hustings by Byng, backed by the Foxites. This culminated in an exchange of letters in the press with Whitbread, who challenged him to a duel which Burdett refused.[14] With both coalition party machines and resources against him Burdett was heavily defeated.

Tooke was blamed for Burdett's refusal of Whitbread's challenge 'which did him great harm'. Lord John Townshend said it was Tooke's system. Long ago at a Westminster election, when Tooke was attacked at a great dinner, Tooke said in a most threatening tone, 'Take care Sir. I here publicly declare that nothing shall ever make me fight – after which avowal every man who values his own character will avoid insulting me lest he should be suspected of picking out the person whom he may venture to abuse with impunity.'[15] Tooke must have been delighted that Burdett had irretrievably broken with the Whigs. Their newspaper the *Morning Chronicle* pitied Burdett, 'who beyond the age of pupillage, can descend to the channel through which another man's venom shall be distributed'.[16]

The Westminster election of 1806 began a week earlier than Middlesex. Sir Samuel Hood, another naval hero and nephew of the Viscount Hood who had represented the constituency earlier, was the Tory candidate, Sheridan the Whig. The radicals, determined to fight the Whig/Tory pact, eventually chose James Paull as independent contender. Son of a Perth tailor, he became a prosperous merchant in Oudh. He returned from India in 1804 determined to get Lord Wellesley, with whom he had quarrelled, impeached for misconduct as Governor General. Paull was in his mid-thirties, a rough, suspicious man who had partially lost the use of his right arm in a duel. The Foxites refused to proceed against Wellesley who was a friend of the Grenvilles. In disgust, Paull turned to the radicals. Burdett nominated Paull and contributed towards his election expenses. Burdett, Cartwright, Bosville and Cobbett, plus many of Tooke's supporters at previous elections, canvassed for Paull. Tooke told Paull that if he were not so decrepit he too would have canvassed through the streets.[17]

There were now about 20,000 eligible voters in Westminster. In the past many had not bothered to vote. Since Tooke first set an example when he stood in 1790, the number turning out to vote had increased due to discontent with harsh wartime conditions and greater political awareness. This time nearly 15,000 votes were cast. Hood and Sheridan got in, but Paull was only 300 votes behind.

While the Westminster radicals backed Paull in a petition challenging Sheridan's election on grounds of bribery, Burdett told the Middlesex electors that he would not contend the seat again while the coalition was in power, and retired to sort out his affairs. Not only had he spent large sums of money on political campaigns, he had inherited estates encumbered with debt and had generously given money to others. He and Tooke devised a plan of retrenchment. Burdett made a will dated 2 May 1807 appointing his brother Jones and his solicitor joint agents to execute the plan. They were to consult 'That trusty, able and beloved friend Horne Tooke upon all and every part of my concerns until my estates are quite cleared'. Unlike Tooke's previous attempt to help Bernard, his plan and advice proved admirable and within a few years Burdett's finances were on a sound footing.[18]

In March 1807, the King dismissed his ministers when they refused to guarantee that they would not make further proposals to remove Catholic disabilities, so another election was held in May. The men who had promoted Paull's candidature decided to contest the seat again. This group, which was not a formal body, became known as the Westminster Committee, very different in composition from the one dominated by Fox and Jebb in the eighties. There were about 26 members, mainly small tradesmen, including several of Tooke's former SCI and LCS colleagues. Most information about the 1807 Westminster election comes from Francis Place who kept detailed records. In general Place is accurate, but he played down his role in the last years of the LCS and exaggerated his own importance in Westminster politics.

Initially the Westminster Committee hoped to run Paull with Burdett, a candidate with far more weight, though it is doubtful if Place wanted to back Paull if he could get Burdett. It is not clear what Burdett's initial intentions or Tooke's real wishes were. Tooke apparently thought that, after Burdett's failure at Middlesex, there was no point in wasting his energy in contending seats where he could not succeed without bribery or corrupt influence. The previous autumn, Paull had been deputed to invite Burdett to succeed Fox at Westminster. Burdett had said that he must consult Tooke and his brother. He had then declined.[19]

While negotiations continued between the Committee, Burdett, Paull and Tooke, Burdett drew up an address to the Middlesex freeholders, published on 29 April, stating that in the 'desperate situation of our affairs' he would not be a candidate for any constituency. The same day, Burdett received from Paull an advance copy of an advertisement announcing that Burdett would chair a dinner meeting to launch Paull's candidature. Paull assumed that, as Burdett had done this the previous autumn, he would be willing to do so again. Burdett was furious. He wrote from Tooke's house protesting that, having declared he had determined 'not to do anything, even for [his] own election', he would lay himself open to charges of inconsistency if he took part in anyone else's.[20]

In the afternoon Place and William Adams, an ex-LCS member who had canvassed for Tooke, trudged out to Wimbledon to interview Burdett. He reiterated that he had told Paull he would not be a candidate and had objected to his name being billed in connection with the dinner. However, when asked if he would accept the seat if returned without his interference, he replied, 'Certainly, this is the right way: electors ought to seek representatives, not candidates solicit electors'. Furthermore, he would 'not spend a guinea nor do anything whatever to contribute to such an election'.[21]

Since Paull had publicly announced that Burdett had agreed to a joint ticket, Burdett's statement that he did not wish to stand cast doubts on Paull's veracity. On 1 May Paull drove in a fury to Burdett's house at Wimbledon. When Burdett refused to apologise, he challenged him to a duel. Smarting under the accusation of cowardice for not accepting Whitbread's challenge, Burdett agreed. The next morning they wounded each other in the leg, then travelled back to London in Paull's carriage. Cline insisted that Burdett must be kept absolutely quiet and receive no communication from the outside world, so for the next fortnight he did not know what was happening.[22]

The following evening, three days before the poll opened, a public meeting reminiscent of the break-up of the SSBR took place. Paull's supporters shouted down Place and his friends, who retired to another room where, respecting Burdett's and Tooke's conditions, they resolved to return Burdett 'free from every sacrifice and expense to himself, upon independent principles, consonant to the genuine spirit of the constitution of England'. A subscription was opened to cover expenses. Nearly £100 was raised immediately, to which Tooke added another £100.[23]

It is impossible now to get to the bottom of the affair. Contemporaries who took up the cudgels on behalf of the protagonists conceded that there were faults on both sides. After the duel, nearly all Paull's committee deserted him and transferred their allegiance to Burdett. Patterson concludes from this that the committee must have been convinced that Paull was a liar and prevaricator and not to be trusted. Paull was known to be in debt and having great difficulty in paying for his election expenses. The following year he lost 1,600 guineas in a gaming house in an attempt to recoup his finances and the next day committed suicide.[24]

Although Tooke was not present at some of the crucial meetings, his influence was considerable. Tooke either genuinely did not want Burdett to stand for Parliament again, or wanted to ensure that, if he stood, he should be backed by a sufficient number of electors to avoid a repetition of his crushing defeat at Middlesex. On his own, Burdett's chances were higher. Tooke had a far more devious personality than Burdett. Having decided that Paull was unscrupulous and only wanted Burdett as joint candidate to trade on his popularity and his purse, Tooke may well have determined to get rid of him by whatever means came to hand. The reasons for Tooke's increasing lack of enthusiasm for Burdett's parliamentary career are obscure. It must have been clear to him that Burdett had far more influence in Parliament than out. Yet in January 1811, four years after Burdett had been elected MP, Tooke was advising Burdett to resign his seat 'as he had often done before'.[25]

The election began on 7 May. There were three candidates besides Paull and Burdett. The Ministry fielded a weaker candidate than in the past, Elliott, a brewer. Sheridan stood for the Whigs, a sad figure, drunken and in debt. Lord Cochrane also stood as an independent. He was an able, colourful personality and naval hero. Although highly critical of the Government, he had little interest in parliamentary reform, his platform being naval abuses. Before the split with Paull, Cochrane had told Burdett that if he did not stand, Cochrane would, and Burdett had welcomed the idea. Cochrane made tentative approaches to the radicals, but they mistrusted him and were unwilling to form a coalition.

The Committee relied for election expenses on subscriptions from individual voters, mostly donations of a few shillings collected by volunteers who traversed the city rounding up electors. The final result was a triumph for Burdett, which was announced to him by a deputation on 23 May. He polled 5,134, Cochrane 3,708, Sheridan 2,645, Elliott 2,137. Both Elliott and Paull, who only received 269 votes, retired before the end. Paull's former election was said to have cost £6,000. This time Cochrane spent several thousands, the Committee only £780.

Directly Burdett had been elected, the High Bailiff put in his bill for £325/15/0. Following Tooke's action in 1796, the Committee refused to pay. Place wanted Burdett to plead that he had not been a candidate since he was elected without his participation. A case was brought before Lord Ellenborough in February 1808. Burdett, on Tooke's advice, employed Clifford as counsel. He argued that Burdett repudiated liability on a principle which Tooke had long maintained: an MP had the right to be elected, and should only be charged for the expense of administering oaths. Lord Ellenborough ruled that Burdett should be considered a candidate as he took his seat. He reduced Burdett's liability to £117/8/2, the cost of administering oaths, plus one fifth of the cost of the hustings for which Burdett's committee had accepted tickets. This was really a verdict against the bailiff and overruled his contention that, even if there had been no agreement with the candidates, he was entitled to recover all costs. The Government, who supported the bailiff, then passed an act making candidates in Westminster liable for the hire of clerks and polling booths. There were wrangles at ensuing elections, and the complex problem was not solved until 1828 when an act was passed putting cities and boroughs on the same footing as counties.

Place complained bitterly at Tooke's, Burdett's and Clifford's handling of the case. He claimed that 'Burdett gladly followed Tooke's advice', given at a Sunday dinner, 'to have as little intercourse with the Committee as possible and cut them on every convenient occasion'. Tooke probably wanted Burdett to maintain his independence and not to be under any obligation to a group of tradesmen. Possibly Clifford mishandled the case, but Tooke and Clifford had far more knowledge of the law than the Committee. They wanted to establish what was practicable. Pressed by Place, who believed that judgement would have been completely in their favour if all the evidence had been produced, they appointed an attorney to help, but he too resisted Place's interference. It is unfortunate that the only detailed account is Place's, simmering with resentment at upper-class disdain. He cited Tooke's objection to making elections too cheap, 'lest every blackguard should become a candidate', as evidence that the trio had 'deliberately cooked up a defence with intent to lose the action, yet say they had defended the rights of the people'.[26]

This was the first election in which public opinion successfully opposed party faction, a crack in the dominance of the Court and great landlords. It was also the first time that artisans and tradesmen combined with members of the professional classes to formulate policy and succeeded in exerting a modicum of power. All the same, the importance of this contest and the credit due to the Committee should not be overrated. A smaller number of voters turned out than at the previous election. In November Paull, without such efficient backing, had gained nearly as many votes as Burdett did in May. Cochrane, to whom little attention was paid, polled a large number of votes, about half Government and half opposition. Maybe some electors had become accustomed to vote for a naval hero, but evidently a majority of Westminster voters would now support any independent candidate in preference to those put up by the Whigs or Tories. It was the culmination of a process which Tooke had initiated and Paull continued. There was no parallel to the Westminster result elsewhere. The main election issue had been the King's treatment by the Ministry of all the Talents. The Tories got back with a huge majority and remained in power for the next 23 years.

Notes on Chapter 14

1 William Tooke's will and chancery suit are covered in Burdett papers Bodleian MSS Eng. Hist. B, pp 197, 198, C 292, 293, Eng. Lett. D, p 97; Law Report 2 Sim 192; Revised Law Reports, ed. Sir F. Pollock 1897 XXIX, p 81; Stephens II, pp 44, 269-77, 414; Patterson I, pp 125-8
2 Stephens II, p 440
3 Brougham MS 6211
4 *Quarterly Review* June 1812, p 327
5 Stephens II, pp 329-30; Todd, pp 192-3; 1886; Woodress, pp 224-33
6 *DOP* II, p 666
7 Stephens II, p 398
8 Paul, C.K., II, pp 105, 144
9 Stephens II, pp 430-4; *DOP* II, p 345; Farington II, p 545
10 Stephens II, pp 354-5
11 Stephens II, p 327; Jones, p 8
12 Burdett MSS Eng. Lett. D 97 f125, D 40 f4-5
13 Patterson, pp 182-3; Add MS 27850 f23
14 Add MS 51544 f44-5, 2.11.1806; Patterson, p 186
15 Gower, *Correspondence* II, pp 223, 232
16 *Morning Chronicle* 31 October 1806
17 Stephens II, pp 317-9; Dictionary of National Biography, Paull
18 Burdett MSS Eng. Hist. A q f56
19 Add. MS 27850 f41
20 Add. MS 27850 f46; 27838 f11-14; Patterson, p 196, Tooke Letter to *Times* 11.5.07
21 Add. MS 27850 f46-7, p 82; 27817 f105
22 Add. MS 27850 f57-8; Patterson, pp 201-6
23 Add. MS 27850 f68-73; Patterson, pp 207-8
24 Patterson, p 195
25 Stephens II, p 410
26 Add MS 27850 f86-105

Chapter Fifteen

Last Years

Tooke's health was deteriorating. Although crippled by rheumatism and confined to his house and garden, he never complained. He derived great happiness from his friends, his family, his home and his books. He became abstemious, but retained his hearty appetite. He was now rather bald and combed his grey hair loosely over his forehead. Although his robust frame had shrunk, he trundled himself adeptly about in a black bath-chair which Jones Burdett had given him.[1]

In January 1808 Tooke appeared to be dying. Burdett spent hours at his bedside, neglected his parliamentary duties, and failed to attend several important Westminster meetings. By November Tooke was able to sit up and chat to a few close friends who called daily; by Christmas he was better, but never regained his former vigour and fell ill again the following August. Burdett wrote to thank his wife for sending venison, at his request, 'to my dear Tooke, who I now fear will never get up again – I really grow quite out of heart about him. Whenever he dies, an able, injured, undauntedly honest man is lost to the Country, whose character will… be an honour and reproach to it. I shall have the melancholy satisfaction of having done him justice, and the never-ceasing recollection of his irretrievable loss.'[2]

Tooke still approved of the new regime in France. Napoleon had decided to incorporate Spain and Portugal into the

Continental System aimed against Britain. When the French invaded, plans were made to hold public protest meetings. Stephens was approached to enlist Tooke's support, as his name and connections would help make the scheme popular. He invited Tooke to dinner with one of the organisers. Long before a suitable moment occurred to broach the subject, Tooke brought it up himself and, to Stephens's dismay, launched into a diatribe against the Spaniards, 'so degenerate ... every change must be for the better'. Only the sword of a more enlightened nation could dispel so despicable and perfidious a reliance on popery and priestcraft. The banners of the holy office were to be unfolded on the side of liberty, and the inquisition was to raise a regiment to combat on its behalf: 'foolish – ridiculous – execrable!'[3]

Between bouts of illness, Tooke made a few last incursions into politics. One cause in which Tooke was much concerned was the affair of seat prices at Covent Garden. The theatre had been burnt to the ground and was reopened in September 1809. All seat prices were raised, and it contained more private boxes with their own separate entrance from which the public were excluded. Theatre-goers raised an outcry which the radicals exploited with alacrity. Leigh Hunt wrote an article pointing out that many people would have stomached higher prices, but not the increase in the number of boxes, which meant that the circle was now reserved for the rich. Management claimed boxes enabled people to eat refreshments or retire if they were bored. In reality, they were an obnoxious foreign import intended for private amusement.

Clifford masterminded opposition with the assistance of Samuel Miller and other members of the Westminster Committee. Protesters in the auditorium wore metal badges with the initials OP (old prices) in their hats and waved banners denouncing boxes which Lords would fill with their mistresses. They succeeded in closing the theatre for ten days and continued to disrupt performances well into November. The management retaliated by bringing Bow Street magistrates on stage. When this failed to intimidate the audience, who stood up and sang 'God Save the King' and 'Rule Britannia', bouncers were introduced into the pit. Clifford, arrested for causing a riot, brought a charge for assault and false imprisonment against the theatre proprietors. Though the judge summed up against him, the jury awarded him damages, to colossal applause from a crowd of several thousand.

Before Christmas the management gave way, former prices were restored and Clifford chaired a reconciliatory dinner for management and audience. Clifford was presented with a blue emblem embroidered with OP in silver, which he gave to Tooke, who put it in a place of honour among his caricatures. Tooke considered it an important victory, for the theatre was 'a great national concern, connected with the morals and… liberties of the people'.[4]

One other dramatic episode took place during Tooke's lifetime which, though he was not directly involved, bears the hallmark of his flamboyant style. It arose from renewed controversy over a question which he always considered of the utmost importance: how far parliamentary privilege should curb freedom of the press. Militant ex-LCS member John Gale Jones ran a debating society, the British Forum. When the Commons held an enquiry into the army's disastrous expedition to Walcheren, strangers were excluded from the gallery. Gale Jones posted placards advertising a debate on whether this exclusion or Windham's attacks on freedom of the press were 'the greatest outrage on public feeling'. In retaliation, on 21 February 1810 the House committed him to Newgate for libel. When Burdett's motion to get him discharged was defeated, Cobbett published an indignant letter in his *Register* which questioned the legality of this action. It was signed by Burdett, but Cobbett had composed its introduction. The House then voted by a narrow margin to commit Burdett to the Tower for breach of privilege. This provoked widespread popular demonstrations. Mackintosh commented, 'Tooke laid a trap for the House of Commons, baited with a baronet, and… the House have bit'.[5]

On Friday 6 April, Burdett declared the Speaker's warrant illegal, came up from Wimbledon and barricaded himself into his town house. When the Serjeant-at-Arms, assisted by troops, broke in, they found him theatrically reading Magna Carta to his son. An armed guard escorted Burdett, who offered no resistance, to the Tower. There were no incidents, but on their return stones were thrown at the escort who fired, killing several people.[6]

Burdett, a popular hero, spent two months in the Tower, visited by admiring deputations and deluged with congratulatory addresses. He was released when Parliament was prorogued on 21 June. Cartwright, with Place and other members of the Westminster Committee, had made elaborate plans for a triumphal procession to Burdett's house in Piccadilly. The Government paraded the 12th Light Dragoons while City dignitaries, bands and spectators massed at Tower Hill and along the route. Burdett, however, had had time for reflection. Wanting to avoid the possibility of riots which would injure the reformers' cause, he skulked off across the Thames by boat and rode with his brother to Wimbledon. It was in many ways a sensible decision, but his supporters, some of whom had travelled far to celebrate, were outraged. Burdett brought public humiliation to the radicals and created resentment among his partisans, thousands of whom tore their cockades from their hats in disgust and dashed them in the mud. When asked to explain his behaviour, he said that his enemies had blamed him for the fatalities when he was taken to the Tower and, if he had been the cause of further bloodshed, it would have haunted him for the rest of his life. He could not warn the Westminster Committee of his decision because they would be unable to keep it secret, and crowds would have surrounded the Tower by water.[7]

So Tooke ended his political career as he had begun it, involved in controversial anti-Government forays in the metropolis. Till his death, he continued to be a target for satire. In one epic after Virgil, Burdett returns from the Tower only to collapse on the appearance of his hoary demonic master. Crying 'Am I in hell?' he calls for a bible. Tooke is horrified; there are none; Brutus and Cataline never read such stuff; Burdett dies. Invariably portrayed as a crooked swindler, Tooke suggests his death should be concealed until he has had time to safeguard the valuable presents Burdett has given to him and the patriotic societies. To save expense, the patriots gather for a midnight funeral at Wimbledon. Tooke rebukes Powell for getting a Latin quotation on a flag wrong.

An epitaph for Burdett appeared in a parody of Gray's 'Elegy'.

Large were his wishes, but his lot severe;
To Tooke he owed his fortune and reverse:
He gained from John, 'twas all his portion – shame,
John gained from him, 'twas all he wished – his purse.[8]

Death of Tooke

Tooke fell ill again at the beginning of 1810. At one point his doctors thought he would not last out the day, and for the first time his will to survive faltered. He had complete confidence in his medical advisers and always said that he 'wished to live no longer than Dr Pearson gave him permission'. At one point he refused to eat; however, thanks to his daughters' devoted nursing and friends' encouragement, he once more rallied, but warned them that this was only a temporary respite. No sooner was he convalescent than he demanded newspapers and books. His daughters read *The Times* and *Morning Chronicle* to him daily. He also wanted so many books read to him that auxiliaries had to be enlisted.[9]

Tooke decided that the time had come to plan his burial. He wanted to be buried in his garden, so a vault was dug at the bottom of the kitchen garden by the wall dividing it from the common. Tooke intended to erect a summerhouse on it from which his daughters could look across the green, dispelling any melancholy atmosphere. Chantrey obtained a large piece of black Irish marble for a tombstone on which Tooke had inscribed:[10]

John Horne Tooke
Late Proprietor, and now occupier of this spot,
was
born in June, 1736,
and
Died in the... Year of His Age,
Content & Grateful.

In the autumn Tooke had another crisis and once more became dropsical. The *Morning Chronicle*, no longer critical of his feud with Fox, hoped that it would be long before the tomb of this 'most distinguished literary and political character' was tenanted. Tooke told Burdett, 'I am now so far on my journey that I do not wish to return back, in order to proceed again by the same road, a few months hence'. A few days later, however, when Stephens rode over, he was surprised to meet Tooke in very good form, being carried out by two servants. They put him in an invalid chair, then with Burdett pulling, his daughters and his nephew John Wildman pushing behind, they bowled along a broad gravel walk to the vault. Pointing to the last line of the inscription on his tombstone, Tooke said how delighted and fortunate he was to have lived so long.[11]

During Tooke's latter years his annual expenditure was about £1,500. He kept detailed accounts, paid all bills promptly, and was able to quote the price of every piece of furniture purchased for his house at Wimbledon. Many elderly people lose their sense of financial proportion. Tooke did not become parsimonious; instead, during his last 18 months, in an attempt to grasp at life, to leave his mark on the future, he embarked on a tremendous splash of expenditure. After a lifetime of worrying how to make ends meet, he felt he could now indulge himself in one last fling. He refurnished his back parlour, where he spent part of the day reclining on a black leather couch, and discarded his normal brown clothes for an elegant suit of peach-coloured cloth. He carried out alterations to the house and grounds which, with his tomb, cost about £1,000. He raised the garden wall, paved the courtyard and papered the house. He planned further grandiose schemes, including a semi-circular drive with gates at each end, but suffered another relapse and talked of them no more. At the same time, he helped cottagers at the back of his garden who were in financial difficulties by discharging their taxes.[12]

Tooke's house still filled with visitors. Conversation, led by Tooke, would roam over many subjects. He was optimistic about the radicals' future, believing that, though there had been few 'friends of liberty', they were now numerous, only needing a focus. However, if the Whigs were to come in, they would turn Tory. 'When measures fail, and the people grumble, a few, who fill some responsible places, go out for a while; and the people are satisfied; but the Government continues the same.' It was not the men that should be changed, but the system. He thought little of the bulk of mankind's judgement, but believed they only 'wanted instruction', for they always meant well, 'even when in the wrong'. Mental superiority sprang from a combination of genius, experience and a knowledge of facts.[13]

Tooke decided to burn his unpublished papers. He must have decided that he lacked the energy to prepare the material for publication, or realised that his theories on the verb – which he had promised to treat in a third volume – would not hold water. A scholarly friend of Tooke's told Stephens that the first word of the third volume was belief, and a large part consisted of a critical examination of the credibility of human testimony. During his last illness he destroyed everything except account books, not only his linguistic writings but a treatise on moral philosophy, a counterblast to Paley, and his correspondence.[14]

Shortly before his death, Tooke was reconciled with his youngest sister, Anne Dickers, with whom he had not been on speaking terms for a number of years, and she formed a close relationship with her two nieces. Tooke had made a will some years earlier, in which he left everything including the Wimbledon property to his elder daughter Mary. It is not clear why Charlotte was excluded, as Stephens said Tooke had no dislike for Charlotte.[15]

Tooke was one of those rare and fortunate men whose character did not deteriorate, nor the appeal of his personality fade as he declined towards his end. He continued to acquire new acquaintance, retained his interest in public affairs and affection for his friends. About a year before he died, his swollen legs began to ooze. Later, due to the time it took, coupled with the intense pain, even Tooke became peevish and irritable and was unwilling to have his legs dressed as often as was necessary. This eventually led to gangrene. Tooke, who never called for sympathy or mentioned his ailments except to play down their disadvantages, pointed to his legs and said, with his normal gaiety, that he should die as he had always wished, in full possession of his faculties. When Stephens dined at Wimbledon in February 1812 there was company as usual – his nephew John Wildman, a JP from Berkshire, Humphry Davy and Chantrey. Tooke discussed the Scottish *literati* and mentioned Wilkes without resentment. The last letter he wrote was to Dr Pearson who had been bitten by a mad dog: 'Though I have foreborne to write because I would not be troublesome, yet I am very anxious about your health. For God's sake let some of your family tell me how you are.'

During Tooke's last days Burdett cared for him devotedly. He sat by his bed for hours and gave him medicine and food. Tooke said to young Sam Miller, 'never did a son attend more to his father than this good creature does to me'. Samuel described the last time he saw Tooke. He had been lifted out of bed and the doctor was binding his legs which had burst in several places. 'You take great pains in binding up my legs,' said Tooke, 'but they will soon run away with me'. So powerful was his mind and spirits that, though for 12 hours he had no sensation in his lower extremities and passed two kidney stones, he made no complaint. Surrounded by his daughters, Burdett, Samuel's father and others, Tooke called Sam and took his hand: 'I have selected you, as the youngest in the company, to hear nearly my last request. I wish you to go to the mount where we used to sit and look over the common and see my new summer house.' Sam was astonished to find Tooke's grave there. When he returned, Tooke asked for his particular attention. 'I am still in possession of my faculties and I die in the same principles I have always entertained. I know that the clergy have requested and are very desirous to come to me, but I have strongly prohibited their admission. Words are put into dead men's mouths and they are made to say what they neither feel or believe, the mind being long gone before the body ceases its functions. Should you at any time hear of my recantation contradict it.' Tooke did not believe in an after-life, but thought, should he be wrong, his record had sufficient merit to be passed by the judges.

Just before he died, he was occupied in correcting a copy of Shakespeare and making notes on the margin. When Burdett called on his last morning, he enquired about a Commons debate on flogging in the army. He remained calm and facetious, said he was happy to die surrounded by those most dear to him, and promised he would not emulate a Strasbourg citizen who, having asked to be allowed a final game of skittles, kept on bowling until the executioner was obliged to creep up behind and cut off his head. He died on the night of 18 March 1812. In spite of his chronic ailments, he had outlived most of his contemporaries.[16]

Tooke had not wanted a funeral ceremony, but requested that the six poorest men in the parish should carry him to his vault and be paid a guinea each. The tomb was prepared, and Burdett invited Tooke's closest friends to attend on 27 March. After considerable disagreement this was countermanded. Bosville wanted to honour Tooke's last request, but his sister and daughters wanted him to have a Christian burial. Hardy had written to Burdett to express sorrow at the death of 'That truly great man... a zealous and faithful friend to the welfare and happiness of his fellow men'. He asked, if it were thought proper, that he attend Tooke's funeral. Hardy was most indignant that Tooke's wishes were not carried out. Burdett told him, 'reasons infinite determined the family and myself.' They feared that, if Tooke were buried in his garden, it would detract from the value of the property, and if it were sold his body would be removed. On 30 March, a procession of mourners and coaches accompanied the coffin to St Mary's Parish Church at Ealing where, after a normal religious service, Tooke was buried in a tomb next to his mother and sister.[17]*

Initially Tooke's daughters offered to sell Burdett his library for £1,000, but as the valuers thought it might go for more he declined, in case it appeared he had not paid the full value. Subsequently he sucessfully bid for the majority of Tooke's books with manuscript notes. The sale lasted four days and was a great success. All the books were sold and fetched high prices, a total of £1250/14/6. Twelve special copies of the catalogue were printed with an engraving of Tooke as frontispiece. The books, ranging from philosophy to horticulture, included works on anatomy and Christianity, histories, political tracts, Bibles in many languages. The majority were connected with his linguistic work, dictionaries and grammars in most European languages, books for the deaf and dumb. There were classical texts, Blackstone, Burke's *Reflections* with Tooke's notes, copies of Napoleon's letters and one of Wilkes's privately-printed works which he had given Tooke after they were reconciled; also a rare translation of the new testament surreptitiously circulated in the reign of Edward III, a present from Burdett.

Heber, a well-known book collector, bought his annotated copy of his treason trial which is now in the British Library. Tooke's copy of Johnson's *Dictionary* with his comments on the margin was bought by Major James for £200. Tooke bequeathed Rogers several of his books, including his annotated copy of Hardy's trial and his old black letter copy of Chaucer's *Boethius* which he had used to write a record of events when in the Tower. In 1840 Crabb Robinson tried to persuade Rogers to leave them

* On 17 June 1919, a memorial tablet was placed in the church recording his championship of the Americans in 1775. It was unveiled by the New England Society of Brooklyn, who paid for the repair of his grave and gave £100 to the Ealing war orphans fund in recognition of Tooke's raising a fund for the widows and orphans of Lexington, and to commemorate the alliance in 1917 of American and British arms. The American Ambassador was unable to be present as he had been invited to luncheon at Ascot by the King, so the Consul General read his speech. Augustine Birrell gave thanks on behalf of Great Britain. Prominent Americans, the Mayor and Corporation of Ealing were present, and schoolchildren led singing of both national anthems. Tooke would have been amused by such a ceremony 107 years after the event.

to someone who would appreciate them or to a library, but Rogers retorted that the auctioneer would find the fittest possessor. 'He who gives money for things values them. Put them in a museum and nobody sees them.' As Robinson feared, the books have disappeared without trace, whereas Tooke's copy of Part I of the *Diversions* with his Tower journal, was handed down by his descendants and kinsmen, until bequeathed to the British Library in 1882.[18]

Tooke's daughters sold the house and moved to smaller quarters. What happened to them is not known, though Mary's will of 1855 shows that she was then living at Chiddingstone, Kent.[19] Bosville and Clifford died in 1813. The Wimbledon circle, which Burdett did not attempt to keep going, disappeared.

Besides innumerable cartoons, there were many portraits and busts of Tooke a few of which survive. A portrait painted by Richard Brompton while Tooke was in the King's Bench prison in 1777 is in Manchester City Gallery. In it Tooke is seated beside a bust of Mercury holding his winged cap to commemorate his 'Letter to Mr Dunning'. A later portrait by Percy was exhibited in 1803. John Raphael Smith painted Tooke shortly before he died, reclining on a couch wearing a loose cap and gown with his manuscripts and favourite books beside him. William Ward made a coloured mezzotint of this in 1811. An engraving of a bust by G. Murray was distributed before Tooke's trial in 1794, and an engraving was made in 1798 of a bust by Mountague Tomkin. By the time of Chantrey's bust, commissioned by Burdett, Tooke was a shadow of his former self, yet the head still has character and power. This is in the Fitzwilliam Museum. Burdett also owned a bust by John Bacon the elder of Tooke in his prime with a poem by Burdett underneath. E. Bocquet made an engraving of this. Both these busts were said to be very good likenesses. There is a watercolour of Burdett as an old man seated in front of Bacon's bust in the National Portrait Gallery. They also have a portrait of Tooke in middle age by Thomas Hardy (the artist, not to be confused with the reformer) from which an engraving was made in 1791. These pictures record Tooke's progress from a lively, moderately attractive young man, to an impressive, vigorous personality with a friendly, shrewd, humorous expression, then on to gentler, frail old age.[20]

Obituaries and Retrospective

There were many obituaries of Tooke, and further articles appeared when Stephens's biography was published the following year. Although estimates of his career and character differed markedly, all conceded that his deathbed was fit for a philosopher. The *Morning Chronicle* criticised the acrimonious severity of his personal animosities, but thought he deserved the nation's gratitude for his fight against injustice. 'He had supported Wilkes and was betrayed; and had united with Pitt and was persecuted. The abuse of power has no greater restraint than the dread of some stubborn mind, which fines and prison cannot subdue. The country has long since come to agree with him over the American war,' and future Ministerial supporters would probably be satisfied 'with classing him among the Hampdens, Miltons and similar disturbers of quiet government and order'.[21]

The *Critical Review* published a laudatory obituary in the form of a review of Stephens's biography whose style it deplored. 'Though… not… among the principal actors on the political theatre during the last half-century, yet he has certainly [made]… his influence strongly felt… in the cabinet, the senate, the courts of law and the people at large.' After praising his devotion to duty while still a clergyman, he 'relinquished his prospects of comfort and affluence' to help Wilkes. In his quarrel with Wilkes, he showed 'more patriotic probity' than did the latter. Referring to his actions in 1771 to ensure publication of the debates in the House of Commons, 'we consider Mr Horne's exertions at this juncture as constituting a very bright portion of his public life and entitling him to the thanks of all lovers of British liberty'. Though he brought much of his ill-treatment on himself, he was rejected for the bar on preposterous grounds, which insinuated that the exercise of clerical functions so tainted a man that it rendered him unfit for other professions by which a learned and conscientious man could earn an honest living. 'His ambition had none of the baser cravings of avarice or selfishness. He who has escaped that taint may well deserve to be chronicled among the political worthies of the age.' 'These praises… have not been spontaneously bestowed; they have been extorted from us by the evidence of facts and the force of truth… they will wear as well, for they have been dearly earned.'[22]

The *Quarterly Review*, hostile to the radicals, contained a long article, ostensibly a review of Reid's *Memoir of Tooke*, which was summarily dismissed: could the British Jacobins not produce a better account of their 'principal ornament and support'? Written by John Ward, First Earl Dudley, and Edward Copleston, Bishop of Llandaff and Dean of St Paul's, it is a brilliant exposition of establishment circles' estimation of Tooke at the time of his death and contains many shrewd comments. To form a correct appreciation of Tooke's character it was essential to remember that Tooke 'laboured under great perpetual, irremovable civil disabilities…'. 'His life was spented in an unavailing and ungraceful struggle to extricate himself from the restraints which his situation imposed upon him.' He wasted 'his strength in an idle endeavour… to pass the magic circle which law and custom had drawn around him'. As he could find no congenial place in society, he consoled himself by waging irreconcilable war against those by whom it was upheld. 'His hand was against every man's hand, and every man's hand was against him… provided he could excite surprise by his paradoxes, and terror by his abuse, he cared little for public esteem.' If he too had been an MP his hostility to leading politicians might have given place to generous rivalry. He had remarkable but limited talents. 'What he saw he saw clearly, but his vision did not extend far.' He behaved as if mankind's fate depended on a Middlesex or a Westminster election. Tooke handled argument with infinite subtlety, ingenuity and dexterity, but lacked Burke's comprehensive mind. 'He was more a sophist than a philosopher… No man ever unjustly provoked him without regretting his rashness for he was armed with supreme weapons, self command and boldness based on habit of victory in such combats. In the ordinary intercourse of life he was kind, friendly and hospitable… never appeared to greater advantage than in conversation.'[23]

Leigh Hunt in the *Examiner* thought Tooke 'one of the acutest politicians of his age, and perhaps the first philologist of his nation. His political character was that of a wrong spirit on the right side of thinking.' And yet, as Lord Brougham said, 'No man out of office all his life and out of Parliament all but a few months… ever acted so conspicuous a part in the political warfare of his times.'[24]

Today Horne Tooke is principally remembered (by the few who have ever heard of him) as the reason why priests of the

Church of England are not eligible to be elected as Members of Parliament. He was excluded out of spite, by a bill drawn up specially for the purpose, such was the degree of hatred and obloquy in which he was held by the governing class.

His most important effect on the course of history may well be his support of Wilkes in the series of Middlesex elections. At that time Parliament was controlled by the aristocracy and the King and was subject to virtually no influence by the law or public opinion. The venality of elections was a byword. Appeals after disputed elections were considered by the whole House, and the candidate who supported the administration was usually declared elected. The substitution of Luttrell for Wilkes was a particularly flagrant example, and led later to Grenville's Election Act whereby disputes were to be decided instead by a more independent committee of MPs. It is unlikely that Wilkes would have won the poll in the first of the elections without Horne's support, and even more unlikely, given his financial problems, that he would have continued to be successful. The money collected by the SSBR, of which Horne was one of the principal founders, was essential. The SSBR was the first of the political clubs whose membership was not confined to aristocrats and landed gentry, and it served as a model for later societies such as the SCI and the associations set up by Wyvill.

In the early part of the eighteenth century, parliamentary debates were considered to be privileged and were not to be published. The reports which did appear in the press were unofficial and of variable accuracy. It was Wilkes and Horne, by challenging Parliament over the affair of the printers, who were largely responsible for putting an end to this state of affairs. This was essential for the development of an informed public opinion, and led to a significant increase in the number of newspapers towards the end of the century.

Support of the American colonists by Tooke and other libertarians was part of his campaign for greater freedom for ordinary people. If British citizens in America were to be subject to arbitrary actions by a legislature in which they had no representation, how could the freedom of the unrepresented in Britain be maintained? Tooke was the only person in Britain to be imprisoned for supporting the Americans.

The reform and widening of political life was always Tooke's main concern. Political apathy by all except an aristocratic elite was a feature of eighteenth-century life; Wyvill's schemes for parliamentary reform foundered for lack of popular support even in the unrepresented cities. Tooke was a prime mover in the SCI whose aim was to spread the word. Its work bore fruit in the founding of the LCS. In his memoirs, Hardy recalled that in 1791 his 'leisure hours were employed in looking over political tracts from... the SCI'. The first few meetings of the LCS were devoted to discussing whether there was any need for parliamentary reform, and whether 'we, who are tradesmen... shopkeepers and mechanics [have] any right to obtain a parliamentary reform?'[25]

However, Tooke was not a democrat like Cartwright or Paine. He wanted to eliminate corruption and imposture, whereby the poor were taxed to pay the sinecures and pensions of the aristocratic politicians. He thought this could be achieved through a wider and more equitably-distributed electorate, a better system of polling and shorter parliaments.[26] He often supported the King as a counterweight to the aristocracy; he might well sometimes have wished that Dunning's famous motion had read, 'the power of the aristocracy... is increasing and ought to be diminished'. Tooke's short period in Parliament was not a success. By then he was too old and infirm and too embittered.

Tooke's career was punctuated by a series of dramatic incidents. He had the unique distinction of being prosecuted for his opposition to both the American and French wars. On both occasions, though not anticipating such severe punishment, he deliberately challenged the Government. Dauntless, ebulliently pugnacious, a shrewd agitator, a resourceful political operator of immense mental and physical energy, he thrived on controversy. He preferred to challenge rather than to woo. Significantly, one of his favourite lines of poetry was 'Flectere si nequeo superos, Acheronti movebo' from the *Aeneid*, 'If Jove and Heaven my just desires deny, Hell shall the power of Heaven supply' (Dryden).

Many people present a more agreeable persona to the world than to their close friends and relations. Tooke, on the contrary, was often rude, cruel and devious in public, yet amiable and benevolent at home. Apparently devoid of feeling, he behaved with great sensibility. He gave generously to good causes. An affable, jovial host, a fount of information yet never boring, he could deflate pomposity wih his caustic wit. Despite his tribulations, he derived enormous enjoyment from life and transmitted his zest to his friends.

One friend said he never heard Tooke defend an opinion in which he was certain Tooke believed sincerely; another complained that his conversation, though fascinating, had no moral effect. Why should it? Tooke was pragmatic, versatile, unemotional; his was not a spiritual, idealistic temperament. He would never ruin the pleasures of the dinner table by parading his principles. Tooke could not have delivered his speeches at the 1796 election without a firm belief in liberty and justice.

The one point on which Tooke's contemporaries were mistaken in his favour was their over-estimation of his future reputation as a philologist. They could not foresee that the *Diversions*, which made an enormous impact when published, would within 70 years be superseded and forgotten. Tooke suffered the fate of others who make original discoveries prematurely, before the right method has been found. Still, Tooke persuaded men to look at words and their meaning in a new way, to appreciate the English language. He helped to make the principles of language more accessible to ordinary people, and to make its political power and importance clearly understood.

Though latterly he appeared somewhat old-fashioned, holding advanced views of a preceding century, all those whose political talents Tooke nurtured were proud to acknowledge their debt to him. Burdett was the last and most important. He was not a politician of the first order, but during the war and for some years afterwards he was the leading radical spokesman and attracted a following of considerable strength.

Tooke preached no new gospel, but he did promote with clarity one important concept – that a patriot's aim should be to promote the greatest possible national happiness. Godwin and Spence wanted to achieve this by abolishing almost all institutions, Tooke by improving existing laws. Tooke did not attempt to elaborate this formula: it was Bentham who came to comprehensive conclusions and produced detailed schemes for the improvement of prisons and codification of the law. Still, Tooke, who had considerable influence on James Mill, was a forerunner of the philosophic radicals, who were not so much inventors as systematic arrangers of ideas.

Tooke tried to promote change at an unpropitious moment, failed and has been forgotten. His countrymen owed him a debt of gratitude for his consistent example in fighting for his beliefs. When hopes for change inspired by the revolutions faded, Tooke kept their promise alive, one of the men who lived dangerously to defend civil liberties. Society needs turbulent irritants, expounders of unfashionable views, with the vigour and self-reliance to take an independent line, who rouse passions and draw attention to faults in the body politic. Tooke had some dubious associates and committed some questionable acts, but he never abandoned the principles which justified his cause. 'My principles… have stood the test of ages and they will keep their ground in the general commendation of the world, till men forget to love themselves; though, till then perhaps, they are not likely to be seen… in the practice of many individuals.'[27] He was a powerful hater, but a sincere patriot with a warm heart. Certain places possess an evocative charm. Who – bar the most conventional – would not wish to have been a guest at Wimbledon and fallen under the Wizard's spell?

Notes on Chapter 15

1 Stephens II, p 413; Mackintosh 1835 II, p 36
2 Patterson, p 130; Add MS 27818 f 96; Hone, p 166
3 Stephens II, pp 369-70
4 *The Examiner*, 24 September 1809; Hone, p 183; Stephens II, pp 373-4; Baer, M, pp 18-36, 145-9
5 Add MS 27850 f156-75; Hone, p 180; Mackintosh II, p 36
6 Add MS 27850 f188-95; Patterson, pp 257-73; Wallas, p 53; Hone, p 186
7 Add MS 27850 f229-39; Burdett MS Eng.Lett.D. 97 f216 Jones Burdett to brother-in-law 17.7.10; Patterson, pp 286-9
8 *The Satirist* 1.8.10, 97-116; *Morning Post*, 20 May 1811
9 Stephens II, p 422
10 Stephens II, pp 383-4; Jones, p 13
11 Stephens II, pp 382, 389; *Morning Chronicle*, 1 October 1820
12 Stephens II, pp 389-90, 441-3, 472, 494
13 Rogers, *Recollections*, p 139
14 Stephens II, pp 372-3; Brougham MS 6211, Miller to Brougham 26 July 1758

15 PRO Prob. 11/1532/199
16 Stephens II, pp 425, 441-6; *Morning Chronicle*, 21 March 1812; Brougham MS 6211, 26.7.58
17 Add MS 27817 f100; 27818 f133-4; Stephens II, p 449
18 Add MS 27817 f204-5; Robinson, p 187, 3.6.40; The catalogue of the sale is in the British Library, with prices
19 Surrey Record Office, Kingston, Acc 620
20 Stephens, pp 502-3
21 *Morning Chronicle* 21 March 1812
22 *Critical Review*, November 1813, pp 460-82
23 *Quarterly Review*, June 1812, pp 313-28
24 Brougham, *Historical Sketches* Second Series I, p 130
25 Add MS 27814 f18-26
26 Horne J., Letter to Lord Asburton 1782
27 *DOP* I, p 1

Bibliography

All material published in London unless otherwise noted.

Newspapers and Magazines

American Quarterly Review, Philadelphia 1827-37
Analytical Review 1788-99
Annual Register 1758-1862
Annual Review and History of Literature 1802-8
Anti-Jacobin 1799-1821
Argus 1789-92
Athenaeum 1828-1921
Blackwood's Edinburgh Magazine 1817-1905
Critical Review 1756-90
Eclectic Review 1805-57
Edinburgh Gazetteer 1792-3
Edinburgh Review 1820-1929
Examiner 1808-36
Express and Evening Chronicle 1796-7
Gazetteer and London Daily Advertiser 1754-96
General Evening Post 1737-90
Lloyds Evening Post and British Chronicle 1757-1805
London Chronicle 1757-1823
London Evening Post 1735-1790
Middlesex Journal 1769-76
Moniteur (*Gazette Nationale*), Paris 1789-99
Monthly Magazine and British Register 1796-1826
Monthly Review 1749-1845
Morning Chronicle 1770-1865
Morning Herald 1780-1869
Morning Post 1772-1937
North Briton 1762-
Notes and Queries 1849-1932
Oracle 1789-94
Original (T. Walker) ed. Jerrold 1832-74
Oxford Magazine 1768-76
Patriote François, Paris 1789-93
Political Register 1767-1772
Public Advertiser (*London Daily Post and General Advertiser*) 1735-94
Quarterly Review 1809-

Satirist or *Monthly Meteor* 1808-14
Sun 1793-9
Tait's Edinburgh Magazine 1832-61
Times 1788-
True Briton 1793-1803
World 1753-

Books, papers and pamphlets

Aasleff, H., *Study of Language in England 1780-1860*, Athlone Press, 1983
Abbott, Charles (Lord Colchester), *Diary and Correspondence*, John Murray, 1861
Abinger MSS, Bodleian Library, Oxford
Adams, M.R., *Studies in Literary Background of English Radicalism*, Lancaster, Pennsylvania, Franklin and Marshall College Studies V, 1947
Adamson, J.W., *English Education 1789-1902*, Cambridge University Press, 1930
Additional MSS in British Library Manuscript Room
Aldridge, A.O., *Man of Reason*, Lippincott, Philadelphia, 1959
Alger, J.G., *Napoleon's British Visitors and Captives*, Constable, 1904
Angelo, Henry, *Reminiscences*, Henry Colburn, 1828
Anon. (Price and Horne), *Facts Addressed to the Landholders…*, 1780
Anon., *An Interesting Address to the Independent Part of the People of England…*, 1777
Anon., *Sir Franctic*, 1809 (by etc. etc. Esquire, Author of Nothing)
Archives du Ministère des affaires étrangères, Paris
Auckland, Lord (W. Eden), *Journal and Correspondence*, 1860-2

Baer, Marc, *Theatre and Disorder in Late Georgian London*, Oxford University Press, 1992
Beattie, James, *The Theory of Language*, 1788
Beinecke, MSS Yale, Osborn Files, New Haven, USA
Belsham, Thomas, *Elements of the Philosophy of the Mind*, J. Johnson, 1801
Bentham, Jeremy, *Chrestomathia*, Oxford University Press, 1983
Idem., *Works*, Athlone Press, 1968
Bewley, C.M.E., *Muir of Huntershill*, Oxford University Press, 1981
Bindman, *The Shadow of the Guillotine*, British Museum Catalogue, 1989
Binns, John, *Recollections*, Philadelphia, 1854
Bland Burges Papers, Bodleian Library, Oxford
Bleakley, H.W., *Life of John Wilkes*, John Lane, 1917
Boswell, James, *Life of Samuel Johnson*, Oxford University Press, 1934
Bowles, John, *Thoughts on the Late General Election*, 1802
Brightwell, C.L., *Memoir of Amelia Opie*, RTS, 1855
Brougham, H.P., *Brougham and His Early Friends* (letters), 1908

Brougham, H.P. (Baron Brougham and Vaux), *Historical Sketches of Statesmen in the Time of George III*, C. Knight, 1839-43
Brougham MSS, University College, London
Brown, F.K., *Life of William Godwin*, J.M. Dent, 1926
Burdett MSS, Bodleian Library, Oxford
Burke, Edmund, *Correspondence*, Cambridge University Press, 1958-78
Idem., *Reflections on the Revolution in France*, 1790
Burnett, James (Lord Monboddo), *Of the Origin and Progress of Language*, Edinburgh, 1773
Byrne, J.C., *Gossip of the Century*, Ward and Downey, 1892

Campbell, John, *Lives of the Chief Justices of England*, John Murray, 1849-57
Idem., *Lives of the Lord Chancellors*, John Murray, 1845
Canning, George, *Journal*, ed. P. Jupp, Royal Historical Society, 1991
Cartwright, F.D., *Life and Correspondence of Major John Cartwright*, Henry Colburn, 1826
Cestre, Charles, *John Thelwall*, Swan Sonnenschein, 1906
Chatham, Earl, *Correspondence of W. Pitt*, John Murray, 1938-40
Christie, I.R., *Wilkes, Wyville and Reform*, Macmillan, 1962
Clayden, P.W., *Early Life of Samuel Rogers*, Smith Elder, 1887
Idem., *Rogers and his Contemporaries*, Smith Elder, 1889
Idem., *Collected Letters*, Oxford University Press, 1956
Idem., *Table Talk*, John Murray, 1835
Idem., S.T., 'Verses Addressed to J. Horne Tooke', 1796, *Poetical Works*, ed. Campbell, Macmillan, 1925
Coleridge, S.T. and Robert Southey, *Omniana*, 1812
Condillac, E. Bonnot de, *Essai sur l'origine des Connaissances humaines*, Paris, 1746
Conway, M.D., *Life of Thomas Paine*, G.P. Putnam, 1892
Cradock, Joseph, *Literary and Miscellaneous Memoirs*, J.B. Nichols, 1828
Creevey, Thomas, *Life and Times*, ed. J. Gore, John Murray, 1934
Idem., *Papers*, John Murray, 1903

Darwin, Erasmus, *Zoonomia*, J. Johnson, 1794
DOP: see Horne, John, *Diversions of Purley*
Douglas, Silvester (Lord Glenbervie), *Diaries*, ed. Bickley, Constable, 1928

Eldon, Lord (Scott, John), *Lord Eldon's Anecdote Book*, ed. Lincoln, Stevens and Sons, 1960
Elliot, Sir Gilbert, *Life and Letters*, ed. Countess Minto, 1874
Erskine, Thomas, *Declaration of Friends of the Liberty of the Press*, 1793

Farington, Joseph, *Diary*, Yale, New Haven and London, 1978
Fearn, John, *Anti-Tooke*, 1824-7
Foster, John, *Critical Essays*, ed. J.E. Ryland, 1856
Fox, C.J., *Memorials and Correspondence*, ed. Russell, 1853
Fox, Henry (Lord Holland), *Memoirs of the Whig Party*, 1852-4
Idem., *Further Memoirs of the Whig Party*, John Murray, 1905
Francis, Sir Philip, *Memoirs*, ed. Joseph Parkes, 1867

George III, *Correspondence*, ed. Fortescue, Macmillan, 1927
Idem., *Later Correspondence*, ed. Aspinall, Cambridge University Press, 1962-70
George, Prince of Wales, *Correspondence*, ed. Aspinall, Cassell, 1963
George, M.D., *Catalolgue of Personal and Political Satires*, British Museum, 11 vols, 1978
Godwin, William, *Cursory Strictures etc.*, 1794
Idem., *The Enquirer: Reflections on Education, Manners and Literature*, 1797
Idem., *Enquiry Concerning Political Justice*, 1793
Idem., *Journal*, Bodleian Library, Oxford
Gooch, G.P. and Stanhope, Ghita, *Life of Lord Stanhope*, Longman, 1914
Goodwin, Albert, *The Friends of Liberty*, Harvard, Cambridge, Mass., 1979
Gower (Lord Granville Leveson Gower), *Private Correspondence*, ed. Granville, John Murray, 1916
Graham, J.A., *Memoirs of Horne Tooke*, New York, 1828
Green, Thomas, *Diary of a Lover of Literature*, Ipswich, 1810
Grey MSS, Priors Kitchen, Durham

Hardy, Thomas, *Memoirs*, 1832
Harris, James (Earl Malmesbury), *Diaries and Correspondence*, R. Bentley, 1844
Idem., *Hermes*, 1751; reprinted Scholar Press, 1968
Hazlitt, William, *Spirit of the Age*, 1825
Idem., *The Plain Speaker* (on conversation of authors), 1826
Idem., *Works*, ed. P.P. Howe, J.M. Dent, 1930-34
Idem., *Memoirs*, ed. P. Quennell, Routledge, 1960
Hobhouse, J.C. (Lord Broughton), *Recollections of a Long Life*, John Murray, 1909
Holcroft, Thomas, *Memoirs*, Longman, 1816
Holland, Lady (Elizabeth Vassall), *Journal*, Longman, 1908
HO (Home Office papers) at Public Record Office
Hone, J.A., *For the Cause of Truth*, Oxford University Press, 1982
Horne, John (Tooke), many of his collected pamphlets can be found in the British Library
Idem., *Address and Declaration*, 1791
Idem., catalogue of his library, 1813, British Library
Idem., *Diversions of Purley (DOP)*, Thomas Tegg, 1840

Idem., genuine copies of all letters... relative to the execution of Doyle and Valine, 1770
Idem., Letter to Browne, Houghton Library, Harvard, USA
Idem., Letter to a friend... Johnson, 1787
Idem., 'Letter to Lord Ashburton', Debrett, 1782
Idem., Middlesex Oration, 1770
Idem., 'Petition of an Englishman', 1765
Idem., proceedings in action for debt between C.J. Fox and J. Horne Tooke, 1792; Tooke's own copies with notes in the British Library
Idem., Sermon, ed. Almon, 1769
Idem., *Tower Diary*, ed. Beedell, Harvey, Leeds Philosophical Society, 1995; and in his copy of *DOP* in the British Library
Idem., *Two Pair of Portraits*, 1788
Idem., Warning to the electors of Westminster, 1807
House of Commons Journal
House of Commons Papers, Scholarly Resources Inc., Wilmington, Delaware, 1975
Hunt, F.K., *The Fourth Estate*, 1850

Johnson, Samuel, *Dictionary of the English Language*, 1755
Jones, George, *Sir Francis Chantrey*, 1849
Jordan's (JS) *Complete Collection of Addresses and Speeches of Fox, Gardner and Tooke*, 1796
Joyce, Jeremiah, Sermon, 1794
Junius, *Letters*, Oxford University Press, 1978

Kyd, Stewart, *Treatise on the Law of Corporations*, 1793, 4

Lamb, Charles, *Letters*, Dent and Methuen, 1935
Lindsey, Theophilus, letters in Rylands Library, Manchester
Locke, John, 'Essay concerning human understanding', 1689
Losh, James, *Diaries*, ed. Hughes, Andrews and Co., Durham, 1962
Lovat-Fraser, J.A., *Erskine*, Cambridge University Press, 1932
Lowth, Robert, *A Short Introduction to English Grammer*, A. Miller, 1762

Mackintosh, R.J., *Memoirs of the Life of Sir James Mackintosh*, ed. R.J. Mackintosh, Moxon, 1835
Manchester MSS, Huntingdon County Record Office
Michigan MSS, William L. Clements Library, University of Michigan
Mill, James, *Analysis of the Phenomena of the Human Mind*, 1829
Milward, R., *Historic Wimbledon*, Windrush Press, 1989
Milton MSS, Northampton Record Office

Morgan, W., *Memoirs of Richard Price*, 1815
Mueller, F.M., *Lectures on the Science of Language*, 1862

Oldfield, T.H.B., *History of the Boroughs of Great Britain*, G. Riley, 1792

Paine, Thomas, 'Rights of Man', J. Johnson, 1791, 2
Parliament, Committee of Secrecy of House of Commons, 1794
Parliamentary Debates, ed. John Wright and W. Cobbett, 1804-1836
Parliamentary History of England, ed. W. Cobbett and R. Bagshaw, 1806-12
Parr, Samuel, *Works*, ed. Johnson, 1828
Patterson, M.W., *Sir Francis Burdett and his Times*, Macmillan, 1931
Paul, C.K., *William Godwin, his Friends and Contemporaries*, 1876
Paull, J., *Refutation Calumnies of John Horne Tooke*, 1807
PC, Privy Council papers kept in Public Record Office, London
Pellew, G., *Life and Correspondence of Addington* (Viscount Sidmouth), 1847
Place, Francis, *Autobiography*, Cambridge University Press, 1972
Political Tracts 1781-2, British Library E 2101
Political Tracts 1716-1841, British Library 8132bb14(7)
Portland MSS, Nottingham University
Prentice, Archibald, *Historical Sketches of Manchester*, 1851

Reynolds, Frederick, *Life and Times*, 1826
Richardson, Charles, *On the Study of Language*, 1854
Rickman, T.C., *Life of Thomas Paine*, 1819
Robinson, H.C., *Diary*, ed. Sadler, Macmillan, 1869
Rockingham Papers, Wentworth Woodhouse Miniments, Sheffield City Archives, by permission of Wentworth Settlement Trustees
Rogers, Samuel, *Recollections*, ed. Sharpe, 1859
Idem., *Table Talk*, ed. Dyce, 1856
Royal Commission on Historical MSS, 4th Report, 1874
Russell, Lady C.C.E, *Swallowfield and its Owners*, Longman, 1901

Shepherd MSS, Manchester College, Oxford
Stanhope, G. and Gooch, G.P., *The Life of Charles, 3rd Earl of Stanhope*, Longman, 1914
Stanhope, Lady Hester, *Memoirs*, 1845
State Trials, ed. W. Cobbett 1783-, R. Bagshaw, 1809-26
Stephens, Alexander, *Memoirs of John Horne Tooke*, 1813
Stewart, Dugald, *Collected Works*, ed. Hamilton, Constable, Edinburgh, 1854-60
Surrey Record Office, Kingston-upon-Thames, Surrey

Thelwall, John, *The Tribune*, 1795
Thelwall, Mrs, *Life of John Thelwall*, 1837

Thompson, E.P., *Making of the English Working Class*, Gollancz, 1963
Timbs, J., *English Eccentrics*, 1866
Todd, C.B., *Life and Letters of Joel Barlow*, G.I. Puttnam, New York, 1886
Townsend, W.C., *Lives of 12 Eminent Judges*, 1846
Treasury Solicitors Files (TS) in the Public Record Office, London
Trevelyan, G.M., *Lord Grey of the Reform Bill*, Longman, 1920
Twiss, H., *Life of Lord Eldon*, John Murray, 1844

Veitch, G.S., *The Genesis of Parliamentary Reform*, Constable, 1913, reprinted 1956

Walker, Thomas, *Review of Some Political Events in Manchester*, J. Johnson, 1794
Wallas, G., *Life of Francis Place*, Longman, 1898
Walpole, Horace, *Correspondence*, ed. Lewis, Oxford University Press, 1937
Idem., *Memoirs of the Reign of George III*, Lawrence and Bullen, 1894
Idem., *Last Journals during the Reign of George III*, ed. F. Steuart, Bodley Head, 1910
Watson, J.S., *The Reign of George III*, Oxford University Press, 1960
Webster, Noah, Letter to Dr Ramsay, New Haven, Conn., 1807
Wharam, Alan, *The Treasons Trials, 1794*, Leicester University Press, 1992
Wilkes, John, *Correspondence*, ed. J. Almon, 1805
Idem., *English Liberty*, T. Marsh, 1769
Idem., *Letters 1774-96*, ed. W. Rough, Longman, 1804
Idem., *Controversial Letters of John Wilkes and Rev. John Horne*, 1771
Wilson, J.M. and Lloyd, A., *Amelia*, Oxford University Press, 1937
Windham, William, *Papers*, Herbert Jenkins, 1913
Woodress, J.L., *A Yankee's Odyssey*, Greenwood Press, New York, 1968
Wordsworth, William, *Early Letters*, Oxford University Press, 1935
Wyvill, Christopher, *Political Papers*, York, 1794-1802

Yarborough, I.M., *John Horne Tooke*, Columbia University Press, New York, 1926

Further Reading

Black, E.C., *The Association*, Harvard, 1963
Brewer, J. and Styles, J. (eds), *An Ungovernable People*, Hutchinson, 1980 (for essays on Wilkites and the law and on the King's Bench Prison)
Brown, P.A., *The French Revolution in English History*, Frank Cass, 1965
Cannon, J., *Aristocratic Century*, Cambridge University Press, 1984
Idem., *Parliamentary Reform*, Cambridge University Press, 1973
Christie, I.R., *Stress and Stability in Late Eighteenth Century Britain*, Oxford University Press, 1984

Cockayne, G.E., *The Complete Peerage of Great Britain*, ed. Vicary Gibbs, St Catherine Press, 1910
Dickinson, H.T., *British Radicalism and the French Revolution*, Blackwell, 1985
Idem., *Liberty and Property*, Weidenfeld, 1977
Dinwiddy, J.R., *Radicalism and Reform in Britain 1780-1850*, Hambledon, 1992
Ehrman, John, *The Younger Pitt*, Constable, 1984-1996
Gilmour, I., *Riot, Risings and Revolution*, Hutchinson, 1992
Halévy, Elie, *Growth of Philosphic Radicalism*, Faber, 1952
Harling, Philip, *The Waning of Old Corruption*, Oxford University Press, 1996
Harris, R. and Taylor, T.J., *Landmarks in Linguistic Thought*, Routledge, 1989
Lecky, W.E.H., *History of England in the Eighteenth Century*, Longman, 1891
Miles, D., *Francis Place*, Harvester Press, 1988
Mitchell, L.G., *Charles James Fox and the Disintegration of the Whig Party 1782-94*, Oxford University Press, 1971
Idem., *Charles James Fox*, Oxford University Press, 1992
Philp, M. (ed.), *The French Revolution and British Popular Politics*, Cambridge University Press, 1991
Pinker, S., *The Language Instinct*, Allen Lane, 1994
Postgate, R., *That Devil Wilkes*, Dennis Dobson, 1956
Prochaska, Alice, *Westminster Radicalism 1807-32*, D. Phil. thesis, Oxford, 1975
Rude, George, *Wilkes and Liberty: a Social Study*, Oxford University Press, 1962
St Clair, William, *The Godwins and the Shelleys*, Faber, 1989
Seaman, W.A.L., *British Democratic Societies in the Period of the French Revolution*, PhD thesis London University, 1954
Smith, Olivia, *The Politics of Language*, Oxford University Press, 1984
Thale, Mary (ed.), *Selections from the Papers of the London Corresponding Society 1792-1799*, Cambridge University Press, 1983
Thomas, P.D.G., *John Wilkes, a Friend to Liberty*, Oxford University Press, 1996

INDEX

POSTSCRIPT
BOOKS
3/2009

8